DATE DUE

10/4	9 AN		

Demco, inc. 38-293

Re ——————————————————————— hts

LANDMARK LAW CASES

&

AMERICAN SOCIETY

Peter Charles Hoffer
N. E. H. Hull
Series Editors

Titles in the series:

The Bakke *Case*, Howard Ball
Reconstruction and Black Suffrage, Robert M. Goldman
Flag Burning and Free Speech, Robert Justin Goldstein
The Salem Witchcraft Trials, Peter Charles Hoffer
The Reconstruction Justice of Salmon P. Chase, Harold M. Hyman
The Struggle for Student Rights, John W. Johnson
Lochner v. New York, Paul Kens
Religious Freedom and Indian Rights, Carolyn N. Long
Marbury v. Madison, William E. Nelson
The Pullman Case, David Ray Papke
When the Nazis Came to Skokie, Philippa Strum
Affirmative Action on Trial, Melvin I. Urofsky
Lethal Judgments, Melvin I. Urofsky

CAROLYN N. LONG

Religious Freedom and Indian Rights

The Case of *Oregon v. Smith*

UNIVERSITY PRESS OF KANSAS

Published by the University Press of Kansas (Lawrence, Kansas 66049), which was
organized by the Kansas Board of Regents and is operated and funded by Emporia
State University, Fort Hays State University, Kansas State University, Pittsburg State
University, the University of Kansas, and Wichita State University.

Library of Congress Cataloging-in-Publication Data

Long, Carolyn Nestor.
    Religious freedom and Indian rights : the case of Oregon v. Smith /
Carolyn N. Long.
        p. cm. — (Landmark law cases & American society)
    Includes bibliographical references and index.
    ISBN 0-7006-1063-4 (cloth : alk. paper) — ISBN 0-7006-1064-2 (pbk. : alk. paper)
    1. Oregon—Trials, litigation, etc. 2. Smith, Alfred Leo—Trials, litigation, etc.
3. Indians of North America—Civil rights. 4. Indians of North America—Religion.
5. Freedom of religion—United States. 6. Drugs of abuse—Law and legislation—
Oregon. 7. Peyotism—Oregon. I. Title. II. Series.

KF228.O74 L66 2000
342.73'0852—dc21   00-043652

British Library Cataloguing in Publication Data is available.

Printed in the United States of America
10 9 8 7 6 5 4 3 2 1

The paper used in this publication meets the minimum requirements of the
American National Standard for Permanence of Paper for Printed Library Materials
Z39.48-1984.

FOR MOTHER

YOU ARE GREATLY MISSED

CONTENTS

It seemed at first no more than the kind of piddling and unfeeling bureaucratic injustice that we all have to bear at one time or another in our lives. Alfred Leo Smith, a recovering alcoholic who had turned his life around, and Galen Black, a coworker at the Douglas County, Oregon, Council on Alcohol and Drug Abuse Prevention and Treatment facility had been denied unemployment benefits by the state of Oregon for being dismissed from their jobs. The cause, according to their employers, was that as substance abuse counselors they had used an illegal drug—peyote. In reply, they argued that they had used the drug during a religious ceremony of the Native American Church (NAC), a pan-Indian group that was recognized as a religious body by state and federal governments. Smith was a Klamath Indian, Black was not, but both claimed that their right to worship was infringed when they were fired and then denied unemployment benefits.

Such a story is unlikely to be the beginning of a landmark law case that would reveal the powerful conflict between law enforcement and freedom of religion, much less lead to a congressional act restoring religious liberty and a series of U.S. Supreme Court decisions, but that is what happened. The Oregon Supreme Court ruled in favor of the two men, but a determined and politically ambitious Oregon state attorney saw the issue not as one of religious liberty but of the state's right to enforce its own drug laws. He appealed the Oregon court's decision to the U.S. Supreme Court. The high court divided over the issues, but a majority found that the state's proscription of peyote was neutral—it bound everyone and fulfilled a legitimate state purpose—and thus Smith and Black's constitutional claims, based on the First Amendment, bowed to the state drug laws.

The story was still not over. A broad coalition of religious groups joined with the Native American Church to press for the Religious Freedom Restoration Act (RFRA) in Congress. Oregon's state legislature beat Congress to the punch, providing a religious exception to the state's drug laws. Two years later, the congressional bill was revised to reassure certain religious groups that it did not apply to abortion and the bill sailed through Congress and was signed into law by President Bill Clinton. A year later, Clinton okayed an amendment to the American Indian Religious Freedom Act (AIRFA) to exempt the use of peyote in religious ceremonies from federal drug laws.

The Supreme Court majority was not done with the issue quite yet. Two years after a nearly unanimous Congress had spoken in favor of protection of peyote use in religious rites, a divided Court ruled that the Religious Freedom Restoration Act violated the constitutional principle of federalism, taking from the states their power to regulate the use of drugs. As this book goes to press, Congress again has before it a Religious Liberty Protection Act. The battle, begun over a decade ago by two men who would not take the ruling of an administrative agency lying down, continues.

Carolyn Long not only tells this story with verve, insight, and caring attentiveness, she gets behind the public record to reveal the human dimension. In interviews with the men who brought the suit and their families, the lawyers on both sides, and the judges, she recovers the courage, perseverance, sadness, and triumph that underlay the complex constitutional give and take. By carrying the tale beyond the end of the suit to the congressional debates, she opens a window into the ongoing struggle between the federal government and the states over basic human rights.

One of the most rewarding aspects about writing this book is that it provided me with the opportunity to come into contact with a cast of fascinating people who were willing to share their valuable time and thoughts about this important Supreme Court decision. This book could not have been written without the wonderful contributions of many individuals along the way. First and foremost, I would like to thank Al Smith, his wife Jane Farrell, and their two children, Kaila and Laylek, who spent several days with me in their lovely home in Breckenheim, Germany, in July 1998. Other notable participants in *Employment Division v. Smith* who graciously agreed to speak with me about this Supreme Court decision include Craig Dorsay, John Echohawk, Dave Fidanque, Dave Frohnmayer, Roy Haber, Barry Joyce, Steve Moore, David Morrison, and Bruce Piper. Former Oregon Supreme Court justices Hans Linde and Robert Jones were particularly helpful about their work on this case at the state level.

I also had the good fortune to speak with a number of incredibly helpful people affiliated with the congressional effort to enact the Religious Freedom Restoration Act and the amendments to the American Indian Religious Freedom Act. Representative Henry Hyde and former representative Steven Solarz provided valuable firsthand information about RFRA's long journey, and David Lachmann and Shawn Bentley offered a behind-the-scenes glimpse at some of the politics surrounding the process. I am also grateful for the insight provided by Nat Lewin, who shared his valuable time to talk about this case and his efforts on behalf of religious liberty. A major player in passage of legislation addressing *Smith* was the participation of the Coalition for the Free Exercise of Religion (CFER). Among this group I would like to thank Steve McFarland, Morton Halperin, Mark J. Pelavin, Oliver "Buzz" Thomas, and David Saperstein. Special thanks go to two individuals associated with this group, J. Brent Walker from the Baptist Joint Committee, for introducing me to members of the coalition and for allowing me access to the valuable archives of CFER, which greatly aided my research, and Douglas Laycock for his worthy insight and scholarship on this subject.

I am indebted to the reviewers who provided constructive criticism on the book proposal and manuscript: Peter Hoffer, Douglas Laycock, Melvin Urofsky, and John Wunder. Most of all, I deeply appreciate the support and encouragement of Mike Briggs, editor-in-chief of the University Press of Kansas, who has been incredibly accessible and kind throughout the process of writing this manuscript. Mike made this process thoroughly enjoyable, and I am grateful he was able to take the time to discuss religious liberty and the battle between the Supreme Court and Congress, as well as offer the occasional respite with conversations about our shared interests in literature and film.

I have been extremely fortunate to interact with several influential academics over the last ten years who have influenced my work in many positive ways: From the University of Oregon, James Klonoski; from Rutgers University, Ross Baker, Dennis Bathory, Charles Jacob, and Susan Lawrence; and from Northern Arizona University, Jacqueline Vaughn Switzer. Special thanks go to my friends and colleagues from Washington State University: Cornell Clayton, Nick Lovrich, Meredith Newman, Paul Thiers, and especially Lance T. Leloup, and to my good buddy and former colleague Brent Steel, now at Oregon State University. Each of these individuals have always offered their encouragement and direction, which is greatly appreciated.

Last but not least, I would like to thank my family for their support and patience during the writing of this book. My father, John Hedding, his wife Gail, and my siblings, Bob Hedding, John Hedding, Dawn Nestor, and Steve Nestor. Special thanks to Cydney Heaviland, who unselfishly helped me in a pinch. My greatest thanks are reserved for Kevin for always being there.

This book is dedicated to my mother, Lynne Hedding, in memory of her love and support.

Prologue

The sacred Indian ceremony was held high in the mountains in the Oregon coastal range near the small town of Myrtle Point. It was sponsored by Barry Joyce, who had led the small intertribal group of four dozen individuals in Native American Church meetings since the early 1970s. Although the group was not formally incorporated as a chapter of the church, it met regularly over the years. Joyce had called this recent ceremony to introduce local Indians, many of whom were active in the alcohol and drug treatment field, to the teachings of the Native American Church. Earlier in the week he invited Stanley Smart, a peyote Roadman who traveled throughout the Northwest performing peyote ceremonies, to lead the meeting at Storm Ranch. Smart, who lived in Nevada, was delighted to come, to be close to the ocean. It was the farthest west he had traveled to lead a church ceremony.

It was a clear, cool, spring evening. At twilight the men and women participants quietly gathered in a large teepee that had been erected earlier that afternoon. A sacred fire was built in a shallow hole in the center of the teepee, surrounded by a crescent-shaped altar of dirt open to the east. A line drawn down the length of the mound symbolized the peyote road, the ethics of the Native American Church. A large "Grandfather Peyote" was placed at the center of the altar.

The group sat on pieces of sagebrush arranged in a circle around the fire. The Roadman was positioned behind the moon-shaped altar opposite the door of the teepee facing east. To his right sat a brother, the Drum Chief, responsible for drumming and accompanying the singing, and to his left, a second brother, the Cedarman, was responsible for placing cedar on the fire at various intervals during the ceremony. The Fire Chief, the Roadman's son, sat by the door of the teepee and minded the fire throughout the evening. The Roadman was surrounded by his ceremonial instruments: a carved and beaded staff, a gourd rattle, a peyote fan made from the feathers of sacred birds, and an eagle-bone whistle.

The ritual began with the ceremonial smoke. The Roadman passed around tobacco and cornhusks in a clockwise direction, and each person hand rolled a cigarette. He made some opening remarks and initiated the communal smoke. The Roadman then opened the ceremony with a prayer. He took a bowl filled with dried peyote buttons and crushed them into a fine powder, which he mixed with water to form a thick paste. The sacrament was passed around the circle in a clockwise direction, and the participants ate a dollop of the bitter-tasting medicine. The Roadman, accompanied by the Drum Chief, then sang a round of opening songs. He shook his gourd rattle and held the ornate staff, focusing on the ancient songs.

As the evening progressed, the Roadman passed the ceremonial instruments among the participants and led the group in rounds of prayers and songs, always in intervals of four. Some sang; others did not, but everyone sat quietly and acknowledged the sacredness of the ceremony. Throughout the evening the Cedarman burned pieces of cedar, and the Fire Chief brought wood from outside to feed the fire. At several intervals throughout the night, the sacrament was passed around and the participants helped themselves. At midnight the Fire Chief brought in a pail of water, which was blessed by the Roadman and passed around the circle. The participants refreshed themselves and took a brief break. After a short time, the ceremony continued. The teepee was filled with rounds of songs and prayers. The evening was long. Occasionally, participants shared their thoughts or talked quietly to themselves. Most sat in quiet contemplation. The atmosphere was peaceful and respectful.

At daylight the Water Woman, the Roadman's wife, went outside and returned with a pail of water, which she prayed over and passed among the group. Some of the people said a few words during this sharing time. One participant, a slender, dignified man with jet-black hair that fell to his waist, spoke of the dilemma he faced two days earlier when he was presented with the difficult choice about whether he should participate in the peyote ceremony or obey his employer, who forbade him from ingesting the sacrament if he intended to keep his job. The man, who looked two decades younger than his sixty-five years, spoke in a quiet tone. He was not judgmental or angry, but rather resigned to the consequences of his actions. He was aware of the risk he is taking, but knew, deep in his heart, that he made the right decision to freely practice his religion.

As the sharing time continued, the Water Woman passed around food and the participants ate a light breakfast. The Roadman then ended the ceremony with a round of songs and prayers. Each person exited the teepee and raised his or her hands to the north, south, east and west to acknowledge the Creator and "to give thanks for the new day that has been given to you." As they left the ranch, several people walked up to the man who spoke of the dilemma he faced in coming to the ceremony. One of them clapped him on the back and said, "Al, welcome to the world of unemployment."

Felix Cohen, the father of federal Indian law, once stated, "The Indian plays much the same role in our American society that the Jews played in Germany. Like the miner's canary, the Indian marks the shift from fresh air to poison gas in our political atmosphere; and our treatment of Indians, even more than our treatment of other minorities marks the rise and fall of our democratic faith." That Saturday evening, March 3, 1983, when Al Smith took the sacrament of his church, as he had done so many times before, he became the miner's canary that Cohen spoke of so eloquently.

CHAPTER I

The Peyote Road

Peyote, a small, leafless, turnip-shaped cactus, is considered sacred medicine by a number of Indian tribes in North America, and has been used in religious ceremonies for centuries. Those who ingest the sacrament contend that peyote is a spirit force that allows them to communicate with the Creator and obtain spiritual enlightenment. Peyotists consume the medicine to absorb God's power. In essence, peyote is used to obtain knowledge. In the United States, members of the Native American Church, an intertribal Christian faith, have used the sacrament in religious ceremonies for over eighty years. Peyotists belonging to the church are guided by the Peyote Road, the religion's ethics, which emphasize brotherly love, care of family, self-reliance, and the avoidance of alcohol. Despite its long history and importance to Indian tribes, however, peyotism is a controversial religion to some, and attempts to eradicate it date back as far as the discovery of the religion itself. A look at the habitat and pharmacology of peyote and its early history sheds light on its use in religious ceremonies and helps explain how peyotism spread to Indian tribes in the United States.

Two major species of peyote have been identified; *Lophophora williamsii* and the less common *Lophophora diffusa*. The natural habitat of both species is primarily an area of approximately sixty thousand square miles in the Chihuahuan desert scrub environment in the high plateau land of northern Mexico and southern Texas. Its natural habitat in the United States is limited to a small twenty-mile strip of land running through four counties of Texas in the Rio Grande valley region. The cactus is commonly found thriving under shrubs and plants, but it can also grow without protection or shade. Peyote grows in various colors depending on environmental conditions, and its appearance varies with age, which is determined by the size and number of ribs on a plant. It forms in various shapes, either as a one- or two-inch single head, or individual peyote, or as a caespitose, which is a clump of heads. If left undisturbed, the caespitose grow in clusters that may resemble particular forms. Some Indian tribes believe that unusual formations, such as those found in the shape of a deer, are a sacred message from God.

The collection and distribution of peyote in the United States is heavily regulated. It is harvested by Peyoteros, who are registered by the state of Texas, and who must keep precise records of the number of peyote buttons harvested and sold. Peyoteros gather the cactus in the wild, and with permission and payment of leasing fees, on private lands. Peyote is harvested by cutting off the exposed tops of the plant. The taproot is left in the soil so it can regenerate, which usually takes several months. Each year fewer than a dozen Peyoteros in the United States harvest approximately three hundred thousand peyote buttons each, which are sold exclusively to the Native American Church. Church members ingest the sacred medicine in several forms. If available, many prefer to eat green peyote, which is peyote that is freshly picked. However, it is most often eaten in dried form or as peyote tea, which is made by steeping dried buttons in water. Those who ingest the sacrament say that it has a very unpleasant, bitter taste that often causes indigestion or nausea.

Lophophora williamsii, which is principally used by members of the Native American Church, contains fifty-five alkaloids, alkaloidal amides, and amino acids that have various physiological and psychological effects. Most notably, it contains the alkaloid mescaline, which can produce a variety of short-term somatic effects, such as an increase in blood pressure, pulse rate, respiration, perspiration, and motor activity. These effects are usually accompanied by psychic manifestations. Peyote produces an altered state of consciousness and users may experience a range of reactions, from a heightened sense of wakefulness and euphoria to colorful visual hallucinations. *L. diffusa* has fewer alkaloids and does not contain mescaline.

After years of early reports on the dangers of peyote, which were often the result of misinformation and government propaganda, more recent medical studies on the religious use of the sacrament conclude that it is safe. There is no evidence of toxicity or short- or long-term harm from use of the medicine. Notably, there have been no recorded cases of deaths attributed solely to the eating of peyote. On the contrary, there is significant anecdotal and scientific evidence that peyote has the power to heal, and that it can help American Indians successfully overcome alcoholism and substance abuse.

———

Peyotism is considered one of the oldest continually practiced religions in the Western Hemisphere. Its use for medicinal and spiritual purposes has been traced to the aboriginal people of the Rio Grande valley in the present-day areas of Mexico and the state of Texas. Anthropologists have identified two distinct forms of peyotism: the "old peyote religion" and the "new peyote religion." Each form is unique to its geographical area and reflects the cultural influences and historical circumstances of the times.

The old peyote religion, also known as the peyote complex or the peyote cult, was originally found in Mexico and in some areas along the Rio Grande. This early religion emphasized the curative aspects of peyote, and the sacrament was primarily used as medicine and as a means to obtain visions in all-night celebrations. Although the peyote ritual differed among Indian tribes, most ceremonies were led by a shaman, who acted as a medicine man to cure those who were ill and to ward off evil spirits. Throughout the ceremony the shaman would lead ritual songs, and the predominantly male participants would join in with a wooden drum and rasp. The ceremonies were held outdoors and there was an emphasis on feasts, ritual dancing, and celebrating. Peyote ceremonies were called for a number of reasons; in some tribes it was a seasonal affair to celebrate the planting and harvesting of crops. Other reasons include rituals to pray on behalf of an ill member of the tribe or to honor a member's death. Anthropologists who study Mexican peyotism characterize it as a tribal affair centered around the actions of the shaman, with an emphasis on curing and doctoring. There is also evidence that the sacrament was used individually by some tribal members, primarily for medicinal purposes.

Mexican peyotism was first documented in the Aztec culture more than four hundred years ago around the time of the Spanish conquest of Mexico. The earliest historical references to peyote are found in the writings of Christian missionaries who encountered its use among Indian tribes native to Mexico. These reports reflected their disapproval of peyote, which they believed was harmful. Some theorize that missionaries were opposed to peyotism because its appeal among Indians made it more difficult to convert them to Catholicism. As Spanish explorers and missionaries moved throughout Mexico during the Spanish Inquisition to Christianize the native people, they also attempted to eradicate peyote. The Roman Catholic Church played a visible role in the antipeyote campaign, believing it to be the "work of the devil." In 1620 the Church issued an edict prohibiting the use of peyote, and promised to "take action against such disobedient and recalcitrant persons as we would against those suspected of heresy to our Holy Catholic Faith." Indians were prosecuted under the edict for the next two centuries.

Peyotism in Mexico flourished despite these efforts to prohibit its use, which ironically may have contributed to its diffusion to the more rural areas of the country. Indians who traveled with missionaries and soldiers also spread knowledge of peyote into areas where it was less known. By the early eighteenth century there were reports that peyote use had spread far beyond its natural habitat, and by the end of the century peyotism was present in most of Mexico. Nevertheless, the Church continued in its effort to Christianize Indians and to warn them of the evils of peyote.

As peyotism traveled throughout the country, the use of the sacrament would vary among tribes as each group incorporated the religion into already existing cultural mores and tribal norms. Most Indian tribes used peyote as medicine, applying it externally to wounds and ingesting it to cure internal ailments and to strengthen the body so that it could resist illness. It was also used as an amulet to protect the wearer from harm. Most of all, however, peyote was used as a sacrament in a religious ceremony. Tribes would often begin with a pilgrimage to the peyote gardens, followed by a ritual of confession and purification that culminated in an all-night religious ceremony.

———

Peyotism would eventually find its way into the United States in the same manner that led to its diffusion throughout Mexico. Although official records are scarce, making it difficult to track its exact origins, the spread of peyotism to tribes indigenous to the United States was aided by the fact that these tribes once lived in or near the area of peyote's natural habitat, or they associated with tribes from Mexico that introduced them to the sacrament. Later, the U.S. policy of isolating Indians to reservations and the attempt to assimilate Indians into white society played a pivotal role not only in spreading peyotism to the United States, but also changing the way the religion was celebrated among tribes living in North America.

Between 1825 and 1840 the United States government removed over one hundred thousand American Indians from over forty officially recognized tribes from the eastern regions of the United States to the present-day state of Oklahoma. Then, as American immigrants moved west, the federal government embarked on its effort to contain the Plains Indian tribes living in and around Indian Territory. This containment policy was carried out through a number of treaties between tribes and the United States where peace was pledged in exchange for tracts of land. Although many of the early treaties were unsuccessful and aggression periodically broke out, by 1867 many of the Plains Indian tribes were confederated and placed on reservations.

The United States entered into a new phase of its Indian policy after the Civil War. The federal government destroyed the power of tribal organizations by transferring previously sovereign tribes into subordinate groups under U.S. rule, and then initiated its effort to "civilize" Indians and assimilate them into white society. The process of assimilation was carried out through forced Christianity and government-imposed white mores considered more acceptable to European American society. Most traditional religious rituals, shamanistic practices, and other cultural activities were banned. Children were compelled to attend sectarian boarding schools, often run by missionaries, and Indian languages and traditional styles of dress and hair were replaced with more "acceptable" fashions. Indians found celebrating their heritage would be tried in the Department of the Interior's Court of Indian Offenses and would be punished by having rations or annuities withheld, or they were jailed. Significantly, because reservations were overseen by government officials and religious missionaries, the process of assimilation was not with white society but with highly ethnocentric segments of society, which made the process even more difficult.

Faced with catastrophic changes in their environment and coerced to abandon their traditional way of life, Plains Indians sought ways to regain control over their lives. Their choices were few; some chose militancy, only to be quickly defeated by the U.S. Army in battles like the Wounded Knee massacre in 1890. Others chose religion. Several religious movements gained popularity at the end of the nineteenth century that allowed Indians to adjust to their circumstances by combining aspects of traditional Plains culture, social solidarity, and an appeal to supernatural means for empowerment. Some religious movements, nativistic and tribal in nature, celebrated Indian culture. Others were Pan-Indian social movements that appealed to larger segments of the Indian population. Two such movements, the Ghost Dance and the peyote religion, were also nativistic, but differed greatly from one another. The Ghost Dance was a militant movement that aimed to break white domination over Indians and ultimately destroy white culture, whereas the peyote religion was more peaceful and allowed a melding of Indian culture and forced Christianity. Because the goal of peyotism was accommodation with the surroundings rather than the opposite, peyotism prevailed. The acceptance of peyotism was also aided by the fact that many of the Plains tribes had had previous contact with Mexican tribes who practiced the religion.

By the end of the nineteenth century, peyotism was spreading rapidly through Indian Territory in the United States. It was first officially documented in 1891 by James Mooney, a young ethnologist living in Indian Territory. Mooney attended several peyote rituals and wrote the first accounts of the ceremony among the Plains Indians. His writings revealed that peyotism in the United States was similar to Mexican peyotism in its use of peyote as a sacrament in a ceremony presided over by a priest, later known as a Roadman or Road Chief, who would lead rounds of singing and praying around an open fire. Mooney noted some differences as well, however. His descriptions were of a pan-Indian ceremony that was strongly influenced by Native American Plains culture. The ceremonies were social rather than ritualistic in character, and resembled a quiet gathering of family and friends. Mooney also detected overtones of Christianity that were not present in Mexican forms of peyotism. The Christian influence and changes in the peyote ritual would become even more overt as the new peyote religion spread throughout the United States.

Comanche chief Quanah Parker and John Wilson, a Caddo-Delaware medicine man, have been identified as significant peyote prophets who introduced a number of Plains tribes to the new peyote religion and incorporated changes to the peyote ceremony that made it even more distinct from the old peyote cult. It was through these two prophets that two distinct forms of the modern peyote ritual developed: the Comanche Half Moon and the Wilson Big Moon, or Cross Fire ceremonies. Both were a combination of Mexican peyotism, Plains Indian traditions and culture, and Christianity. The Half Moon ceremony, which also came to be known as the Quanah Parker Way, is characterized by an emphasis on Indian legends in prayers, the use of tobacco, and a teepee ceremony where participants sit on sagebrush cuttings in a circle around a crescent-shaped altar. Wilson's ceremony differs in the shape of the altar, which is in the form of a horseshoe rather than a crescent, and a strong Christian influence through the presence of the crucifix and the Bible. Wilson also helped develop the ethics of the Peyote Road, which includes abstinence from liquor, restraint in sexual matters, matrimonial fidelity, and prohibitions against angry retorts, falsehoods, vindictiveness, vengeance, and fighting. The Road emphasizes brotherly love, and members are instructed to be honest, truthful, friendly, helpful, and to care for one another and their family. Both ceremonies emphasize the sacredness of peyote, which is seen as a gift from God that has the power to heal and the power to teach the difference between good and evil. The sacrament aids members in their effort at revelation, and helps them follow a spiritually and physically pure life.

By 1910 most tribes located in the United States had come into contact with the peyote religion, and it grew in popularity, particularly among tribes new to Indian Territory. It is estimated that between 35 and 90 percent of tribal members were practicing peyotists, with the exception of the five "Civilized Tribes" from the East, most likely because of their fidelity to Christianity and assimilation into white society. The peyote religion allowed Indian tribes to adjust to new surroundings after being forced to relocate and undergo the politics of assimilation. For many, peyotism allowed the preservation of Native American culture, so followers were able to retain some sense of moral and religious cohesiveness.

———

As peyotism grew in popularity in Mexico and North America, efforts to suppress the religion became more prevalent. Christian missionaries and church leaders led the antipeyote campaign with the full support of federal Indian agents working in Indian Territory. Government and church officials opposed the religion because it hindered their efforts to assimilate Indians into the general population. Most non-Indians were unfamiliar with its long history and banned use of peyote along with other native practices. Peyotism also hindered efforts to impose Christianity on Indian populations. Additionally, some individuals were frightened by peyote's effects on the user. Many believed it was a harmful drug that could result in personal injury and have a negative effect on society. Support for federal and state legislation outlawing the transport and use of peyote was also fueled by ignorance and a lack of empathy for Indians suffering the trauma of removal and assimilation.

The earliest federal effort to restrict peyote in Indian Territory was indirect. Antipeyotists in Oklahoma attempted but failed to prohibit the ingestion of peyote under an 1897 prohibition law against articles that produce intoxication. There were also attempts to prosecute peyotists under vaguely written state laws, but these efforts were thwarted in the courts. Undaunted, some Indian agents acted on their own to achieve the same ends. There are examples of agents resorting to threats and intimidation to harass peyotists, and several acted unilaterally to block or destroy shipments of the sacrament to reservations.

By the turn of the century, antipeyotists had teamed up with mainline church leaders and representatives from the Bureau of Indian Affairs to lobby for federal legislation that directly proscribed peyote. In 1907 and 1910 draft legislation outlawing peyote was sent to Congress, but the bills were never introduced. Bills were introduced in 1915 and 1916, but the measures did not make it very far in the legislative process. The most serious attempt occurred in 1918 when Congress held extensive hearings on the dangers of peyote. It was at this point that peyotists formally organized to oppose the legislation. They held petition drives, wrote letters to members of Congress, and sent delegates to Washington, D.C., to lobby for the preservation of their religion. At the hearings, several ethnologists, including James Mooney from the Smithsonian Institution's Bureau of American Ethnology, appeared to oppose the bill. They introduced evidence on the historical use of peyote in religious rituals, and in the case of Mooney's testimony, provided a firsthand account of peyote ceremonies and the positive effect the sacred medicine had on numerous tribes. Their efforts were unsuccessful in the House of Representatives, which passed the bill, but the measure was stopped in the Senate.

Efforts to enact antipeyote legislation continued for several more years, although each attempt failed. There was even a strategy to pass riders to the Indian Bureau Appropriation Act to allot

{ *Religious Freedom and Indian Rights* }

funds to stop the traffic of peyote, but this was unsuccessful as well. Antipeyotists did achieve several minor legislative victories, however. In 1915 the Department of Agriculture issued a regulation prohibiting importation of peyote "on the ground that it is an article dangerous to the health of the people of the United States," and peyote was defined as a narcotic in the Narcotic Addict Farm Act of 1929 and the federal Food, Drug and Cosmetic Act of 1938. The post office also successfully banned shipment of peyote through the mail from 1917 to 1940. But the measures had little actual effect on access to peyote and the popularity of the religion.

Unable to enact federal legislation prohibiting peyote, antipeyotists turned their attention to state legislatures, and this approach was more successful. Once again, church and government officials were involved in this effort. Some members of Congress also persuaded state lawmakers to introduce legislation after failing at the federal level. In 1917 laws prohibiting the transportation and use of peyote were enacted in Utah, Nevada, and Colorado. In 1920 Kansas passed a similar law, followed in 1923 with antipeyote legislation in Arizona, Montana, North Dakota, and South Dakota. In 1929 peyote was outlawed in New Mexico and Wyoming, and in 1933 Idaho joined the list of states proscribing the cactus. Several states enacted statutes prohibiting peyote, only to repeal them later. Iowa had such a law on the books from 1924 before rescinding it in 1937, as did Texas between 1937 and 1954. Antipeyote laws only interfered with the transportation of the cactus, however, and did little to stop the practice of the religion. States could not feasibly stop peyotism in Indian Territory because they did not have jurisdiction on Indian reservations. Moreover, because transportation was difficult to regulate, there were few arrests and even fewer successful prosecutions of peyotists in the state courts.

The antipeyote campaign prompted peyotists to reassess their political strategy. They understood that many non-Indians were ignorant about the religious use of the sacrament and that Christian religious leaders viewed peyotism as a threat to their mainstream beliefs. Several tribes believed that a formal church organization would give legitimacy to their cause and provide a way to inform others about peyotism to combat the propaganda that had shadowed the religion for years. Some early peyotists belonged to a loosely organized association, the Peyote Society, later known as the Union Church Society, but the association was not legally incorporated and there are scarce records of its existence. Then, in 1914 the first American Indian church, the First Born Church of Christ, was incorporated in the state of Oklahoma. It was a small, strongly Christian religious organization, but membership was limited to one tribe and there was not an effort to nationalize the church. Moreover, although it had been partially formed to protect the peyote religion, there is no mention of peyote in the organization's bylaws.

Peyotists knew they needed to cooperate on a larger scale and create a national organization to defend their religious freedom. They noted the success of other religious groups, such as the Methodists and Baptists, which incorporated their churches, held national conferences, and planned legislative and political strategies to protect their religious rights. In the summer of 1918 a number of peyotists from the Cheyenne, Oto, Ponca, Comanche, Kiowa, and Apache tribes held a conference to discuss organization of a Pan-Indian church that would specifically protect the use of peyote as a religious sacrament. Later that year, on October 10, 1918, at a meeting held in El Reno, Oklahoma, the Native American Church was formally incorporated. Those who formed the church intended to reach out to all of the Oklahoma peyotists and named it the Native American Church to emphasize intertribal solidarity. Article II of the articles of incorporation reads:

> The purpose for which this corporation is formed is to foster and promote the religious belief of the several tribes of Indians in the state of Oklahoma, in the Christian religion with the practice of the Peyote Sacrament as commonly understood and used among adherents of this religion in the several tribes of Indians in the State of Oklahoma, and to teach the Christian religion with morality, sobriety, industry, kindly charity and right living and to cultivate a spirit of self respect

and brotherly union among the members of the Native Race of Indians including therein the various Indian tribes of the State of Oklahoma.

Branch churches were established in each of the Indian tribes in the state, and church members were governed by the "General Council of the Church" which consisted of two trustees elected by local church branches.

After fifteen years the Native American Church reached out to Indians outside the state of Oklahoma, and in 1934 the Oklahoma charter was amended to allow out-of-state church branches. In 1944 it became a national organization, "The Native American Church of the United States," which held its first conference the following year. After several years, however, some tribes in Oklahoma expressed their desire to return to the smaller state organization, and so in 1949 the church split into two groups. The Oklahoma state group became the Native American Church and retained the church's original 1918 charter. In 1950 the national group was incorporated as the Native American Church of the United States. In 1954 it became an international organization when it incorporated the Native American Church of Canada, and its name was officially changed to the Native American Church of North America in 1955. Separate organizations were also formed in the Navajo Nation and in South Dakota.

Today, the Native American Church is a confederation of four large organizations; the NAC of North America, which has forty-six chapters in twenty-four states, Canada, and Mexico; the NAC of Navajoland, which has ninety-two chapters in the Navajo Nation; the NAC of Oklahoma, with seventeen chapters in the state of Oklahoma; and the NAC of South Dakota, with several chapters within the state. Each chapter has its own charter and articles of incorporation, and is governed by its own bylaws, but all belong to the Native American Church. There is some variation in the bylaws; for instance, some chapters limit church membership to individuals with at least one-quarter Indian blood; others do not restrict membership to Indians as long as the person has expressed a genuine interest in the religion.

Most chapters endorse the ethics of the Peyote Road, which are often printed on church membership cards.

The Native American Church has grown significantly in membership over the years. In 1925 there were approximately 13,000 peyotists; the present number is estimated to be at least 250,000 and perhaps as many as 400,000 members from over seventy different Indian tribes. The largest number of peyotists belong to the NAC of Navajoland, and the NAC of North America has the widest scope, with members throughout North America. This group is also the most visible politically and is largely responsible for any litigation activities. The church continues to thrive and provides a means of interaction between groups to help protect the practice of peyotism for members in North America.

———

In the mid-1960s, changes to federal laws regarding drug classifications had an effect on the legality of peyote in the states and nation. In 1965, in part because of the increase in the illegal use of hallucinogens during this decade, the Food, Drug, and Cosmetic Act was amended to add hallucinogens, including peyote, to the definition of "Depressant and Stimulant Drugs," and many states followed suit. Peyote was later classified as an illegal Schedule I substance in the Comprehensive Drug Abuse and Prevention Control Act of 1970. Schedule I drugs are identified as substances that have a "high potential for abuse" with no accepted medical use in the United States. Other Schedule I drugs include heroin, cocaine, and marijuana. An aggressive lobbying effort on the part of the Native American Church paved the way for an exemption to the peyote proscription for Native American Church members, reflecting limited progress in the federal government's recognition of the sacrament's role in the religious ceremonies of American Indians. Section 21 CFR 1307.31 states, "The listing of peyote as a controlled substance in schedule I does not apply to the non-drug use of peyote in bona fide religious ceremonies of the Native American Church."

States have enacted their own laws that similarly classify controlled substances, and a number of these laws are identical to the federal statute. However, not all of the states have similar exemptions for the religious use of peyote by members of the Native American Church. There is a great deal of variety among the states; twelve states, Alaska, Mississippi, Montana, New Jersey, North Carolina, North Dakota, Rhode Island, Tennessee, Utah, Virginia, Washington, and West Virginia, have an exemption similar to the federal law, and seven states, Iowa, Kansas, Minnesota, South Dakota, Texas, Wisconsin, and Wyoming, have full exemptions for the religious use of peyote. Three states, Colorado, Nevada, and New Mexico, do not limit the religious exemption to members of the Native American Church but extend an exemption to any bona fide religious use of the substance. Idaho exempts peyote use only on reservations. As a result, state legislative exemptions provide only limited protection for the peyote religion. The remaining two dozen states have laws prohibiting peyote, usually classified as a Schedule I drug, even if used for religious purposes. After attempts by the Native American Church to carve out legislative exemptions failed, several of these laws were challenged in state courts. Church members argued that the laws violated their free exercise of religion, protected by the First Amendment of the Constitution. However, the results were mixed. In cases where the church was allowed to present expert evidence on the safety of peyotism and the lack of an adverse impact on the state's drug laws, the religious claimant prevailed, and peyotists were granted a judicially created exemption. In other cases, the religious challenge was unsuccessful.

The first example of a judicially created exemption to a state antipeyote statute occurred in 1960 in *Arizona v. Attakai*. The case involved a challenge by a Navajo woman who was arrested for illegal possession of peyote. The defendant was represented by attorneys from the American Civil Liberties Union (ACLU), who argued that the law violated the free exercise clause of the First Amendment as well as religious guarantees in the state constitution. Attorneys asked the court to use the highest level of scrutiny to evaluate the religious claim. They recommended the application of the compelling government interest balancing test used in other First Amendment challenges to laws interfering with freedom of speech, press, and assembly. This test, also referred to as "strict scrutiny analysis," requires the court to balance the religious liberty claim against the interests of the state. Only when the state interest is compelling and the state law is narrowly drawn to best protect liberty rights would it be upheld.

Several expert witnesses appeared at the Arizona trial, including University of Colorado professor Omer Stewart, an authority on the peyote religion, who testified to the long history and safe use of peyotism by members of the church. The judge ruled in favor of the defendant, finding the statute unconstitutional as applied to the case. He wrote, "The use of peyote is essential to the existence of the peyote religion. Without it, the practice of the religion would be effectively prevented." The judge dismissed the state's argument that peyote was harmful, noting that "The manner in which peyote is used by the Indian worshiper is not inconsistent with the public health, morals, or welfare. Its use, in the manner disclosed by the evidence in this case, is in fact entirely consistent with the good morals, health and spiritual elevation of some 225,000 Indians." *Arizona v. Attakai* was upheld by the Arizona Supreme Court on appeal.

A similar legal challenge was successful several years later in California. The case, *People v. Woody*, also concerned a request for a religious exemption to the state's antipeyote law. The ACLU, which represented the three Navajo defendants at the request of the Native American Church, used a strategy similar to *Attakai*. The attorneys presented testimony from expert witnesses who defended peyotism and challenged the state's argument that an exemption to the law would adversely affect the state's enforcement of its drug laws. Nevertheless, the county court found the defendants guilty, declaring that "the Native American Church must forsake its peyote rituals in deference to the unqualified legislative command of prohibition." The court of appeals upheld the decision, but it was later reversed by the state's highest court. The California Supreme Court used strict scrutiny analysis to evaluate the constitutionality of the law, balancing the state's interest in drug enforcement against the religious liberty claim. The court determined that peyote was the "essence of religious expression," and that its use by church members posed "only slight danger to the state and to the enforcement of its laws." It concluded,

> We know that some will urge that it is more important to subserve the rigorous enforcement of the narcotic laws than to carve out of them an exception for a few believers of a strange faith. They will say that the exception may reduce problems of enforcement and that the dictate of the state must overcome the beliefs of a minority of Indians. . . . We preserve a greater value than an ancient tradition when we protect the rights of the Indians who honestly practiced an old religion in using peyote one night at a meeting in a desert hogan near Needles, California.

Attakai and *Woody* would later be cited by other state courts facing similar religious challenges to state antipeyote laws. For example, in 1967 the Native American Church set up a test case in Texas to challenge the state law forbidding peyote possession. In *Texas v. Clark*, the state court declared the law unconstitutional as applied to a Native American Church member, holding that peyote was "the sole means by which the members of the Church are able to experience their religion," and that the defendant "used the peyote in good faith in the sincere and honest practice of Peyotism, a bona fide religion." The state would later enact a statutory exemption for the religious use of peyote by members of the Native American Church. Further, in *Arizona v. Whittingham* (1973) and *Whitehorn v. State of Oklahoma* (1977) state appellate courts overturned the convictions of church members convicted for peyote possession after they determined that the state had not proven a compelling reason why the exemption should not be granted.

However, not all judicial challenges were successful. In *Montana v. Big Sheep* (1927) the state supreme court upheld the constitutionality of the state's antipeyote law, ruling that peyote use, even for religious reasons, was a threat to the interests of the state, and in *North Carolina v. Bullard* (1966) the state court reached the same result, concluding that the First Amendment did not protect acts that threatened public safety. At times, the state courts would not even consider evidence of religious motivation. In Oregon, where peyote is classified as an illegal Schedule I drug, a state trial court judge evaluating an arrest for peyote possession refused to allow a religious defense. The case, *Oregon v. Soto* (1975), left the issue of a religiously inspired exemption unresolved in the state of Oregon.

In sum, legislative and judicial protection for sacramental peyote use differed from state to state, resulting in a patchwork of laws and unequal access to religious freedom depending on where one lived. Action from the federal government was slow in coming, and when Congress finally did respond with federal legislation, the result turned out to be a paper tiger.

———

After years of insensitivity to native cultural and religious practices, in 1978 Congress held hearings on the need to protect Indian religious freedom. Later that year it enacted the American Indian Religious Freedom Act, which declared that "it shall be the policy of the United States to protect and preserve for American Indians their inherent right of freedom to believe, express, and exercise the traditional religions of the American Indian, Eskimo, Aleut, and Native Hawaiians, including but not limited to access to sites, use and possession of sacred objects, and the freedom of worship through ceremonial and traditional rites." Notably, the law identified some of the problems Indian people faced from the federal government, including a "lack of knowledge or the insensitive and inflexible enforcement of federal policies and regulations." AIRFA gave the impression that the federal government would be more vigilant in the protection of Indian religious freedom. Section 2 directed the president to have federal departments evaluate policies and procedures and to recommend any legislative action to protect traditional religious rights. The law appeared to be a significant victory, given the lack of protective state legislation for American Indians. After its passage, there were even some administrative regulations and policies put in place to allow input regarding how land use would affect American Indians. Actual changes were limited, however. The act did not have any "teeth" because it did not create any judicially enforceable rights; although Congress announced its *desire* to protect Indian religious freedom, AIRFA did not put any mechanisms in place to ensure this protection. Several years later, the inadequacy of the federal law would become even more clear.

CHAPTER 2

God v. Caesar

Al Smith's life has not been easy. As a young child he was the unwilling recipient of the U.S. government's policy to deprive American Indians of their native heritage and assimilate them into U.S. society. Years of forced Christianity and indoctrination about "appropriate" behavior in a white world would separate him from his cultural traditions and sense of self. As a young man he lived on the city streets and was unwillingly drafted into the army to fight a foreign war, only to come home several years later to a life of alcohol abuse. In 1954 Smith's sense of identity as a Klamath Indian and member of an Indian nation was stripped away when the federal government enacted its termination policy, which ended the government-to-government relationship of the United States with 109 Indian tribes and bands in the United States, 62 of which are native to Oregon. For Smith's tribe, the Klamath Termination Act included abrogation of its 1864 treaty with the United States, the nullification of all federal responsibilities owed to tribal members, the abolishment of its tribal government, and the loss of millions of acres of resource-rich land in return for a small lump payment. The act was adopted without the consent of the tribe and members were not prepared for the fact that in the eyes of the federal government, the Klamath Indian tribe no longer existed.

But Smith was strong. He was not one to be forced to do anything against his will, and throughout this destruction of his native identity, he rebelled against the government, the Catholic Church, and his own demons. From an early age Smith fiercely struggled against attempts to assimilate him into white society and fought to live his life the way he wanted. The road was not easy, but throughout this journey his independent spirit helped him survive a number of trials and tribulations, and would eventually lead him to the U.S. Supreme Court.

———

"Baby Boy" Smith was born on November 6, 1919, in Modoc Point, about ten miles outside Chiloquin, a small river town in the Klamath Indian Reservation. The reservation is located on 2.2 million acres of land, one-tenth of the Klamath's original territory, in southwestern Oregon at the foot of the Cascade Mountains. He was later christened Alfred Leo Smith, named after two uncles. As a young child Smith lived with his two sisters, Lavina Gail and Rosetta, and his mother Delia on his grandmother Emma's forty-acre ranch and farm on the Williamson River. He never knew his father and did not have a consistent male role model in his life. Smith remembers his early childhood fondly, especially the times he spent with his grandmother fishing on the river and paddling through the Klamath marsh gathering wocus, the seed of the water lily, a staple of the Klamath diet. He also spent a lot of time in the country looking for native plants with his family and picking huckleberries in the mountains near Crater Lake.

However, these early years were not without misfortune. His sister Lavina was killed when she was only a toddler after she "hitched a ride" on the back of their grandmother's car, fell off, and was accidentally run over. There was also the limited freedom of life on the reservation. Smith recalls what it was like to "be only a number," and "live in a kind of prison." He has vivid memories of government prohibitions on his behavior, such as "not being allowed to go out and hunt or practice native rituals," and the draconian measures to enforce compliance with government rules such as the withholding of food rations. In spite of these hardships Smith is quick to recall the happier times as a young child living in the Klamath basin. "My happiness was going up and down the river in the canoe. Being with my grandmother and my mom."

The pleasant memories were short-lived. When he was around seven years old, Smith was loaded up with a group of native children and taken into the town of Klamath Falls, where representatives from the Bureau of Indian Affairs enrolled him in Sacred Heart Academy, a Catholic school. It wasn't his choice, or his mother's choice. Rather, "The government enrolled me in the school. It is amazing how the reservation people in charge treated human beings." It was typical at this time for native children to attend parochial schools. In fact, by the time he was born, the U.S. policy of assimilating Indians into white society was firmly in place and schools were a major instrument of reform. Smith found Catholic school difficult. He was told how to dress, how to speak, and what to believe. He was not allowed to explore his native culture or spirituality, and felt stifled by the sectarian atmosphere. Smith resisted these efforts to wean him from his native roots and indoctrinate him with a white religion and white culture so he could better "fit" into a white society. He recalls, "They said they were reeducating me, but they were really breaking me from my native traditions. No one spoke the language or taught the Klamath culture. Instead, we were given Catholic religion every day."

After attending Sacred Heart Academy in Klamath Falls for two years, Smith was transferred to St. Mary's Catholic School in the small timber town of Albany, Oregon, located two hundred miles north of Klamath Falls. The school housed both native and white students, and the process of assimilation continued. Smith struggled in school, and his situation was further complicated because of the distance from home. He would attend St. Mary's in Albany for several years before being shipped off in the seventh grade to a Catholic boys' home located outside of Beaverton, a suburb of Portland. By the time Smith reached the Catholic boys' home he had "had enough of moving from one city to another," and decided to run away with another student and "try to make it in Portland." The two were able to reach the Portland Heights area overlooking the city before the police found them, loaded them into the patrol car, and brought them to the county jail, where they were given cookies and milk. The priest from the boys' home came and hauled them back to school. Smith was locked in a room with his friend and chased around by the priest, who beat the boys with a strap and threatened them if they ever chose to run away again.

The threats didn't work. Smith had endured enough and wanted to be with his family. After he was sent back to the boys' dormitory, he woke up his friend, Skinny Chipps, also a Klamath Indian, and said to him, "Skinny, I'm going home, do you want to go with me? And he woke up, we got dressed, snuck out of the building, and went across the road to the railroad tracks because we had to get off the highway." Smith and his friend walked along the tracks for several miles to Oregon City, where they waited for a Southern Pacific freight train to hitch a ride back to the Klamath Reservation. He knew the train would be coming in very slowly when it passed through Oregon City, but that it wouldn't be making a stop. Smith laughs, remembering, "I knew I could catch it easily, but Skinny—he wasn't too fast and I had to help him catch this train." They traveled on the train for one hundred miles until they got to Eugene, where they were discovered and unceremoniously kicked off. They later managed to sneak back on again and make it back to Klamath Falls. And so, he said, "We made our escape."

Their freedom was short-lived. After Al and Skinny returned home, Indian agents from the Bureau of Indian Affairs came to their homes and took them far away to a federal boarding school in Stewart, Nevada, to "get us an education," and no doubt make it less likely that they could run away again. It was an all-native school and was not affiliated with the Catholic Church. Smith recalls feeling a little more comfortable in that environment, although he disliked its distance from home. He spent several years at the Stewart Indian School, where he would excel in varsity sports, especially basketball. During his sophomore year the team made it to the state championships, where they placed second. It was a high point for Smith, but his troubles at school continued. By this time he was drinking alcohol and acting as a bad influence on his friends. "You know," he said, "Klamath Indians are kinda like troublemakers. They are always stepping out first. Let's do this, and let's do that. Come on, chickens."

By the time he was sixteen, Smith and some of his friends, Skinny Chipps, Lou Johnson, and Marvin Issacs, all Klamath Indians, and several friends from the Bettey tribe, which also resides on the Klamath Reservation, were drinking regularly, which led to numerous problems with the school authorities. Most notably, Smith recalls rounding up his friends to raid a nearby farmer's barn because he knew the owner had a stash of homemade wine. They found a huge barrel of wine, rolled it out into the countryside, and drank and camped out for the night. It was quite a sight, he remembers, "Out on the sagebrush you could see a number of little fires where we were all drinking homemade wine and spending the whole night having a good time."

After that episode Smith was kicked out of Stewart, Nevada, and sent back to Salem, Oregon, located three hundred miles north of the reservation, to attend Chemewa Indian School his junior year. Brushes with the school authorities became more frequent. He describes himself as "just a live wire . . . always drinking, sneaking into my girlfriend's room, things like that." One evening during the Christmas holiday after he had been drinking most of the day Smith tried to find the girls' dormitory to visit some friends. He miscalculated, however, and ended up in faculty housing. He disturbed one of the English teachers, "a cute little gal," and woke up the next morning to the police and the school superintendent. He was told to get dressed and get the hell out of there. "They loaded me up with another kid, took us out of Salem, and told us that if we ever showed up at the school again we would be arrested."

Smith returned to the Klamath Reservation for the remaining part of the winter and then struck out on his own in the spring. He considered going to college in Kansas, but ultimately wound up in Portland, Oregon. His drinking escalated, and within a short time he was a practicing alcoholic living on the streets in Skid Row, an area of Portland where the homeless converge. It was generally an unpleasant experience, but Smith was also relieved to be rid of the constant indoctrination of white culture and religion. In Portland he was independent, and although he was still quite a distance from his native home, at least he no longer had to endure the government's attempts to transform him into a person it would feel more comfortable with.

Smith lived on the streets for a couple of years before being drafted into the army in 1941. His troubles with the army began immediately. He found himself in the stockade because of his drinking during basic training, and then went AWOL after being granted a brief leave to return to the Klamath Reservation for the funeral of his sister Rosetta, who died from a ruptured appendix after being kicked in the stomach during a bar fight. The military police tracked him down in Reno and sent him to St. Louis, where he was jailed. He was later transferred to North Dakota and then to New York before being shipped over to Liverpool, England.

In Europe Smith's struggles with alcohol continued, and he found himself in military stockades in England and Ireland for a variety of mishaps that occurred when he was drunk. Throughout this time "there were bombings all the time, and the war was going on" but Smith was oblivious, living through the war in an alcohol-induced haze. After going AWOL once again in Northern Ireland, Smith was captured and exasperated army officials placed him in a sanitarium on the army base. However, as he had done so many times as a youth, he was able to escape from the mental health facility one afternoon. He fashioned a key out of his toothbrush, recruited a buddy, and found his way out. They stole some army fatigues off a clothesline and hitched a ride into town, where they had a drink to celebrate their good fortune. Smith would eventually be picked up again for being AWOL and drunk, and this time was sentenced to five years in Greystone Prison in southern England. At one point the army gave Smith the opportunity to reenlist rather than spend five years in prison. "And for a split second I thought, hey, I can get out of here, versus five years. But knowing me and my inability to stay sober—I didn't know the word, alcoholic—I just knew I couldn't make it without a drink, so I said, thanks, but no thanks." His decision didn't go over well with the officers, who thought he would jump at the chance. "The army wanted people to obey—like soldiers," he states, "so they got pissed off at me. They got angry. They slammed the door and said I could rot." To Smith, it was a choice of one form of incarceration over another; in his mind, hardly a choice at all.

Smith later received a dishonorable discharge for alcoholism and was sent back with a "whole boatload of prisoners" to a federal penitentiary in upstate New York. Reflecting on his experience in the army, he observes, "So I went back the same way I came over. I came over against my will, in a type of prison, and they shipped me back the same way." He spent about a year in prison before being released. "One day they called me in, gave me a black suit, brown army shoes, a tan shirt, ten dollars, and said adios." It was 1948, and Smith left New York to go to Chicago "to buy some new clothes, to get drunk, to get on the streets, to get laid, all that stuff." After three weeks he woke up in a flophouse with the shakes and a stained suit. In his pocket was a train ticket back to Oregon. He loaded himself on the train and took the northern route back to Portland.

In Portland, Smith would meet and marry his first wife, Dorleen, and have three children, Mark, Maureen, and Matthew. He occasionally worked odd jobs to support his family and continued his battle with alcohol abuse, periodically finding himself back on Skid Row. In the fall of 1950 Smith's frequent drinking binges finally took a toll on his health. He was temporarily working picking apples up in Hood River, a small agricultural community east of Portland, when he got into a car wreck while making a wine run in a heavy storm. The car was totaled, but he and his friends managed to salvage some of the wine and make it back to Hood River. They drank all evening, and Smith woke up the next morning coughing and spitting up blood.

Realizing Smith was ill, the orchard owner paid him for his apple picking and bought him a bus ticket back to Portland. Smith found his way to a Portland hospital, where he was diagnosed with severe internal injuries and tuberculosis. He was transferred to a TB hospital in Salem with extreme symptoms, and was in such poor health that for several weeks it was not clear whether he would outlive the disease. The doctors were unable to completely stop the internal hemorrhaging, and could not operate to collapse his lung because he was so badly battered from the accident. They had to use an alternative treatment, giving Smith massive doses of streptomycin several times a day to stop the bleeding. He later underwent two operations: one to remove three ribs and another to saw several ribs in half so the doctors could collapse his lung and refashion his rib cage.

Smith was in the hospital for over a year. For the first six months he was bedridden while he recovered from surgery. He was later moved to a dormitory where he was "fattened up." He recalls how the nurses would take him out into the sun each day for a few minutes to help him regain his strength. Smith was, as one might expect from his past history, less than a model patient. He frequently got into fights with the nurses because he wanted to stay outside, and he was eventually kicked out of the hospital "because I wasn't behaving." Smith would later fully recover from tuberculosis, but he still bears the aftereffects of the disease. He has a permanently collapsed lung and has lost his sense of balance and his night vision owing to the high doses of streptomycin.

In 1952 Smith returned to Portland to be with his family. He was sober for several years and it was a period of relative calm in his life. In 1954 Smith faced the difficult decision about whether he would vote to terminate the Klamath tribe's relationship with the federal government. The tribal government opposed termination and the Bureau of Indian Affairs also objected to the plan, but many Klamath Indians, unaware that they would lose their land, tribal sovereignty, and sense of cultural identity, voted to terminate. Smith had felt disconnected from the tribe for years. Like many Klamath Indians, he did not fully understand the implications of the agreement and he signed the forms to end the Klamath tribe's relationship with the federal government. The 1864 treaty between the Klamaths and the United States was abrogated, the Klamath tribal government was abolished, and the federal government was absolved of all responsibilities toward the Klamath people in exchange for a lump payment of $43,000. Like many of the Klamath people, Smith did not see the money for several years.

In 1956 Smith once again fell prey to alcohol and his unwillingness to obey the law. One evening when he was arrested for drinking in public and generally "misbehaving" he unwittingly created a situation that would lead him to the path to recovery. Before Smith was sentenced for his drinking offense he investigated the judge who would preside over his case, and discovered that the judge was involved in a number of community activities, including serving on the board of a halfway house. Smith suspected he might be open to an alternative sentence to jail time, and so when he appeared before him, he decided to play on his good nature. Always the schemer, Smith gave the judge the pitch that he thought would keep him out of jail. "I told him, 'Your honor, I finally found out what's wrong with me, I'm an alcoholic. I can't quit drinking. Every time I get sobered up, I find myself locked up in these jails, and I'm tired of being locked up.' I knew I was conning the judge, but I didn't want to be locked up again." He told the judge he had heard about Alcoholics Anonymous, and that he thought he should give it a try. The suggestion worked, as Smith hoped it would. The judge sentenced him to six months of Alcoholics Anonymous, and he stayed out of jail.

For the next several months Smith went to individual alcoholic counseling, and then to regular AA meetings where he learned the nature of the disease of alcoholism and the steps that would lead him to recovery. He stopped drinking and "became a sober, loudmouthed member of AA in those recovery meetings for six months. And I even gave them a seventh month."

Then Smith took a road trip to San Francisco and went on a drinking binge. He found some Klamath people at a bar and "met a gal that I wanted to make a move on. She was drinking and asked me to drink." He later found himself wandering alone in the streets and ended up in an alley sleeping between some cardboard boxes. The moment of truth came the morning after the binge when Smith realized he was shaking himself down to see if he had enough money for a jug run. "I remember telling myself, if you think you're sick now, just wait, because you will get sicker. I knew that if I didn't stop drinking now, I never would. So I said, that's enough of that. It was my last binge." He returned to Klamath Falls and sobered up with some friends who were working for the railroad. Smith later returned to AA and embraced sobriety. "I finished my last drink and my last drunk in 1957. I've been sober ever since."

———

In 1960 Smith entered a new phase of his life. He left his family and Oregon and moved to California and lived in an apartment on the Santa Monica pier. He worked several odd jobs, had a short-lived second marriage, another daughter, and learned to surf. Throughout this time he remained active in Alcoholics Anonymous and helped others struggling with alcohol and substance abuse. In 1967 he moved back to Portland and got a job at B. P. John's Furniture Refinishing. One day several leaders from the African American community approached Smith and asked if he could help them secure funding for an alcohol and drug rehabilitation center. Apparently, "they heard about Al Smith, and I had eleven years of sobriety at that point." He helped them complete the paperwork for a federal grant, and after the group received the funding, Smith was hired to help set up the treatment center and hire the other staff. Smith recommended his friend, John Spence, a fellow Native American, to direct the program. The Portland Alcohol and Drug Treatment Program quickly grew. The group approached the mayor, Neil Goldschmidt, for assistance. He allowed the group to set up rehabilitation centers in some vacant houses in the city, and they opened several drug and alcohol treatment facilities, including separate houses for women and American Indians. Spence successfully wrote grants, and Smith and the "gang" hit the streets to help people interested in sobriety. They were very proactive about helping individuals struggling with alcohol and substance abuse. The gang would follow up on requests for help, go to the drunk tanks in the jails, and visit Smith's "old stomping grounds" on Skid Row and other areas frequented by alcoholics and drug addicts. They even approached the police to ask for suggestions on how they could reach out to people in need of assistance. "We did great work, getting guys off the street and getting them help."

At one point representatives from the Bureau of Indian Affairs came to visit the Portland program, and in 1972 Smith was hired by the bureau to serve on the American Indian Commission on Drug and Alcohol Abuse and travel across the country and help develop Indian drug and alcohol treatment centers. He moved to Arvada, Colorado, and worked for the national program for two years, primarily going into reservations and urban settings to set up Native American alcohol and drug treatment centers.

Early into his employment on the American Indian Commission on Drug and Alcohol Abuse Smith experienced an event that would have a significant impact on his life. The director, Bob Moore, sent Smith and some of the other counselors to Wyoming for a week to visit a medicine man to "Indian educate us." Prior to this visit Smith had not made a serious attempt to explore his Indian roots. In Wyoming he attended his first sweat lodge ceremony. He recalls not being able to comprehend the prayers or songs that were part of the ceremony. "I had no understanding of what I was becoming involved in. But my spirit was so thankful to me for taking me to that ceremony." Smith and the others also participated in dozens of native ceremonies and learned about Indian culture. He spent most of this time with the medicine man leading the ceremonies, asking numerous questions and reconnecting with some of his traditions. Smith learned a great deal that week and left Wyoming wanting to learn more. "That was my introduction to a whole new spiritual path. It was a new perspective, a spiritual awakening."

On the drive back to Colorado, Smith recalls seeing an eagle perched on top of a telephone pole. Overcome, he pulled off of the road. He was fifty-three years old and had never seen an eagle before. He saw the vision as part of his purification, a symbol of his return to his Native American roots. "I thought to myself, all right, you are on the red road, Indian, the Native American road. Tunkashila (Lakota for "Great Spirit"). You are on your way back on the red road. Talk about a high." Once he returned to Colorado, Smith approached his job with newfound vigor. He continued traveling throughout the United States and Canada to help tribes develop alcohol and drug treatment programs, and was often invited to sweats and other native ceremonies where he continued his personal education.

Smith left the Bureau of Indian Affairs in the winter of 1976 to return to the Klamath basin. For eleven months he lived at a seventy-two-acre camp on the Williamson River owned by Edison Chiloquin, a Klamath Indian. Chiloquin was well known and respected by the Klamaths as the only tribal member who refused to give up his ancestral land and sign the termination agreement. The federal government sent him a check, but he never cashed it and embarked on a lengthy battle with the federal government to have his land formally returned. In 1985 he succeeded. The small plot is all that remains of the Klamath Indian Reservation. There were other Klamaths that initially refused to sign, but over the years bureaucratic snafus and mismanagement of the trust funds that controlled their original annuities persuaded them to relent and give up their rights to the land. Chiloquin held fast. He refused to give up his land and lit a sacred fire on his property that burned constantly to invite native people to the camp to visit and reconnect with their traditional roots. The camp was run by Max Baer, a Lakota Indian who was also a member of the American Indian Movement. Smith and the other visitors lived in earth lodges, swam in the river, and shared their experiences. Smith used the camp as an opportunity to continue his education about Indian traditions. He learned the Lakota language, Lakota songs, and Lakota sweats and prayers. The camp also provided participants the opportunity to face their addictions in a supportive environment, and Smith drew on his personal and professional experience with alcohol addiction to help others. "We were down in Klamath, my homeland, where other Klamath people were sobering up, attending the camp, singing the songs, going to sweat lodge ceremonies, and being with each other." Smith and others would also go into the city of Klamath Falls and help Klamaths being hassled by the city.

Smith left the camp in 1978 to work as a treatment counselor at Sweathouse Lodge, a Native American alcohol program in Foster, Oregon, a small town outside Corvallis. The lodge served an all-native clientele and Smith helped incorporate Native American treatment modalities as part of the counseling repertoire. The lodge hired a medicine man, Devere Eastman (also known as Brave Buffalo), a Lakota Indian who Smith first met after he sobered up in Portland. Eastman ran sweat lodge programs several times a week and taught other Indian cultural activities to the clientele. Smith continued to learn about native traditions, and was soon traveling with other Indians to locations across the state to teach others about the ceremonies. "It was a great learning time: Learning how to drum, learning how to sing, learning how to hold sweats. It was part of the education that I've been going through all my life. Getting educated and educating other people, coming into contact with a lot of people who know less than I do, and helping them."

One day one of Smith's friends at Sweathouse Lodge, Herb Powliss, a Paiute Indian who was involved in the American Indian Movement, invited Smith to attend a meeting of the Native American Church. Smith was intrigued by the church, but did not know much about it, and he and the others at Sweathouse Lodge had a difficult time deciding whether they should attend the religious ceremony, and if so, whether they should take the sacrament. They were unfamiliar with peyotism, and Smith was concerned the ritual might affect his sobriety. He brought these reservations to his friend, who told him, "It's a sacred ceremony you are going to." When Smith told Powliss that he had been told that peyote was a drug, his friend responded, "Well, it's not dope. It's a sacred sacrament. Our ancestors were praying with that medicine."

After much soul searching, Smith and the others decided to attend the meeting of the Native American Church. It was one of several Indian ceremonies held at the Makah Nation in Neah Bay on the Olympic peninsula in Washington State. Before the church meeting Smith repeated his concerns about peyote to the Roadman, Powliss's son, who would lead the ceremony. "I told him, 'I'm a recovering alcoholic. I don't want to be in relapse.'" He said, "You don't understand; this is not a drug. This is a sacred medicine used for centuries by native people to come in communication with the Creator in their prayers. It's for healing; it's for doctoring; it's a sacred medicine." Relieved, Smith attended the ceremony and ingested the sacrament. "I remember the ceremony, and how they fed us peyote. The Roadman mixed it with water, to make it soft, and it was mushy, and then force spooned it to all of us. One, two, three, four, everything in fours. We prayed, and sang songs. . . . Of course I threw up, because peyote is very bitter. I don't recall a lot of the experience, I recall only that I got sick. The night was long, and the medicine was strong. I didn't understand the songs, because they were not Lakota songs, so the first time was a difficult experience. The first time was not a spiritual experience for me. However, it was an awakening."

Most important to Smith was that he did not relapse into alcoholism. "I took the medicine—the communion, the sacrament, and I survived. I didn't have to go back and have a relapse. And again my spirit thanked me, that acknowledging the sacred ways of our people, of our ancestors, was good."

Smith returned to his work at Sweathouse Lodge and attended Native American Church meetings several times each year. Often, the Roadman at the ceremony was Stanley Smart, a Paiute-Shoshone Indian from Ft. McDermitt, Nevada. Smart had been a Native American Church member since his youth and was trained by his father, a Roadman who was trained by his father decades before. For the last thirty years Smart had traveled around the West conducting teepee ceremonies of the Native American Church, including ceremonies at the Sweathouse Lodge. The church ceremonies were a healing time for Smith. "I learned to handle the medicine, to only take a little, to take vegetables with it. I wanted to take enough to at least, in a good way, use the medicine." He also learned more about the church and the importance of the peyote ceremony. "I watched quite a bit. I was interested, and wanted to become a member. It is the same today. I still want to learn more about the church. Because I will never learn all there is to learn about the Native American Church."

Smith continued with his work at Sweathouse Lodge, which included traveling across the state introducing people to sweat lodge ceremonies and the incorporation of Native American culture into the treatment of substance and alcohol abuse. He met his future wife, Jane Farrell, on one of those trips at a powwow in Siletz, and a year later they were together. They later married and Smith left Sweathouse Lodge to travel with Farrell across the West before they returned to the Rogue Valley, near the Klamath Reservation. In 1982 their first child, Kaila Rose, was born. After the birth of his daughter, Smith knew he had to go back to work to support his family, and so he called some of his former associates in the drug and alcohol treatment field and told them he was looking for employment as a counselor. They told him of an opening at the Douglas County Council on Alcohol and Drug Abuse Prevention and Treatment (ADAPT) facility, a private, nonprofit alcoholism and drug treatment center located in Roseburg, Oregon.

———

ADAPT was founded in 1969 with few patients and a small staff. By 1983 it had grown in size to twenty-three staff members, with an annual budget of over $600,000. At the time Smith was looking for employment at ADAPT, the executive director was John Gardin, a specialist in substance abuse and family counseling and a doctoral candidate in clinical psychology at the University of Tennessee at Knoxville. When he was at ADAPT, Gardin was very active in professional boards and task forces in the field of addiction, and at one point served as president of the Alcoholism and Drug Addiction Program Directors Association of Oregon.

Bruce Piper, who began working at ADAPT as a clinical supervisor in 1983 and is currently the executive director, explained that since ADAPT began in 1969, it has taken the position that "the only responsible and prudent course of recovery for an alcoholic and/or addict is total abstinence." He describes the facility's treatment philosophy:

> It starts with the belief that is consistent with the American Medical Association, that alcoholism and drug addiction are a disease, and what that means, practically speaking, is that once somebody has crossed some kind of invisible biological and or psychological line, that their ability to go back and use any kind of mind altering substance is compromised in such a way that there is no predicting what will happen if they do that again. In fact, the only reasonable prediction is that they will use in some manner that will produce very deleterious consequences in their lives. Whether that be an occasional bender, or that every time they drink, they black out. . . . So once somebody has

crossed that line, the only reasonable choice for them and the only moral choice and ethical choice as a helping individual is to counsel abstinence. And to model abstinence.

From its onset, ADAPT was committed to hiring a mix of recovering and nonrecovering staff to offer a range of counseling treatments, including counseling from staff who had personally struggled with substance or alcohol abuse. Piper notes that many clients respond to people who have successfully struggled with the disease. It is particularly important, states Piper, that former drug or alcohol addicts model abstinence because they do not come to the job with a graduate degree in psychotherapy or social work. "Although most counselors have a repertoire of different counseling models to use," he stated, "the recovering person is limited to modeling recovery."

In the early 1980s, prior to hiring Smith, ADAPT evaluated how well the facility addressed the needs of the community. One thing it discovered was that there were significant alcohol and substance abuse problems in the Indian communities in southern Oregon. Native Americans were the largest minority group in Douglas County, and ADAPT was investigating alternative treatment modalities in anticipation of bringing these treatments to the facility to better serve this population. Part of this investigation included sending the staff out to learn more about the cultural mores and traditions of the native community to be better informed about American Indian culture. Piper describes an outpatient staff retreat to Charleston, a small town near the city of Coos Bay, where the staff took part in a Native American sweat lodge ceremony. "We all participated in the ceremony to experience it, and to expand our awareness of alternative treatments that some other people are doing to learn to work with folks that we may want to work with." After the ceremony, the executive staff spoke of the need to hire an Indian counselor familiar with alternative treatment modalities.

With twenty-five years of sobriety and his years at Sweathouse Lodge, Smith was an ideal candidate for the job. He had a personal history with alcohol addiction he could use to connect with

ADAPT clients to show that there is a way out of alcohol dependency, and he had experience with alternative treatment modalities that he could use to treat ADAPT's clientele. Smith was thrilled about the job and ADAPT was excited about hiring Smith.

Smith started working for ADAPT in August 1982. When he was hired, he signed a standard personnel policy that governed staff behavior. Under the category of "Personal Integrity" several policies addressed employee behavior and substance abuse. One section required all employees to "Refrain during all working hours and work-related hours from the use of any and all alcoholic beverages and/or other mind-altering substances unless prescribed by a physician. Work-related hours include preworking hours, lunch periods, and on-call time." Another section required employees to "Demonstrate exemplary behavior in order to enhance work with clients. This includes, invariably, the avoidance of all substance abuse." The personnel policy also gave the executive director the right to suspend with notice and to terminate, with counsel from the Personnel Committee, "any staff member who misuses alcoholic beverages and/or other mind-altering drugs." Although the policy referred to the *misuse* of alcohol or drugs rather than the *use* of alcohol or drugs, Piper mentions that given the center's treatment philosophy, it was "well understood" and "common knowledge within the agency" that any use of drugs and alcohol by a recovering addict is tantamount to abuse, and that this was verbally communicated to employees hired by ADAPT. The need for total abstinence among recovering counselors is so strong, Gardin would later observe, "that if a recovering alcoholic counselor working for ADAPT were to receive wine at communion, that would be grounds for termination."

When Smith began working for the facility, he was told by the executive staff that they would support him fully in his effort to reach out to American Indians in the area struggling with alcohol and substance abuse and to tailor his treatment approach to the special needs of the clientele. The staff accommodated his desire to set up a sweat lodge on property owned by another staff person located near the facility and actively encouraged clients to participate in the sweat lodge ceremonies and other native practices.

Smith was pleased he was given the opportunity to incorporate some of his native teaching methods from his previous work at Sweathouse Lodge. He encouraged patients to attend the ceremonies, and the lodges were open to all patients and personnel at ADAPT. Soon, Smith said, "the lodges were full." He received a lot of personal gratification from passing on what he had learned about his native culture to others and enjoyed teaching other staff members about Indian traditions.

One person drawn to the sweat lodge ceremonies and interested in exploring alternative treatment modalities was Galen Black, a non-Indian. Black started working for ADAPT in September 1982 as an intern, and was promoted to the position of drug and alcohol rehabilitation counselor in June 1983. Like Smith, he was in recovery for alcohol and drug addiction, although he had only been sober for a year and a half before working at the facility. Black became acquainted with Smith and learned about his treatment approach while transporting in-patients at the facility to the weekly sweat lodge ceremonies. He decided to participate in the sweats, initially because he wanted to better understand "his clients' spirituality." Black was intrigued with Smith's use of Indian cultural activities and sweat lodge ceremonies in the treatment of alcohol and substance abuse, and he reached out to Smith to learn more about his treatment approach. Black also investigated the subject on his own outside of work.

Eventually Smith would tell Black about his experiences with the Native American Church and the peyote ceremony. Black decided he would like to join the church, and for approximately six months before his departure from ADAPT, he regularly attended Native American Church ceremonies. However, he did not ingest peyote as a sacrament during this time. Like Smith, Black had concerns about whether peyote was considered a drug and whether it might jeopardize his sobriety.

In early September 1983 members of Sweathouse Lodge invited Smith to attend a teepee ceremony that was to be held the following Saturday, September 10, at the lodge grounds in Foster, Oregon. Smith told Black about the ceremony and Galen asked if he could join him. He also had a conversation with Smith about whether the use of peyote might affect his sobriety. Smith told Black about his own reservations several years earlier and how he also struggled with the decision, but told Black that each individual must make his or her own decision to take the sacrament.

Smith and Black decided to go to the ceremony in Foster. However, at the last minute, Smith fell ill and was unable to attend. Black then went to the ceremony on his own. At the ceremony he ingested a small amount of peyote as a sacrament, but not enough to cause any hallucinogenic effect. Although Black understood his employer had a rule proscribing the misuse and abuse of alcohol and or other mind-altering substances because he signed the policy when he was hired by ADAPT, like Smith, he did not understand his ingestion of the communion to constitute "abuse or misuse of drugs."

After several ADAPT staff members discovered that Black ingested peyote at the religious ceremony, he was confronted by Gardin, the executive director. Black admitted that he ingested the sacrament and was reprimanded for "displaying poor judgment." Gardin told him he would be subject to appropriate disciplinary action. Several days later Black was placed on indefinite mandatory sick leave and was told that he would have to undergo an evaluation by a social worker to determine if his use of peyote should be considered a relapse into drug use.

After his discussion with Black, Gardin called Smith into his office to ask him about the Native American Church and the peyote ceremony. Smith recalls, "They started asking me these questions: what is the Native American Church, what is the philosophy of the Church? They asked me all these questions, and I shared with them, the best that I could, my interpretation of what I believed the Church was all about." Gardin also asked Smith if he had ingested peyote while he was an employee at the facility; Smith said that he had not. The executive director used the opportunity to warn Smith that use of peyote was considered misuse and abuse of a mind-altering substance under ADAPT's personnel policy and that he would be discharged from his job if he used the sacrament, even if it was part of a religious ceremony.

On October 3, the social worker who evaluated Black reported that he considered Black's use of peyote to be a relapse into substance abuse, and advised that he undergo treatment for drug and alcohol abuse or intensive personal counseling. Gardin then informed Black that to remain employed at ADAPT he would have to receive treatment for his relapse at a residential treatment center in a nearby city and undergo counseling. Black refused treatment, contending that his use of peyote was part of his religious freedom and should not be considered the "misuse or abuse of substances." He was then discharged from his job for engaging in misconduct under the personnel policy.

Later that day ADAPT's board of directors met to specifically discuss Black's dismissal and the appropriateness of the company policy regarding use of drugs and alcohol by recovering addicts. The board agreed that the existing policy was inadequate, and that it would be necessary to formulate additional rules that specifically addressed this issue.

———

Upon his termination from ADAPT, Black went to the state of Oregon's Employment Division for the Department of Human Resources in Roseburg and filed an application for unemployment benefits. His petition was reviewed by a representative for the Employment Division, who investigated his dismissal from ADAPT. On November 4, 1983, Black received a letter denying his application for unemployment benefits. The representative concluded that Black was terminated from his job for violating ADAPT's known company policy regarding professional integrity, and was thus appropriately discharged for misconduct connected with work. Black's actions were characterized as a "willful violation of the standards of behavior which an employer has the right to expect of an employee." The decision was based, in part, on Oregon Revised Statute 657.176, which provides "An individual shall be disqualified from the receipt of benefits if the authorized representative designated by the assistant director finds that the individual . . . has been discharged for misconduct connected with work." An administrative rule, OAR 471-30-038 defines misconduct as "An act that amounts to a willful disregard of an employer's interest, or recurring negligence which demonstrates wrongful intent." Although the rule provides exceptions for "isolated instances of poor judgment, good faith errors, unavoidable accidents, absences due to illness or other physical or mental disabilities, or mere inefficiency resulting from lack of job skills or experience," Black's actions were not classified under these exceptions.

Black next filed a request for a formal hearing to review the denial of benefits, which was held on December 5. An independent referee, Robert Gruber, presided over the hearing attended by Black, representing himself, and John Gardin, representing ADAPT. At the hearing Gruber reviewed Black's employment history and personal struggle with drug and alcohol abuse, ADAPT's policy regarding the use of drugs and alcohol by recovering employees, and the appropriateness of the Employment Division's denial of unemployment benefits. Part of the hearing addressed Black's reasons for ingesting peyote at the church ceremony, which he characterized as a "personal decision."

On the same day as the hearing, nearly two months after Black was discharged from his job for using peyote, ADAPT issued a memorandum to all employees "clarifying" the agency policy regarding the use of alcohol and drugs by ADAPT employees. The memorandum stated:

> In keeping with our drug-free philosophy of treatment, and our belief in the disease concept of alcoholism, and the associated complex issues involved in both alcoholism and drug addiction, we require the following of our employees:
> 1. Use of an illegal drug or use of prescription drugs in a non-prescribed manner is grounds for immediate termination from employment.

Gardin insisted that the memorandum was not a new rule regarding the use of drugs and alcohol, because this policy was communicated orally to every employee upon hire, but rather served as a reminder about the company's standards for professional conduct. However, it was the first time ADAPT's policy regarding the use, rather than misuse of drugs, was placed in writing, and it was obviously written in response to ADAPT's concerns about Black's actions.

Several days after the hearing Gruber entered his decision on the appropriateness of the Employment Division's denial of Black's unemployment benefits. He disagreed with the original claims officer's assessment that Black was correctly discharged for misconduct under Oregon law. Rather, he believed Black's behavior should fall under the exceptions to the administrative rule as an "isolated instance of poor judgment." Although Gruber agreed that Black's use of peyote was "a cause for great concern by the employer," he did not describe it as misconduct as defined in the administrative rule. As a result, he reversed the administrative decision disqualifying Black under ORS 657.176 (2)(a), and ruled that Black was entitled to unemployment compensation benefits.

ADAPT filed an application for review to the Employment Appeals Board (EAB) on December 20, 1983. Before it handed down its ruling, the board received legal advice on the merits of Black's request for unemployment compensation from the Oregon attorney general's office. Because the attorney general is the legal adviser for every state agency, officer, and employee, it was appropriate that the office provide a reading on the case. A representative from the office gave the EAB the same advice that the Employment Division's general counsel already provided: That Black was fired for misconduct and was therefore not eligible for unemployment benefits under Oregon law. The attorney general for the state, Dave Frohnmayer, saw this as a simple case of employee misconduct: "He made a deal with ADAPT. The deal was, you don't use substances. You may not agree with the treatment philosophy, but ADAPT could not have been clearer. That this was an abstinence program. A deal is a deal. You knew it when you signed up. You signed up for this, and now you want to get paid money when you get fired when you don't follow the policy. . . .

It looks as though this would be rewarding behavior that would be unlawful. That is criminally unlawful to everyone else."

On January 27, 1984, in a decision joined by Jerry E. Butler and Glenn E. Randall, the chairman of the EAB, Ross Morgan, reversed the referee's decision. The board determined that Black was aware of ADAPT's rules and policies that specify that employees avoid substance abuse, that Black knew peyote was an illegal substance and an optional part of the Native American Church ceremony, and that despite this, he made a decision to ingest the substance in violation of the employer's rules. The board concluded that Black willfully disregarded ADAPT's interests, that his termination for violation of ADAPT's rules was appropriate, and that he should therefore be denied unemployment benefits. The EAB refused to consider Black's actions as an "isolated case of poor judgment," noting that, "considering the seriousness of the claimant conduct in violating the employer's rules we find the exculpatory provisions of the Rule cannot come into play."

Black received a certified copy of the EAB decision in the mail on February 3, 1984. The decision also notified Black that its decision was subject to judicial review if he filed a petition with the Oregon Court of Appeals within thirty days of the date the decision had been mailed. Galen Black knew it was time to get legal assistance. He was unemployed, he had no savings, and no immediate source of income. He made an appointment to visit the Roseburg office of Oregon Legal Services (OLS).

CHAPTER 3

Religion and the Supreme Court

There are two main religion clauses in the federal Constitution, both in the First Amendment: the establishment clause, which prohibits laws "respecting an establishment of religion," and the free exercise clause, which forbids laws "prohibiting the free exercise thereof." Simply stated, the religion clauses protect our freedom to worship from governmental interference. The Supreme Court's religion jurisprudence is far from simplistic, however. The two clauses appear to be separate but they actually overlap, and there is often tension between the two, although each works to protect religious freedom. The Supreme Court has not attempted to formally reconcile the two clauses, and as a result, although some religion cases involve both establishment and free exercise issues, the Court's First Amendment religion jurisprudence has developed along two separate tracks. It also developed slowly; most of its religious freedom decisions were handed down in the last seventy years.

The fact that the Court's jurisprudence advanced along two separate tracks complicates rather than clarifies the Court's interpretation of the religion clauses of the First Amendment. This is because the Court has left unanswered questions such as whether a strict interpretation of the establishment clause calling for separation between church and state would mean that any accommodation of religion to allow free exercise would also violate the establishment clause. However, until the Court formally reconciles the two clauses or attempts to lay out strict guidelines to guide its jurisprudence in a manner that addresses this tension, as some have suggested, then the Court's jurisprudence is best described separately because it developed on a case-by-case basis.

When the Oregon State Employment Division's Employment Appeals Board decided that Galen Black was appropriately denied unemployment compensation for engaging in misconduct, the agency's actions potentially violated Black's constitutional right to freely exercise his religion. One interpretation of the facts was that Black willfully violated the Alcohol and Drug Abuse Prevention and Treatment center's personnel rules prohibiting the "abuse or misuse of drugs" and that he was appropriately fired for misconduct, which justified the state's denial of unemployment compensation under Oregon state law. A contrary interpretation, however, was that Black's use of the sacrament was in accordance with his sincere religious beliefs—an exercise of his religion—and that he was unconstitutionally denied unemployment benefits by the state. Because the First Amendment protects the right to freely exercise one's religion against government interference, the courts would have to determine whether the state's denial of benefits violated the Constitution. A review of the U.S. Supreme Court's free exercise jurisprudence would provide guidance in this matter.

The Supreme Court has decided relatively few free exercise cases over the last one hundred years. Moreover, in many of these cases it specifically avoided articulating the meaning of the free exercise clause, choosing instead to protect religious conduct within the context of the other First Amendment guarantees. The Supreme Court initially decided a trio of cases at the end of the nineteenth century that removed any possibility that the free exercise clause would be used to defend the exercise of religion, and then avoided any significant developments in its jurisprudence for several decades. Then, beginning in the late 1930s, several justices on the Court endorsed the doctrine that some constitutional freedoms, particularly the free speech, press, and assembly guarantees under the First Amendment, were "preferred freedoms" deserving of special protection by the Court because of their importance to a democratic society. In order to properly protect these freedoms, a majority of the Court applied the "compelling government interest test" to evaluate the consti-

{ *Religious Freedom and Indian Rights* }

tutionality of government regulations that interfered with preferred freedoms. Under this test, the interests of the state are balanced against the interests of an individual, and the state has the burden of proving that the government regulation fulfills a compelling government interest that is achieved in a manner least restrictive to constitutional rights. In the context of religious liberty challenges, what the preferred freedom doctrine meant was that cases that also implicated freedom of expression would be protected at a high level of scrutiny.

In 1961 the Warren Court handed down a decision that suggested that religious exercise might also be deserving of a higher level of protection under the First Amendment. Although the religious challenger lost, the decision laid the foundation for a ruling two years later when the Court declared that the exercise of religion was also a preferred freedom, and that challenges to government action that burdened religion should be subject to the same high level of protection granted to other First Amendment guarantees. The Court announced that religious challenges to laws that directly burdened religious exercise, or indirectly burdened religious exercise through the application of neutral, generally applicable laws, should also be subject to the compelling government interest test. If government was unable to prove that it had a compelling interest in the law, achieved in the least restrictive manner, then the religious challenger should be provided an exemption to that law. The Burger Court then applied this high level of scrutiny to free exercise challenges that came before it for the next two decades. Although only a handful of cases were decided and the free exercise claimants did not always prevail, the Supreme Court was consistent in its evaluation of free exercise cases.

————

The Court's earliest attempt to define the meaning of the free exercise clause occurred in 1878 in *Reynolds v. United States*. The appellant, a Mormon, was convicted of violating a federal antipolygamy statute. He defended his behavior as necessary according to the tenets of his faith, and argued that he should be exempt from the statute because his conduct was constitutionally protected under the free exercise clause of the First Amendment. A unanimous Supreme Court rejected this interpretation. It introduced the "belief-action distinction," reasoning that although the free exercise clause absolutely protected religious beliefs, it did not protect religious conduct. The Court agreed with the state's contention that the practice of polygamy was a danger to societal norms, and that an exemption to the law in this instance "would be to make the professed doctrines of religious belief superior to the law of the land, and in effect to permit every citizen to become a law unto himself. Government could exist only in name under such circumstances." The belief-action distinction was reaffirmed in two later cases involving the practice of polygamy and members of the Mormon Church. In each case the Court rejected the notion that the free exercise clause required religiously inspired exemptions to general laws, and refused to use the First Amendment to defend behavior it considered criminal. The result of the Mormon polygamy decisions was the rule that religious conduct was placed completely outside of the protection of the First Amendment, removing any possibility that the free exercise clause might be used to defend the "exercise" of religion.

Because this belief-action distinction precluded any successful conduct-based religious challenges under the First Amendment's free exercise clause, religious claimants eventually looked to other constitutional guarantees to safeguard religious activity. In a series of cases decided between late 1930 and 1960, the Supreme Court considered constitutional challenges to state and local laws that also affected religiously motivated behavior. The cases raised a number of First Amendment concerns, including whether the contested regulation violated the free exercise of religion clause, and in most instances the Court found protection for religiously motivated behavior in the free speech, press, and assembly guarantees of the First Amendment.

For instance, in two early cases, *Lovell v. Griffin* (1938) and *Schneider v. New Jersey* (1939) the Court considered the constitutionality of antihandbill distribution ordinances that required prior approval from city officials. The laws were challenged by

48

members of a small religious sect, the Jehovah's Witnesses, a group known for its vigorous proselytizing activities. The Witnesses argued that the regulations violated their right to free speech, press, and religious exercise under the First Amendment. In each case the Court determined that the city ordinances violated the free speech and press guarantees of the First Amendment. Although both cases involved claimants who stated that they were acting according to the tenets of their religion, the religious orientation of the appellants was of little significance to the Court. The decisions foreshadowed the Court's reliance on the speech and press clauses of the First Amendment to protect religious conduct. This was because the Court's focus was on the constitutionality of the statute, rather than the nature of the expressive activity. The cases were handled well within the context of free expression, making an independent examination under the free exercise clause unnecessary.

The free exercise clause of the First Amendment did merit separate attention by the Supreme Court in 1940 in *Cantwell v. Connecticut*. The case involved the arrest of several Witnesses convicted under a state law prohibiting door-to-door solicitation and for disseminating religious literature without first obtaining a license from a city official. In the majority opinion, the Court stated for the first time in its history that some religiously motivated actions were constitutionally protected. Although it recognized that the state may in a general and nondiscriminatory way regulate the times, places, and manner of solicitation on its streets, it also clearly stated that the government could do so only in a manner that was protective of religious liberty. In *Cantwell*, the Court evaluated the state law using a modified "clear and present danger" test. It determined that the ordinance, although neutral on its face, was not narrowly drawn because it allowed a public official considerable discretion in the distribution of licenses, and therefore ruled that it unduly infringed on the religious practices of the Witnesses because the state could have used less drastic and intrusive methods while also protecting religious liberty.

Cantwell was a significant development; the Court's use of heightened scrutiny to evaluate the ordinance foreshadowed the compelling government interest test the Court would later adopt in free exercise cases. The Court also used this opportunity to expressly extend the free exercise protections of the First Amendment to the states under the due process clause of the Fourteenth Amendment. However, a review of the Court's reasoning reveals that it closely resembles free speech analysis—the ordinance was declared unconstitutional because it gave the state the opportunity to exercise prior restraint—so the Court did not endorse an affirmative right to religious conduct.

For over two decades after *Cantwell*, the Court evaluated the constitutionality of a number of state and municipal restrictions on religiously motivated practices. The cases were appealed to the Court in two different forms, either, as in *Lovell* and *Schneider*, a free exercise challenge combined with claims to freedom of speech, press, or assembly under the First Amendment, or solely on the grounds that the contested regulation violated the free exercise clause. Interestingly, the manner in which the case was appealed to the Court had a direct effect on how the Supreme Court framed the First Amendment issue in each case and the outcome of the decision: Cases involving multiple First Amendment guarantees were successful, and those appealed only under the free exercise clause were unsuccessful.

In the several cases involving appeals under several First Amendment guarantees, the Court invalidated a number of neutral, generally applicable statutes, including prohibitions on the distribution of handbills with commercial advertisements (*Jamison v. Texas* [1943] and *Largent v. Texas* [1943]); door-to-door proselytizing (*Martin v. City of Struthers* [1943]; *Murdock v. Pennsylvania* [1943] and *Follett v. Town of McCormick* [1944]); solicitation without a license (*Marsh v. Alabama* [1948]); the use of sound amplification devices without permission (*Saia v. New York* [1948]); and a requirement that individuals obtain permission from city officials before holding meetings in a public park (*Kunz v. New York* [1951] and *Niemotko v. Maryland* [1951]). In some of these cases, the Court concluded that the government regulation violated each one of the contested First Amendment clauses. In others, it would focus on one particular clause. Often, the Court relied on *Lovell* and *Schneider*, where it avoided any consideration of the free exercise clause, as controlling precedent to support the Court's decision to protect the religiously motivated conduct under the broad umbrella of the First Amendment. A review of the Court's reasoning illustrates that the decisions rested heavily on free speech or free press considerations, and in none of the cases did the Court authorize religion-based exemptions to the laws. The success of the appellants was also owing to the fact that the contested regulations were usually overly broad and prohibited most forms of communication, including those that were the result of an individual's religious beliefs.

Although the Court's consideration of these cases as free expression may have contributed to the success of the religious challenges, there was one major disadvantage with the Court's strategy: It made it tremendously difficult to assess which First Amendment clause controlled the decision or determine the independent meaning of the free exercise clause. This was further complicated by the Court's somewhat haphazard approach to this category of cases. It often chose not to classify these as free exercise decisions, but rather as speech, press, and assembly decisions that only incidentally concerned religious practices. Occasionally, the Court completely ignored any mention of the free exercise clause, even if the religious claimant appealed the case on religious grounds.

In contrast to the success of religious challenges to time, place, and manner restrictions on freedom of speech that also incidentally hindered religious practices, in the cases appealed and decided by the Supreme Court exclusively on free exercise grounds, the religious challenge was unsuccessful. The appeal was either dismissed for want of a substantial federal question or the religious claimant failed in his challenge to the government's regulation. If one includes the Mormon polygamy decisions, not a single free exercise appeal was successful. The Court declared that a free exercise challenge to a statute forbidding snake handling (*Bunn v. North Carolina* [1949]), a zoning ordinance barring the erection of a church and a parochial school in a residential area (*Corporation of Presiding Bishops v. Porterville* [1950]), a compulsory Sunday closing law (*Friedman v. New York* [1951]), and a denial of unemployment compensation benefits to a Sabbatarian who refused to work on Saturdays (*Heisler v. Board of Review* [1952]) did not present a substantial federal question. One similarity among these free exercise cases was that they each involved activity motivated by an individual's religious beliefs that was not communicative in nature. Because the Court chose not to hear these cases, it avoided articulating what types of religious conduct were protected by the free exercise clause independent of the other First Amendment guarantees.

In cases where the Court did render a decision on the basis of a free exercise appeal, the free exercise claimant lost. For instance, in *Prince v. Massachusetts* (1944) the Court upheld the conviction of a Jehovah's Witness who allowed her niece to distribute religious literature in violation of a Massachusetts child labor law that proscribed the sale of merchandise by minors on the streets, and made it unlawful for any person to furnish material to minors to sell, or for parents and guardians to permit minors to work in violation of the law. In a series of three cases in the late 1920s and early 1930s involving conscientious objectors who requested a free exercise exemption to mandatory naturalization pledges and military science classes, the Court ruled against the claimants on statutory grounds, ignoring the objector's free exercise challenge (*United States v. Schwimmer* [1929], *United States v. Macintosh* [1931], *and Hamilton v. Regents* [1934]).

The best illustration of how the Supreme Court's protection of religious conduct differed depending on whether a free exercise claim was argued alone or in conjunction with other First Amendment guarantees is a comparison of the Court's decisions in two cases involving religious challenges to compulsory flag salute statutes, *Minersville School District v. Gobitis* (1940) and *West Virginia State Board of Education v. Barnette* (1943). This comparison reveals how in the absence of a well-developed free exercise jurisprudence, the Court was unsympathetic to a lone free exercise appeal in *Gobitis*, whereas three years later in *Barnette* the Court found protection for religiously motivated conduct in the free speech clause of the First Amendment.

In *Gobitis*, where the respondents challenged the law as a violation of the free exercise clause, Justice Felix Frankfurter, joined by seven other justices, ruled that because the regulation was neutral and not directed toward the students' religious beliefs, it did not violate the First Amendment. Frankfurter, who strongly opposed special treatment for religious exercise, established that the free exercise clause did not require the state to provide exemptions to general legislation passed for secular reasons. If the law was reasonable, Frankfurter concluded, it outweighed the religious challenge. However, three years and three new justices later, Justice Robert Jackson and five other members of the Court framed the case more broadly to include freedom of conscience, and determined that one's conscientious objection to the flag salute implicated the free speech clause of the First Amendment, a preferred freedom that required greater protection by the judiciary, irrespective of the individual's religious motivation. By limiting the relevancy of religion, the Court distinguished *Barnette* from *Gobitis* and classified the former as a free speech case, where it was appropriate to use the compelling government interest test to assess the constitutionality of the law.

As this review of cases illustrates, during the sixty years of the Supreme Court's free exercise jurisprudence, the definition and application of the free exercise clause as a protector of religious conduct had not progressed a great deal since *Reynolds*. If the religious activity was communicative in nature, however, the Court used the free speech, press, and assembly guarantees of the First Amendment to justify a higher level of judicial scrutiny and invalidate laws that restricted religious practices.

The Court did not directly address its free exercise jurisprudence until 1961 when it considered three cases involving constitutional challenges to "blue" or Sunday closing laws. The free exercise argument was best articulated in *Braunfeld v. Brown*, where a group of Orthodox Jewish merchants challenged a Pennsylvania criminal statute that forbade the sale of certain commodities on Sunday. The merchants, whose religious beliefs required that they not conduct business from sundown Friday to sundown Saturday, alleged that the law infringed the free exercise of their religion because it caused them substantial economic hardship and placed them at a severe competitive disadvantage because it effectively forced them to choose between their religious beliefs and complying with the law in order to stay in business.

Chief Justice Earl Warren wrote the plurality opinion. He agreed that the law placed an indirect burden on the appellants' ability to freely practice their religion, but that it was a consequence of the religious adherent's choice, rather than the action of the state. His inquiry did not end with this assessment, however. He noted, "To hold unassailable all legislation regulating conduct which imposes solely an indirect burden on the observation of religion would be a gross oversimplification." To evaluate whether such a burden was constitutionally permissible, Warren stated, the Court must balance the interests of the state against the requested exemption to the general law. "If state regulates conduct by enacting a general law within its power, the purpose and effect of which is to advance the state's secular goals, the statute is valid despite its indirect burden on religious observance unless the state may accomplish its purpose by means which do not impose such a burden." Using this test, Warren determined that the state's interest in providing a day of rest from labor was justifiable, and that an exemption to the law would result in enforcement problems. He also added that an exemption could potentially violate the establishment clause because it might give some merchants an economic advantage over competitors, and the state might have to conduct inquiries into the sincerity of some claims for exemptions to eliminate false religious claims for individuals wishing to circumvent the law.

Although the religious claimants lost in *Braunfeld*, it was a significant evolution in the Court's jurisprudence. The Court determined, following a line of reasoning that began in *Cantwell*, that religious conduct was protected under the First Amendment's free exercise clause, even if the conduct was only indirectly burdened by a government regulation. The Court also attempted to fashion a standard to evaluate free exercise challenges to neutral, generally applicable laws. Warren suggested that the Court consider the nature of the government's interest in passing the regulation and determine whether that interest might be fulfilled in other, less restrictive manners, as well as whether the government might still achieve this interest if it granted an exemption to the neutral, generally applicable law.

The decision is also important because of the strongly worded dissent by Justice William Brennan, which was a precursor to the next stage in free exercise jurisprudence. He argued that religious exercise was a preferred freedom and that the Court should therefore use the same high level of scrutiny used in free speech cases—the compelling government interest test—to evaluate laws that burdened one's religion. Using this standard, he suggested that the state interest in a day of rest was not significant enough to justify a substantial, although indirect burden on the appellant's religious freedom, and that the Jewish merchants should be granted an exemption to the law.

Two years after Brennan called for a higher level of protection for religious liberty in his dissenting opinion in *Braunfeld v. Brown*, the Supreme Court entered a new phase in its free exercise jurisprudence. This change was tied to the development of a constitutional standard promulgated in the 1963 decision, *Sherbert v. Verner*. The decision completely reformulated free exercise doctrine, because for the first time a majority on the Court declared that the free exercise of religion was a preferred freedom, subject to the highest level of judicial scrutiny, regardless of whether the violation of that liberty was the result of a direct or indirect government action. In *Sherbert* the Court introduced the "*Sherbert* standard"—a multitiered, progressive test similar to strict scrutiny analysis—to the evaluation of free exercise challenges. Under this standard, if the state was unable to prove that the regulations served a compelling state interest, achieved in the least restrictive manner, the religious adherent should be granted an exemption to the law.

Sherbert involved a free exercise challenge to a denial of unemployment compensation benefits. The appellant, a member of the Seventh-Day Adventist Church, was fired from her job because she refused to work on Saturdays, the Sabbath of her faith. She was later denied unemployment compensation benefits because her refusal to work on Saturdays violated the state's Unemployment Compensation Act requiring claimants to be "able" and "available" for work. The state defended the law as necessary because of the difficulty of finding people to work on weekends, and because it had an interest in preventing fraudulent claims for unemployment compensation benefits.

In the majority opinion for the Court, Brennan introduced the new balancing test. At the first tier, he explained that it was necessary for the Court to evaluate the situation to determine whether the state action placed a burden on the religious claimant's ability to freely exercise her religion. Once a burden was established, at the second tier the Court must determine whether the uniform application of the regulation served a compelling government interest, achieved in the least restrictive manner. At the third tier, the Court would consider if an exemption to the law would undermine this compelling interest. If the state was unable to prove that its interest was affected by the exemption, the Court would rule that the individual was entitled to a religiously based exemption to the law.

Using this standard, Brennan determined that the South Carolina law forced Sherbert to choose between exercising her religious rights and forfeiting unemployment benefits, or abandoning her beliefs in order to accept work. Because this choice punished Sherbert for her religion, he explained, the law implicated the free exercise clause. He then concluded that the state interest justifying the law was not sufficiently compelling to warrant such a burden on Sherbert's religion, and that the state's concerns could be realized in a manner more protective of First Amendment rights. He therefore ruled that Sherbert was entitled to an exemption to the statute because the state could not prove that it would adversely affect its interest. Brennan added that this did not necessarily implicate the establishment clause because the Court was merely equalizing the treatment of Saturday observers with those who were not penalized by the unemployment act. This decision, he stated, "reflects nothing more than the governmental obligation of neutrality in the face of religious difference, and does not represent that involvement of religious with secular institutions which it is the object of the Establishment Clause to forestall."

For the first time in its history, the Court expressly applied a higher level of scrutiny to a neutral statute that indirectly burdened an individual's religious values. The rule of law after *Sherbert* was that if a government action oppresses, even unintentionally, a sincerely held religious belief or practice, the state had the burden of proving that the regulation fulfilled a compelling state interest, achieved in the least restrictive manner, and that granting an exemption to the law would undermine this interest. If it was unable to do so, the state was constitutionally compelled to grant the religious claimant an exemption.

The next time the multitiered *Sherbert* standard was formally used was in *Wisconsin v. Yoder* (1972) a decision handed down almost a decade later at the beginning of the Burger Court. This heightened level of scrutiny was then applied to all of the free exercise challenges that came before this Supreme Court. At times the Court determined that the state was constitutionally compelled to provide a religiously inspired exemption to a neutral, generally applicable law that had the incidental effect of burdening an individual's free exercise of religion. At other times it did not. Although the application of this level of scrutiny led to a variety of results, the Burger Court was consistent in its use of the *Sherbert* standard in free exercise challenges.

There were three decisions where the Burger Court ruled in favor of the free exercise claimant. In *Yoder*, the Court invalidated a state's refusal to exempt Amish students from a neutral, generally applicable criminal law that required children from the age of seven through sixteen to be enrolled in school during regular school hours. Chief Justice Warren Burger, who wrote the majority opinion, reiterated Brennan's earlier argument in *Sherbert* that the Court focus primarily on the effect of the generally applicable law on the religious adherents, rather than tacit acceptance of the governmental action because the state had not directly infringed on the free exercise rights of the Amish. He noted, "A regulation neutral on its face may, in its application, nonetheless offend the constitutional requirement for government neutrality if it unduly burdens the free exercise of religion." Burger determined that the Wisconsin law "would gravely endanger if not destroy the free exercise of respondents' religious beliefs," and concluded that the state interest in the law, educating children and citizenship, was not sufficiently compelling to justify the infringement on their free exercise rights, and that this interest would not be undermined by granting the Amish respondents an exemption to the law.

Next in *McDaniel v. Paty* (1978) a unanimous Court ruled that a state law that prohibited members of the clergy from being elected to the state legislature or from serving as a candidate in a state constitutional convention violated the First Amendment. There were several decisions of the Court, and Burger's plurality decision applied the *Sherbert* standard to evaluate the constitutionality of the law. He concluded that the law placed a burden on the challenger's religious exercise and that the state's interest, avoiding potential establishment clause violations, was not compelling enough to outweigh this burden.

The third example concerned a fact situation similar to *Sherbert*. In another decision by Burger, *Thomas v. Review Board of the Indiana Employment Security Division* (1981), the Court ruled that the denial of unemployment benefits to a Jehovah's Witness who quit his job at a munitions factory because he believed he could not engage in the production of materials that would be used to create weapons placed a substantial burden on the appellant because it forced him to choose between fidelity to his religious beliefs or unemployment compensation. Burger was unpersuaded by the state's concerns about fraudulent claims and its desire to avoid investigating the veracity of an individual's religious beliefs. The chief justice noted that less restrictive alternatives were available to serve these interests of the state. According to Burger, an exemption to the law would allow the state to treat Thomas's claim in a neutral fashion, because his access to unemployment benefits would thereupon be equal to individuals with other religious beliefs. His decision was joined by seven other members of the Court. The lone dissent was provided by Justice William Rehnquist, who announced that the free exercise clause did not protect individuals from the application of neutral, generally applicable laws. "Where, as here, a State has enacted a general statute the purpose and effect of which is to advance the State's secular goals, the Free Exercise Clause does not in my view require the state to conform that statute to the dictates of the religious conscience of any group." Rehnquist suggested that the Court overturn *Sherbert* and *Thomas*, noting, "We cannot afford the luxury of deeming preemptively invalid, as applied to the religious objector, every regulation of conduct that does not protect an 'interest' of the highest order."

Application of the compelling government interest test did not necessarily mean that religious adherents always prevailed. In several other cases decided during the Burger Court years, the free exercise challengers lost their request for an exemption. Although the Court applied the *Sherbert* standard, the state was able to prove that a religiously inspired exemption would undermine its compelling interest in the uniform application of the government regulation, and the request for an exemption would be denied. The loss of a free exercise challenge is not surprising; application of a higher standard of scrutiny does not guarantee that an individual will win his or her challenge to the government regulation. One possible explanation can be found in the Court's less than stringent adherence to the strict requirements warranted by the compelling state interest test. The Court either interpreted the government interest very broadly, or it chose not to consider whether the state used the least restrictive means to achieve this interest. At the same time, the Court appeared to give little attention to the legitimacy of the government action or the necessity of the government action in light of the law's effect on an individual's request for an exemption. The result of this change was that it was easier for the state to fulfill its burden of proof that it had a compelling interest in the law.

These changes to the second and third tiers of the standard were introduced in four cases where it was fairly easy for the government to prove that it had a compelling interest. In *Gillette v. U.S.* (1971) the Court ruled that the government's interest in maintaining a fair and efficient manner of raising armies was compelling enough to deny a conscientious objector's request for an exemption. In *U.S. v. Lee* (1982) a unanimous Court denied an exemption request by an Amish farmer and carpenter who refused to withhold Social Security taxes from his employees' paychecks or pay the employer's share of Social Security taxes on quarterly tax returns. The Court concluded that the fiscal vitality of the Social Security system was a compelling interest, and that religious exemptions could lead to numerous claims that would ultimately undermine the integrity of the Social Security fund. In a similar case, *Tony and Susan Alamo Foundation v. Secretary of Labor* (1985) a unanimous Court rejected a nonprofit religious foundation's challenge to the requirements of the Fair Labor Standards Act, which the foundation believed infringed upon their employees' right to exercise their religion. The Court determined that there was no constitutionally recognizable burden on their free exercise rights, and therefore dismissed the request for an exemption. In the fourth case, *Bob Jones University v. United States* (1983) the Court upheld the IRS's denial of tax-exempt status to a religious college engaged in racial discrimination. In his majority opinion, Chief Justice Burger found the government had "a fundamental and overriding interest in eradicating racial discrimination" that outweighed the burden on the petitioners' exercise of their religious beliefs.

Although this brief review reveals that some free exercise challenges were unsuccessful, it is important to note that up to and including its 1985 term, the Burger Court consistently applied the *Sherbert* compelling government interest test announced over two decades earlier. Moreover, in each free exercise decision, the Court cited *Sherbert* and *Yoder* as controlling precedent. What this would mean for anyone considering a First Amendment free exercise challenge to the state of Oregon's denial of Black's unemployment compensation was that if this denial of benefits placed a substantial burden on his ability to exercise his religion, the state must justify its decision by proving its actions served a compelling government interest, achieved in the least restrictive manner, and that an exemption to that decision would jeopardize this compelling interest. Moreover, the precedent cases of *Sher-*

bert and *Thomas*—which also concerned the denial of unemployment compensation benefits to individuals whose conduct under the statute allowed the denial of benefits—would be instructive.

———

Galen Black's case also potentially raised an issue under the establishment clause of the First Amendment. The state of Oregon could argue, for instance, that to award Black unemployment compensation when it would deny benefits in other instances involving similar situations would constitute preferential treatment toward members of the Native American Church. Therefore, to maintain neutrality in the application of the law, the state might contend that it was necessary to deny compensation to Black to avoid violating the constitutional prohibition against the establishment of religion. This issue would also be considered in the courts when it reviewed the state's denial of unemployment compensation in Black's case. As with a potential free exercise challenge, an establishment clause challenge would require a review of the Supreme Court's interpretation of the meaning of the establishment clause under the Constitution, and an assessment of its jurisprudence.

Over the years, the Court's interpretation of the establishment clause of the First Amendment has been guided by at least three distinct approaches to the meaning of the clause, each of which is rooted in differing perspectives regarding the intent of the framers of the First Amendment: the concept of strict separation, the accommodationist or nonpreferential approach, and lying somewhere in the middle, the concept of neutrality. Separationists believe that the establishment clause mandates strict separation between church and state, or an impregnable "wall" as described by Jefferson in his letter to the Danbury Baptist Association, and Madison's Memorial and Remonstrance Against Religious Assessments. Under this theory, government and religion should operate in separate spheres and not influence one another. Strict separationists believe that most forms of government assistance would constitute a violation. For instance, a time-release program in which a religious instructor comes on the premises of a public school to provide religious training would be struck down as violating the establishment clause.

On the other hand, accommodationists believe that although there should be a degree of separation between church and state, there can be some government involvement in religion as long as it does not benefit one religion over another. For example, government actions that incidentally benefit religion or a religious organization are permissible. Adherents to this theory point to intersections of religion and government at the Founding, such as the declaration of the Thanksgiving Day proclamations, as an example of the framers' intent to allow some accommodation of religion. An example of the accommodationist principle would be to allow students to be released from school to obtain religious instruction off the school premises. Neutrality is best described as a compromise between these two interpretations. Advocates suggest that government cannot directly benefit or impose a burden on religious exercise, but rather must remain neutral.

In the mid-1940s, at the beginning of its establishment clause jurisprudence, a majority of the Supreme Court endorsed the concept of separation, in theory if not in result. However, during the Warren and Burger Court years, at various times a majority of the Court endorsed the theory of neutrality or accommodation, and as a result, the Court's establishment clause jurisprudence developed in an ad-hoc, confusing fashion.

———

One of the few areas of agreement found among judicial scholars and Supreme Court justices is that the establishment clause forbids a state-sponsored religion or church, and prohibits government from preferring one denomination over another. Beyond these issues, few agree on what constitutes an establishment clause violation of the Constitution. The Court's decisions have been described as "unprincipled," "confusing," and "illogical." Over the years the Court has attempted to establish clear standards to guide its jurisprudence, but this has largely been unsuccessful and the Court has failed to provide a "bright line" to help determine results. However, there are some general themes running throughout the establishment clause decisions of the War-ren and Burger Courts. Overall, these decisions illustrate the Court's struggle to clearly articulate the meaning of the estab-lishment clause and the extent to which it will allow government and religion to overlap without violating the Constitution's anti-establishment principle.

The Court's first major establishment clause decision, *Everson v. Board of Education* (1947), addressed whether public funding for bus transportation to parochial schools violated the First Amend-ment. The decision is notable for several reasons. First, the Court used this opportunity to incorporate the establishment clause to the states under the due process clause of the Fourteenth Amend-ment. Second, the majority decision by Justice Hugo Black in-cluded a thorough review of the framers' intent behind the establishment clause, which the Court failed to do in its examina-tion of the free exercise clause. Borrowing the phrase from Jeffer-son, Black announced the need for a "wall of separation between Church and State." Notably, his interpretation of the meaning of the clause was endorsed by the entire Court. And third, the ma-jority decision illustrated that even this clearly articulated vision of the establishment clause can result in differing conclusions re-garding whether government action violates the Constitution. Black, joined by four members of the Court, concluded that this form of government aid did not breach the wall of separation, thus permitting use of state tax dollars to reimburse parents for transportation costs incurred transporting their children to reli-gious schools, whereas four justices in dissent believed it did. As Justice Jackson wrote in his dissent, "the undertones of the opin-ion, advocating complete and uncompromising separation of Church and State, seem utterly discordant with its conclusion yielding support to their commingling in education matters." He went on to liken it to Byron's Julia, who "whispering 'I will ne'er consent'—consented." The Court's future establishment clause cases would continue to result in opinions that were seemingly at odds with one another, as justices belonging to either the separa-tionist, accommodationist, or neutralist camps interpreted the es-tablishment clause in diametrically opposed fashions.

The Supreme Court eventually did craft some guidelines to help guide its decision making in establishment clause cases. First, in *Abington School District v. Schempp* (1963) the Warren Court announced a two-part test to evaluate the constitutionality of the state law at issue; the government action must have a secular legislative purpose, and its principal or primary effect must neither advance nor inhibit religion. *Schempp* concerned the constitutionality of mandatory Bible readings, which the Court struck down as a violation of the second part of this test, finding that the "primary effect" of Bible readings was to advance religion. Later, during Burger's tenure as chief justice, the Court would add a third criterion to its evaluation of whether government action violated the establishment clause; that it not foster excessive government entanglement with religion. Then, in *Lemon v. Kurtzman* (1971), which concerned the constitutionality of salary supplements for the teaching of secular subjects in parochial schools, the Court formally announced a tripartite test incorporating the three criteria to strike down state aid. The "*Lemon* test" as it is known, was then used in future establishment clause cases. The test gave the appearance of a principled approach to establishment clause cases, but it has yielded less than consistent results, and the "wall of separation" metaphor first articulated in *Everson* has broken down over the years as the Court's doctrine has evolved.

However, the Supreme Court was fairly consistent in its rulings regarding nondenominational school prayers and readings. In 1962 it determined that a state-composed prayer violated the establishment clause [*Engel v. Vitale*] and one year later handed down *Schempp*. More recently, the Court ruled that a voluntary moment of silence violated the establishment clause in *Wallace v. Jaffree* (1985). A majority of the Court also invalidated an anti-evolution statute and a state law forbidding the teaching of evolution unless accompanied by the teaching of "creation science" in *Epperson v. Arkansas* (1968), although it has allowed the study of the Bible as part of a secular educational program.

The Burger Court's establishment clause decisions involving challenges to government financial support for religious institutions, especially parochial schools, on the other hand, has led to widely divergent results, reflecting the indeterminacy of the *Lemon* test. Some themes have emerged from this line of cases, however; aid that is given directly to students and parents to promote the education of children is usually upheld as constitutional, whereas aid given directly to the schools has been found to violate the establishment clause. For instance, the Court allowed state-funded services such as standardized objective tests, diagnostic services, and outside counseling in *Meek v. Pittenger* (1975) and *Wolman v. Walter* (1977) and taxpayer deductions for school tuition and expenses to schools, including parochial schools, in *Muller v. Allen* (1983). On the other hand, cases involving a direct payment of aid or materials to a religious institution were usually found to constitute state sponsorship of religion, violating the establishment clause. For instance, the Burger Court ruled that states may not reimburse the salaries of teachers and supplemental material for the teaching of secular subjects in *Lemon v. Kurtzman;* provide state tax relief only for children in parochial schools in *Committee for Public Ed. v. Nyquist* (1973); or use public school teachers in parochial schools, in *Grand Rapids School District v. Ball* and *Aguilar v. Felton* (1985).

Despite these two general themes, there are decisions that are difficult to reconcile, such as *Wolman*, which allowed the use of public funds for textbooks, testing, and remedial services, yet disallowed instructional material purchases and field trip transportation, and *Pittenger,* where the Court upheld the loaning of textbooks to students but struck down the loan of other types of instructional material such as maps, audio and video equipment, and "auxiliary services" such as counseling on school premises. The Court's explanation of these mixed results was that it only invalidated funding for material or services that could potentially be used for sectarian purposes because it was concerned teachers might use the aid to invoke religion in their instruction, thereby violating the establishment clause. To some observers, however, the difference between permissible and impermissible commingling of government and education was minimal.

Another theme running through the Burger Court's establishment clause decisions was its willingness to be much more lenient in cases involving aid to college students, who are considered "less impressionable and less susceptible to religious indoctrination." The Court decided several cases that allowed the accommodation of religion in college funding, such as *Tilton v. Richardson* (1971), where it upheld a federal grant for the construction of college buildings used for secular purposes in sectarian institutions, and *Hunt v. McNair* (1973), which validated the use of bond revenue for similar construction. Other cases include *Widmar v. Vincent* (1981), where the Court ruled that use of facilities by student groups, including religious groups, did not violate the establishment clause because of the "equal access" principle, which requires that religious and nonreligious groups be treated equally.

Outside the parochiaid cases, the Burger Court applied the *Lemon* test to establishment clause challenges to the tax-exempt status of religious institutions and to religious symbols and displays on government property. In most instances, the Court allowed the accommodation of religion. For instance, in *Walz v. Tax Commission* (1970), a majority ruled that property tax exemptions to religious institutions did not violate establishment clause because it concluded that entanglement problems would be worse without the exemption. And, in *Lynch v. Donnelly* (1984), the Court determined that a nativity scene combined with symbols of the Christmas season in a shopping district withstood constitutional scrutiny because of the context of the display. On occasion it failed to invoke the *Lemon* test altogether, however, such as its ruling in *Marsh v. Chambers* (1983) when it determined that a state's practice of opening its legislative session with a prayer did not violate the establishment clause because the tradition extended back to the Founding, and because the First Congress also began its session with a prayer, a practice that continues today.

By 1985, different majorities on the Burger Court had endorsed either the neutralist or accommodationist position in the evaluation of establishment clause cases. In most of the decisions during Burger's tenure, the Court applied the *Lemon* test to evaluate situations where government and religion came together in a manner that implicated the establishment clause. However, as noted earlier, the results were less than consistent, leading to frustration not only for members of the Court, but also for judicial scholars attempting to understand the Court's establishment clause jurisprudence.

At the very least, however, the Court's line of establishment clause decisions did raise the potential that the state of Oregon's denial of unemployment compensation to Galen Black was done to avoid preferential treatment for adherents of the Native American Church.

CHAPTER 4

"Thou Shalt Not Ration Justice"

Galen Black walked into the Roseburg Oregon Legal Services office shortly after the Employment Appeals Board made its decision denying his request for unemployment compensation. He introduced himself to David Morrison, the lead attorney, and told Morrison his story. Black had little idea where this road would lead him, but he did firmly believe he was wrongfully terminated from his job for exercising his religion, and that the state unfairly denied him benefits. "What I recall," said Morrison, "was that he was desperate for someone to help him. He was a very typical legal aid client, a low-income guy who was getting stepped on by someone who was bigger, more powerful, and wealthier than he was."

Morrison did not immediately take the case. He told Black that he needed to think about it, and that he would get back to him. Legal aid lawyers usually turn away more people than they can help because the demand for free legal assistance is always greater than the supply. Morrison observed, "As a legal aid lawyer, you are always trying to figure out how you can leverage limited resources to provide maximum service to the largest number of people." It is a problem that has plagued legal aid for the poor since the turn of the century, when legal assistance was offered by local charitable organizations. Today, assistance is provided through a federally funded program with a limited budget. Judge Learned Hand once noted, "Thou shalt not ration justice," but this is exactly what lawyers for the Legal Services Corporation must do each day.

The Legal Services Corporation was created in 1974 as a private, nonprofit organization authorized to receive and distribute federal funds to local legal aid clinics and national support centers to provide legal services for the poor. The corporation's mission statement declares its intent to "serve best the ends of justice and assist in improving opportunities for low-income persons." It was previously organized as the Legal Services Program, created as part of Lyndon Johnson's War on Poverty from 1965 to 1974, when its primary goal was to focus on the legal causes of poverty and the use of litigation as a means to change the system in ways that would benefit the poor. Since its creation, LSC has grown in budget and number of clients served; however, funding is limited, and only a fraction of the poor receive legal assistance. Legal services field offices are governed by a local board of directors comprised of attorneys, community members, and representatives for the poor, which sets the priorities for the office and helps determine the allocation of resources. Each office has a degree of latitude in the selection of clients, which is often difficult because of inadequate resources.

David Morrison, the lead attorney for the Roseburg legal aid office, recalls the moment Galen Black approached him about his situation at the Douglas County Alcohol and Drug Abuse and Prevention Treatment program. Black's case presented what appeared to be a very straightforward, yet important legal question about protection for religious liberty in America. It also was a typical situation where "the little guy was getting squashed by the big guy," which really interested Morrison. One of the reasons he went to work for legal services in the first place was because he was raised in a politically active household in which one of the strongest values imparted to him was a strong belief in social justice and what one could do to achieve it. "And that," he states, "was a gift that was given to me."

Morrison's early exposure to politics led him to the University of California, Santa Cruz, where he earned a degree in American History. He decided to pursue legal studies after reading an article about how the law could be a good vehicle for people who are interested in social change. "My interest in the law came from a very political perspective, because of my background as a student in the antiwar Vietnam era. My goal was to obtain the tools and the credentials of a lawyer and to use those and to try and address social problems—and it sounds corny—social injustices." Morrison graduated from Antioch School of Law in Washington, D.C., and was hired as general counsel at California's newly established Department of Housing to help bring affordable housing to the poor. After several years he moved to Roseburg, Oregon, a small town of approximately fifteen thousand located in Douglas County, to help open its first legal aid office. Like most legal aid field offices in rural communities, it was small, with two lawyers, a paralegal assistant, a receptionist, and a significant number of poor in need of assistance. Morrison states,

> What we saw in Roseburg was a community in which various existing interests had had a free run on exploiting the poorer members of the community, and so we basically felt like we came in and we cleaned up the town. We sued landlords, we sued used car dealers, we sued debt collectors. All of them had never, ever been challenged before in the way they were treating people. And you just wouldn't believe some of the stuff that was going on.

Morrison discovered that one of the greatest advantages of working for legal services was the degree of freedom it provided him as an attorney. "Just having had the opportunity to do that kind of work and to be able to choose cases free of my own economic concerns gave me more freedom than I will ever have as a private businessperson. And, it was that freedom that allowed me to take first Galen Black's case, and then Al Smith's case."

Morrison's first step was to petition the Oregon Court of Appeals for judicial review of the Employment Appeals Board's denial of unemployment compensation to Black. The Oregon Court of Appeals, an intermediate appellate court, is considered a "case deciding" rather than "lawmaking" court, and primarily corrects errors in the application of principles of law in cases that are appealed from state district or circuit courts and from judicial review of orders from administrative agencies. Morrison filed the petition on March 2, 1984, naming Raymond P. Thorne, the assistant director of the Department of Human Resources, and ADAPT as the respondents in the case. Morrison then planned his legal strategy. At the same time, events were taking place at ADAPT that would change the dynamics of the case.

———

In another area of Roseburg, Al Smith was facing a difficult decision about whether he should continue his participation with the Native American Church. He knew the peyote ritual played a central role in the tenets of the church and that he had a right to practice his faith, but he was mindful of ADAPT's actions against Galen Black, and was concerned his attendance at church ceremonies would jeopardize his employment as well. Smith's meeting with Gardin after Black was fired, when he was specifically warned that any use of peyote would be grounds for termination, was in the forefront of his mind. There was also ADAPT's recent Policy Statement on Alcohol and Other Drug Use by Employees instituted on December 5, 1984, which clarified that any use of substances in a nonprescribed manner would be grounds for termination. Smith was painfully aware, based on Black's experience, that his supervisors would not consider exempting his religious use of the sacrament from this policy.

Smith was torn. He benefited from the spiritual guidance he received from practicing his faith. He knew his past use of peyote had not jeopardized his sobriety, and in fact believed the opposite—that his church attendance helped him maintain his sobriety. Smith had a strong desire to continue with the church and to include the peyote ceremony as part of his worship. It was also a difficult time for him because members of the local church were trying to persuade him to continue practicing his religion, including use of the sacrament. Some members of the local branch, and Stanley Smart, the Roadman who presided over the ceremonies, believed Smith's use of the sacrament might result in a successful challenge to the constitutionality of the state law proscribing peyote possession. In the only state court case that addressed this issue, *Oregon v. Soto* (1975), the trial judge did not allow the American Indian defendant to offer any evidence regarding his religious motivation for possessing the sacrament, leaving the possibility of a judicially created exemption to the state law unresolved. Smart argued that a religious defense would give the state court the opportunity to carve out such an exemption for church members, who would then be able to freely practice their religion without fear of arrest and prosecution.

Smith would not allow anyone to pressure him into a decision; it was his to make, and it came down to a choice between going to church and losing his job or giving up his religion so he could provide for his family. The prospect of unemployment weighed heavily in Smith's mind. He thought to himself, "I have to work. I have a wife and a baby at home." He discussed the situation with his wife, Jane. She recalls the conversation.

> He was in a dilemma because he had already been threatened that if he went to the ceremony he would most likely get fired. Al knew up front he would probably lose his job. It was really difficult for him because it was a matter of principle. Do I not go to this ceremony because my boss threatened me with losing my job, to maintain a salary to take care of a family and a young baby, or do I stand on principle? In its presentation it became a moral ethical decision.

Smith still hadn't made up his mind about whether he would attend the church ceremony when he went to work on Friday, March 2, 1984. That day he received what he thought was a sign that he should go ahead with his religious activities, including the peyote ceremony. Someone had placed twelve eagle feathers in a manila package in his mailbox at work. The eagle is a sacred symbol to American Indians. It is considered "a messenger to the spirit world" that allows the "living to communicate with their creator." Eagle feathers signify power and are also a sign of blessing. To Al Smith, the eagle feathers represented the answer to his dilemma. Although there was no indication of who sent the feathers and they were not accompanied by a note, in his heart Smith knew the eagle feathers were sent as a message that he should go to the Native American Church ceremony and take the sacrament as part of his worship. (Ironically, years later Smith learned the story behind the eagle feathers that were left at his work. They were never intended for him, but had been left in his mailbox to give to another person. However, Smith still feels the feathers were a sign that he pursue his interest in the Native American Church and ingest the sacrament. "I believe to this day that it happened for a reason.")

After Smith received the eagle feathers, he informed his employers at ADAPT that he "needed to go to church" as an exercise of his religious freedom. ADAPT's executive director, John Gardin, responded that he was free to attend the meeting, "but that if he did ingest peyote during the ceremony he would be expected to resign or be terminated immediately." Smith recalls that Gardin also tried to convince him that taking the communion was a mistake. "They told me, don't ingest any peyote, because it was a drug. That it would jeopardize my sobriety. I told them on Friday, I would see them when I got back. I told them I was going to the teepee ceremony after I received the eagle feathers."

———

Smith attended the ceremony the next day and returned to work on Monday. He informed Gardin that he had taken the sacrament as part of his worship. The executive director then asked Smith if he wished to resign from his job. Smith declined, and insisted that he had not done anything wrong by attending church. Gardin next offered Smith the option of participating in the Employee Assistance Program to address his substance abuse, but Smith responded that the assistance program was unnecessary because he had not suffered a relapse. He did not, he said, "need rehabilitation for going to church." Smith was then terminated from his job. Gardin wrote him a letter informing him that he had engaged in employee misconduct by ingesting an illegal drug in violation of company policy.

After he received notice that he was fired from his job, Smith sought advice from friends about what he should do. He knew it would be difficult to prevail before the Employment Appeals Board, which turned down Black's request for unemployment compensation. He also needed outside assistance because he was not in a financial position to fight the state of Oregon in court. Smith initially contacted the Native American Rights Fund (NARF) for advice on how he should proceed with his case against ADAPT for wrongful termination, and against the state of Oregon if his request for unemployment benefits was denied. But Smith was unable to get assistance from NARF. He was told that NARF primarily represents Indian tribes rather than individuals and that it only took cases of "national significance." Nor did NARF offer any real advice to him. He was also unable to get any support or even acknowledgment from the national organizations of the Native American Church, which did not recognize the loosely organized Oregon church group. Smith found it difficult to be turned down by these Indian rights organizations. Although the legal process was just beginning, Smith was already weary. "I needed some help. I was tired, exhausted, trying to get some help with the case." He finally received guidance from the Eugene chapter of the American Civil Liberties Union, which had been in contact with Galen Black after his dismissal from ADAPT. Dave Fidanque, the executive director, offered Smith moral and advisory support, and assured Smith the ACLU would remain involved in the case as it went through the state courts. He recommended that Smith seek assistance from David Morrison at the Roseburg legal aid office to help him through the series of administrative appeals that lay ahead and hopefully avoid a lengthy court battle. Smith called the Roseburg legal aid office to set up an appointment.

———

Morrison was immediately impressed with Smith and his obvious dedication to his religious faith, and was stunned that ADAPT had not made an exception for Smith, especially given his long-term sobriety and past safe use of peyote. Morrison also knew the case's significance went far beyond Smith's personal circumstances. He believed it provided a good opportunity for a discus-

{ *Religious Freedom and Indian Rights* }

sion about Indian religious freedom and clarification on the legality of peyote use by members of the Native American Church in Oregon. "I think it was a gut, instinctual feeling. It just didn't feel right that this guy could be denied his unemployment benefits for participating in a religious ceremony. The attitude that the employer had was so rigid and so categorical. One of the things I have found in my career, is that if I sense that there is a conflict or a dispute where one side is just really being a jerk, it makes it easier to take the case."

The legal aid lawyer was familiar with the circumstances of Smith's termination and ADAPT's personnel policy because of his work on Black's petition to the Oregon Court of Appeals. He knew the first step would be to persuade the board to award Smith unemployment benefits. Because Black had gone through the administrative appeals process without legal counsel, a religious liberty argument had not been clearly presented to the Employment Appeals Board. Morrison believed he could persuade the board that a denial of unemployment compensation to Smith would violate the First Amendment to the Constitution.

With Morrison at his side, Smith duplicated Black's efforts to procure unemployment compensation from the state of Oregon. He initially filed a petition for compensation, which was denied on March 22, 1984, and several days later filed a request for a formal hearing to review the denial of benefits. On June 6, 1984, the hearing was held before Robert Gruber, the independent referee who previously presided over Black's hearing. Morrison accompanied Smith, and John Gardin represented ADAPT. Although Eldon Caley, a Roseburg attorney, had been hired to represent ADAPT in Black's request for judicial review of the board's decision in his case before the state Court of Appeals, this time Gardin appeared alone to defend ADAPT.

There were two significant differences between Black's hearing and Smith's hearing before the independent referee. First, because Smith had been a member of the Native American Church for approximately five years, he was more familiar with the tenets of the religion and was better able to articulate the philosophy behind the peyote ceremony and his own reasons for taking the sacrament. Second, Morrison had the skill and outside resources to present a vigorous defense of Smith. He was assisted by individuals from the Native American Program at Oregon Legal Services (NAPOLS), a nonprofit organization that provides legal services to low-income Indian people and tribes in Oregon. NAPOLS provided Morrison scholarly data on the Native American Church and the importance of the peyote ceremony in the treatment of substance abuse problems.

Smith's hearing followed a format similar to Black's hearing. Gardin began with an explanation of ADAPT's treatment philosophy and personnel policies regarding substance abuse. He repeated the information first presented in Black's hearing; that the treatment center follows a strict abstinence policy in accordance with its treatment philosophy, and that this information is conveyed both in writing and verbally to employees upon hire. Gardin also testified that staff members who are in recovery must act as role models for clients, and that they had a duty to respect ADAPT's rules, particularly rules that mandate abstinence from alcohol or controlled substances. Smith's termination was appropriate, Gardin stated, because he specifically warned Smith he would lose his job if he ingested peyote. Morrison remembers that he was very surprised with Gardin's position regarding Smith's use of the sacrament. "What I recall is that same rigid, unbending categorical refusal to make any exceptions to this rule. And the irony here was that ADAPT was encouraging exploration of treatment modalities? I always felt that their position was internally inconsistent and not intellectually honest."

In his appearance before the referee, Smith defended his long-term membership in the Native American Church and his decision to ingest the sacrament. He also responded to Gardin's assessment that he had abused drugs. He told the referee that he was sincerely practicing the central ritual of his church, and that he did not consider this ancient form of worship to be drug abuse. Smith also added that he did not violate the personnel policy that was in place when he was hired because the treatment center had changed its policy after the situation with Galen Black, from a prohibition of the *abuse and misuse* of drugs and alcohol by recovering employees, to the *use* of drugs and alcohol by recovering employees.

Morrison ended the hearing with a comprehensive First Amendment argument about why Smith's decision to practice his faith was protected by the federal Constitution. He argued that the state's denial of unemployment benefits burdened Smith's free exercise of religion, and that this violated the First Amendment to the Constitution because, using the balancing test announced in prior Supreme Court decisions in *Sherbert v. Verner* and *Thomas v. Review Board*, the state did not have a compelling interest that justified the denial of benefits. The legal aid lawyer argued that the circumstances in Smith's case closely paralleled the situation in these previous Supreme Court decisions, which were resolved in favor of the claimant. He also included into the record the affidavits supplied by NAPOLS that supported the position that Smith's use of peyote was not a relapse into substance or alcohol abuse, and that the peyote ritual was an essential part of the religious ceremonies of the Native American Church. Affidavits were presented by Terrence T. Gorski, a drug and alcohol relapse specialist; Robert Bergman and Omer Stewart, two scholars familiar with the importance of the peyote ritual to members of the Native American Church; Emmerson Jackson, president of the Native American Church of North America; and Stanley Smart, the Roadman who conducted Smith's peyote ceremony.

Gorski, who had extensive experience in clinical training for alcoholism and drug abuse counselors, stated that the use of peyote in a religious ceremony of the Native American Church was analogous to the use of wine in the Catholic ceremony, and that if used infrequently in a religious context toward spiritual ends and if the user did not obsess for peyote between ceremonies or suffer adverse life consequences, that use of the sacrament did not constitute a relapse into abuse. Bergman, an associate professor of psychiatry at the University of Washington, who was employed at the Indian Health Service in Arizona and New Mexico for ten years and was chief of Mental Health Programs for the Indian Health Service nationally from 1969 to 1975, testified about the safety of sacramental peyote use. He remarked that he had "treated hundreds, perhaps over a thousand persons who were members of the Native American Church," and that the peyote ceremony was "the single most effective manner of treatment for Indian alcoholism and other drug abuse." Bergman conceded that the peyote ceremony may not be the best treatment for everyone, but he believed that it was the best treatment for Native Americans, and that "thousands of Indian people have gained control of a drinking problem through the Native American Church." He also stated that if church members were prohibited from practicing their religion or the use of peyote, "that denial would itself threaten the individual's sobriety."

The other affidavits addressed the history of peyote use by members of the Native American Church. Stewart, an anthropology professor at the University of Colorado and the leading scholar on the peyote religion, who had previously testified in the *Arizona v. Attakai* and *People v. Woody* state court cases as well as other disputes involving the Native American Church, described peyote as "essential" to the church ceremony. "It assists the participants in maintaining a feeling of well-being throughout the ceremony and in gaining spiritual fulfillment." Stewart shared Bergman's conclusion that peyote was useful in the treatment of alcoholism. "I believe it is fair to say that nothing has been shown to be as effective in combating the negative effects of alcoholism as the use of peyote in an Indian religious ceremony." Reverend Jackson agreed, stating that one of the fundamental purposes of the church was to promote the morality and sobriety of its members. Smart, who had known Smith for several years, testified to the sincerity of Smith's religious beliefs and the importance of peyote to the practice of the religion and the treatment of substance abuse. "Without peyote, there could be no religious aspect to the ceremony . . . [it] has beneficial effects on recovered or recovering alcoholics, by providing spiritual strength to help with their problem. In addition to the religious and health benefits of the teepee ceremony, a major result is to encourage participants to avoid the use of alcohol in their daily lives."

ADAPT presented affidavits from specialists that countered

the expert advice offered on Smith's behalf. Joseph R. Steiner and John L. Desmet, both active in the treatment of drug and alcohol abuse, testified that peyote use constituted a relapse for people in recovery, and John Gardin presented evidence that described ADAPT's justification for the strict company policy.

Steiner, a certified alcoholism counselor and president of his consulting service that provides supervision, consultation, and training for treatment programs in Oregon, disagreed with Gorski on the issues of relapse and safe use of peyote. He concluded that peyote increases the likelihood of an episode of drinking or renewed use of drugs, and cautioned that the use of any substance, even for religious purposes, "must be strictly avoided, as costs may be far too high." The affidavit offered by Desmet, director of the Alcohol Dependence Treatment Program at the Veterans' Administration Medical Center in Roseburg, who had trained "thousands" of individuals on the subject of denial, shared Steiner's conclusion that any use of drugs constituted a greater risk of relapse. Desmet also characterized Smith's use of the sacrament as unsafe, and theorized that it was possible that Smith had suffered a relapse from using peyote because he purposely placed himself in a position that harmed the treatment center, thus creating an occupational hazard, and he harmed himself by the loss of his job.

> A counselor who offers himself as a role model and yet who knowingly places himself in a position which increases his likelihood for relapse certainly impairs his credibility significantly with his clientele and in my opinion is no longer an asset to an organization. . . . I believe equally that an employer has a reasonable right to hire the paraprofessional, recovering staff member who will support the goals of the agency, which are not only abstinence, but taking all reasonable and prudent measures necessary to reduce the chance of relapse, not increase the chance for relapse.

Gardin's affidavit included documentation of ADAPT's treatment philosophy, which since 1969 has been that the "only course of recovery for an alcoholic and/or addict is total abstinence," and emphasized that counselors must model abstinence because they serve as role models, and it would be "counterproductive within this field to preach total abstinence as the most prudent and responsible course of recovery, and then have a counselor on staff who is unwilling to abide by that principle."

Morrison and Smith left the hearing believing they presented a solid case. The legal aid lawyer thought his First Amendment argument was consistent with Supreme Court precedent, and that Smith persuasively defended his religious faith. When asked about his personal reaction to Smith's testimony, Morrison responded, "I will answer that by telling you that his testimony at the unemployment hearing in this little tiny closetlike room in the back of the state employment office on Pine Street in Roseburg was one of the most moving experiences I've ever had. And I know at that point why I am taking this case."

––––––

After the hearing, Morrison believed Smith might prevail, but he also knew it was likely, based on the results of Black's case, that the EAB could also deny Smith's request for unemployment compensation, which would begin a lengthy battle in the Oregon courts. In light of this possibility Morrison suggested that Smith pursue an alternative strategy—a federal discrimination case against ADAPT for terminating him from his job for exercising his religion. Smith agreed. In his mind there was little doubt that ADAPT forced him to choose between his right to worship and his job. He chose his religion, and lost his job. He set up a meeting with a representative from the Equal Employment Opportunity Commission (EEOC) to see if he had a legitimate case under Title VII of the Civil Rights Act of 1964.

The Civil Rights Act of 1964, the most comprehensive civil rights measure enacted since Reconstruction and one of Lyndon Baines Johnson's greatest achievements as president, provides statutory protection for civil rights and liberties. The law broadly protects equal access of all Americans to public facilities, prohibits job discrimination, and authorizes Congress and the federal courts with appropriate remedies to order compliance with the law, including the authority to withhold federal funds if necessary. More specifically, Title VII of the act prohibits employers from discriminating on the basis of race, color, religion, sex, or national origin in the hiring, classification, training, or promotion of employees. The act also created the Equal Employment Opportunity Commission, an executive branch agency, to investigate complaints of discrimination and to seek compliance with the law. Several years later the EEOC was given the authority to use federal courts to enforce the act, and the courts were authorized to use any appropriate remedies to order employers to compensate employees who have suffered discrimination. Significantly, in Title VII cases, when an individual charges that he or she has suffered discrimination, the burden of proving nondiscrimination falls on the employer. This makes it easier to prevail under this legislative remedy than when making a constitutional challenge. When one initiates a case contending that he or she has suffered discrimination in violation of the equal protection clause of the Fourteenth Amendment, the burden shifts, and the employee must prove that the employer intentionally discriminated. Thus, the Civil Rights Act of 1964 actually provides greater protection against job discrimination than the Constitution of the United States.

Smith met with representatives at the EEOC's Seattle district office and explained the circumstances that led to his dismissal from ADAPT. The EEOC then investigated his claim, and on July 18, 1984, the district director, Donald W. Muse, believing there was sufficient evidence to pursue a case against the private treatment center, filed a case against ADAPT. He charged the treatment facility with violating Title VII of the act for purposely discriminating against Smith on the basis of his religion when they terminated him from his job in March. Muse then sent a letter to ADAPT laying out the EEOC's case against the facility. The letter recognized that Smith was a sincere member of the Native American Church and acknowledged that the sacramental use of peyote was an essential part of church ceremonies. It also noted that the federal government was committed to accommodating this religion, as illustrated by the exemption of nondrug use of peyote from the Controlled Substances Act of 1970.

The EEOC rejected ADAPT's defense that its abstinence policy was not discriminatory because it applied its personnel policies in an "evenhanded way" to apply to all recovering staff, in any situation, rather than targeting any individual for his or her religion. (Gardin, the executive director of the facility, once stated that the policy was so strict that it "even proscribed recovering alcoholic counselors from receiving wine at communion.") Muse responded, "This reasoning evidences a misunderstanding of the requirements of Title VII, and of the protection of freedom in religious practices, which is based on *individual* belief and activity rather than *comparative* treatment." The EEOC also cast aside ADAPT's second justification for its stringent personnel policy—that it was necessary in order to protect the credibility of recovering staff persons who would be counseling clients the policy of abstinence. Muse found no evidence that the counseling process was negatively affected because Smith had been fired immediately, thus limiting his access to clients.

In rejecting these two points, the district director concluded that there was reasonable cause to believe ADAPT violated Title VII of the Civil Rights Act of 1964 when it terminated Smith from employment for ingesting peyote. He recommended that the parties come together collectively to resolve the matter rather than go immediately to court. Muse enclosed a "Notice of Conciliation Process" and then sent representatives to both Smith and ADAPT to help them negotiate a settlement. A similar letter was later sent on behalf of Galen Black, who by this time had duplicated Smith's challenge under Title VII.

———

On July 23, 1984, several days after Muse charged ADAPT with a violation of Title VII of the 1964 Civil Rights Act, the independent referee assigned to Smith's unemployment compensation case handed down his ruling on Smith's request. Robert Gruber determined that Smith was appropriately discharged for misconduct in connection with his employment, because although he did not technically violate the employer's written policies, "the evidence at the hearing clearly showed that the claimant had been specifically informed that this ingestion of peyote would be a violation of the standards of behavior which the employer expected." However, he concluded that Smith should not be disqualified from receiving unemployment benefits because such action would violate his right to the free exercise of religion under the Constitution. Gruber referred to the balancing test announced in *Sherbert* and *Thomas*, and found that the state interest, which was "limited to protecting the undue depletion of the unemployment insurance fund by payment of benefits to those who would be otherwise disqualified," was not compelling enough to warrant the burden on Smith's free exercise of religion. He reinstated Smith's award of unemployment benefits.

The next day ADAPT appealed the referee's decision to the Employment Appeals Board, which handed down its decision a month later. In a decision written by Ross Morgan, the chair of the EAB, and joined by Jerry E. Butler, the board agreed with Gruber's determination that Smith had been appropriately discharged for misconduct, but disagreed with the referee's conclusion that he was entitled to unemployment benefits. In a brief statement, Morgan reasoned that because Smith's ingestion of peyote was unlawful in Oregon, the "compelling state interest is in the proscription of illegal drugs, not merely in the burden upon the Unemployment Compensation Trust fund." He modified the referee's decision to disqualify Smith from benefits because state law allowed the denial of benefits to those terminated for misconduct. It was a majority decision. The third member of the board, Glenn E. Randall, dissented from the ruling without opinion.

Morrison was disappointed, but not surprised. He had been hopeful that the additional evidence presented before the referee would compel the board to consider the constitutional question that was prompted by its denial of benefits to Smith, but he also knew the argument would fare better in a judicial proceeding. Morrison was already in the midst of preparing his legal brief on behalf of Galen Black before the state court of appeals, and was pleased when Smith decided to join this fight.

Al is such a compelling person . . . and he wanted to pursue this case. After the hearing, he told me how he had received eagle feathers in his mail, and how they were a symbol to him. A symbol that he had been chosen by his community or his people to pursue this case no matter what needed to be done. You just don't have many clients that get eagle feathers in the mail. It was a very unique, very special experience. And he had had a life in which he had obviously paid his dues, and he had survived all of that, and it was almost as if it was all for this purpose.

Morrison filed the petition for judicial review of the EAB's order denying Smith unemployment compensation, and prepared his legal appeal on behalf of Galen Black and Alfred Smith before the Oregon Court of Appeals.

CHAPTER 5

The Oregon Battle

Of the one hundred million court cases filed in the United States each year, over 99 percent are heard in state courts, which means that most Americans will experience the judicial process in their home state. It is also likely that the experience will be brief; most cases never proceed past the lowest level court. The Oregon state court system is organized in a simple, hierarchical fashion. At the lowest level are circuit courts, which are trial courts of general jurisdiction that are arranged according to geography. At the next level sits the Oregon Court of Appeals, the intermediate court, which handles appeals from the circuit courts and state administrative agencies. The court of last resort is the Oregon Supreme Court, which has both mandatory and discretionary jurisdiction as designated in the state constitution and statutes. If a case originating in the state system involves a federal question of constitutional law, it may be appealed to the United States Supreme Court, but its review is discretionary. Few will take their case "all the way to the Supreme Court" despite this clarion call; even fewer will be selected for review by the Court.

Galen Black's case would be the first to move through the state judicial system. Because Oregon's Employment Appeals Board is a state administrative agency, David Morrison prepared Black's case before the Oregon Court of Appeals. Morrison knew the decision in Black's case would give him an indication of Al Smith's chances of prevailing in court, so he prepared the case with Smith's upcoming appeal in mind. Most of his attention was focused on Smith, and Black's role in the two cases, Morrison recalls, "Faded into the twilight. It was not strategic, or a conscience decision on my part. It really happened on its own. It is just that the Native American Church holds such a special place in our religious freedom jurisprudence. Somewhere along the way it was clear that the argument was stronger on behalf of Al Smith than Galen Black." The brief he prepared was for Black, but Morrison knew this would be Smith's battle from now on.

Morrison worked alone on the legal brief that he would present to the Court of Appeals. "A legal aid lawyer at this level, on the ground level," he stated, "does everything." Although he does not consider himself a First Amendment specialist, Morrison did not find the legal issues particularly challenging and he believed the EAB's ruling denying Black unemployment compensation clearly violated the free exercise clause of the First Amendment. "It was pretty straightforward law, and so I didn't feel as though I was getting myself into some really difficult legal scholarship that presented conceptually or intellectually hard problems."

Morrison had written dozens of legal briefs, so he was familiar with the process. He followed the guidelines provided in the Oregon state's Rules of Appellant Procedure, which governs the format and presentation of the legal arguments submitted to the court. The main text of the brief consists of "assignments of error" which direct the court to the mistakes in the administrative ruling that are open to judicial review, followed by arguments persuading the court to overturn these errors.

Morrison filed his legal brief on October 31, 1984. His primary argument was that Black's ingestion of peyote was part of a bona fide religious ceremony, and that his actions were protected by the First Amendment to the U.S. Constitution. He contended that the state of Oregon could not deny unemployment compensation to individuals for exercising their religion unless they had a compelling reason to justify such a denial. Morrison also characterized the state's denial of unemployment compensation as "particularly offensive" because the exercise of Black's religion during nonworking hours did not interfere with his ability or willingness to perform his job. The legal aid lawyer cited *Sherbert v. Verner* and *Thomas v. Review Board*, which also involved states' denial of unemployment compensation as relevant Supreme Court precedent.

Referring to *Sherbert*, he stated, "In this highly sensitive constitutional area, only the gravest abuses, endangering paramount interests, give occasion for permissible limitation by the state." Looking at the specifics of Black's case, Morrison concluded that Oregon did not fulfill this high threshold requirement.

Morrison was comfortable with the constitutional argument. The fact situation in *Black v. Employment Division* closely resembled the precedent cases that were decided in favor of the religious claimants. Because Morrison was confident with the federal constitutional argument, he did not bother arguing that the board's actions also violated article I, section 2 of the Oregon State Constitution, which reads, "All men shall be secure in the Natural right to worship Almighty God according to the dictates of their own conscience," or section 3, "No law shall in any case whatever control the free exercise, and enjoyment of religious opinions, or interfere with the rights of conscience." He admits, "It was probably laziness that I did not go to state issues, to be quite frank about it. But the federal law was so clear that I thought, why go looking for work? My thinking was, you've got *Sherbert*, what else do you need? And it was more than one case; there were later decisions where the Supreme Court reaffirmed that rule."

The task of defending the respondent, the Employment Division, fell to the state attorney general's office, which represents all state agencies in court. A separate brief on behalf of ADAPT was submitted by Eldon F. Caley, a Roseburg attorney who was hired by the treatment center shortly after Morrison appealed the EAB decision to the state Court of Appeals.

Jeff Bennett, the assistant attorney general, prepared the state's brief. Appearing with Bennett on the brief were Dave Frohnmayer, the state attorney general, and the state solicitor general, James E. Mountain Jr. The attorney general's office was familiar with the case, having advised the EAB earlier in the year that a denial of unemployment benefits was appropriate. The state's brief focused upon the EAB's justification for the denial of unemployment compensation. Bennett established that Black was not fired for his religious activity, but rather that he was terminated for misconduct for violating a personnel policy that prohibited the use of alcohol or substances. He also cast doubt on Black's justification for ingesting the substance, arguing that the respondent failed to fully articulate a religious interest that would allow him to invoke the constitutional protection provided by the free exercise clause of the First Amendment. Bennett characterized Black's decision to ingest peyote as "personal" and "voluntary" and contended that it failed to meet the threshold requirement that ingestion of peyote was mandated by his religion.

Bennett then argued that even if the ingestion of peyote was a legitimate exercise of Black's religion, that the state could still justify the denial of unemployment benefits if it had a compelling interest for doing so. Citing *Sherbert*, he reasoned, "That interest must be found in the statute that created the burden." Bennett maintained that the state had a compelling interest in protecting the integrity of the Unemployment Compensation Trust Fund, "particularly from depletion by those who are undeserving due to their own conduct, e.g. those who quit or are fired without good reason." He insisted that the incidental burden the denial of unemployment compensation placed on Black's religious practice was clearly outweighed by this compelling state interest. At this point in time it was the only interest articulated by the state. And it was identical to the state's justification for denying unemployment compensation benefits in *Sherbert* and *Thomas*.

The brief filed by Caley provided additional facts into the record regarding ADAPT's treatment philosophy, personnel policies, and rationalization for terminating Black. Caley also introduced two additional justifications for the state's denial of unemployment benefits. He reasoned that the state also had a compelling interest in eradicating drug use and in avoiding a violation of the establishment clause of the state and federal constitutions. To support the state's need to control drugs, Caley cited the 1975 Oregon Court of Appeals decision, *Oregon v. Soto*. In *Soto*, the court affirmed the conviction of an American Indian arrested for possession of peyote on the grounds that the state had a compelling state interest in banning dangerous drugs. Because the judge had not allowed evidence to be submitted regarding the defendant's religious motivation, Caley argued that *Soto* established the precedent that the state could legitimately ban peyote, even if used for religious purposes. This court, Caley stated, should make a similar ruling in *Black*. He also suggested that accommodation of Black's religious exercise through an award of benefits risked violating prohibitions against the establishment of religion because the state would be carving out an exception to the willful misconduct rule in the employment disqualification statute, which violated the principle of religious neutrality mandated by the U.S. and Oregon constitutions.

Both respondents asked the Court of Appeals to uphold the decision by the Employment Appeals Board to deny Black unemployment compensation benefits because he had been appropriately discharged from work for engaging in misconduct.

———

In the state of Oregon, oral arguments at the Court of Appeals are scheduled approximately two months after the last legal brief is filed. However, oral arguments are not mandatory, and attorneys may stipulate to submit the case on the briefs. Morrison and the Attorney General chose to waive the oral presentation. *Black v. Employment Division* was then submitted to a panel of three judges, which considered the case. At the departmental conference the panel decided to refer the case to a full court conference, and on June 6, 1985, a majority of the judges present at conference determined that the case should be considered by the Oregon Court of Appeals sitting en banc.

As Black's case was moving through the Court of Appeals, Morrison was also proceeding with Smith's case. The Court of Appeals granted judicial review of the EAB's decision denying Smith unemployment compensation, and several weeks later the attorneys representing the parties prepared and submitted their legal briefs. Morrison submitted the brief on behalf of the petitioner, Smith; Frohnmayer, Bennett, and Mountain submitted a brief on behalf of the Employment Division, and Caley submitted a brief on behalf of ADAPT. Each of the briefs was similar in content to the briefs submitted in *Black*; the only significant changes were reflected in the facts of the case, which addressed Smith's participation in the Native American Church, reasons for ingesting peyote and the circumstances surrounding his termination from ADAPT. The assignments of error, and the state's and Caley's responses were the same.

———

Several months later, on October 16, 1985, the Court of Appeals handed down its decisions in *Black v. Employment Division* and *Smith v. Employment Division*. In *Black* a majority of the court, sitting en banc, reversed the Employment Appeals Board decision denying Black unemployment compensation and remanded the case back to the administrative agency. It was a majority decision. Three judges wrote a brief dissent. A three-judge panel in *Smith* handed down a per curiam opinion that reversed and remanded the case to the EAB for further consideration in light of the constitutional finding in *Black*.

Judge Rossman, writing for the majority in *Black*, accepted Morrison's presentation of the legal question in the case. He announced that the case was controlled by the Supreme Court decisions in *Sherbert* and its progeny, and that the compelling government interest balancing test would be used to evaluate whether the Employment Appeals Board's denial of unemployment compensation benefits to Black, because of his religious use of peyote in a Native American Church ceremony, violated his right to the free exercise of religion. Rossman first acknowledged the burden on Black's free exercise of religion. "It is beyond dispute that to deny someone unemployment benefits for engaging in bona fide religious conduct places a substantial burden on the exercise of his rights." Next, applying the *Sherbert* balancing test, he determined that the only interest advanced by the state, the preservation of the insurance fund for deserving individuals, was not compelling enough to overcome the burden on Black's free exercise beliefs. Rossman cited both *Sherbert* and *Thomas* as controlling precedents where the United States Supreme Court had rejected the state's interest in the integrity of an unemployment compensation fund over a free exercise challenge.

{ *Religious Freedom and Indian Rights* }

The decision also addressed whether Black's use of peyote was a practice deserving of constitutional protection. Rossman acknowledged, "To some, peyotism might seem unconventional. However, we cannot ignore a fundamental constitutional principle simply because the facts of the case surround an obscure church whose mode of worship may be controversial and little understood . . ." However, because the court was unable to determine from the record whether Black's decision to ingest peyote was a religious act or not, the case was remanded to the EAB to answer this point.

At the end of the majority decision, Rossman turned his attention to the relevance of *Soto*. Although the 1975 decision did not involve the disbursement of unemployment compensation benefits, the three dissenting judges in *Black* used *Soto* to argue that the state also had a compelling interest in protecting the public from the use of illegal drugs, and that this factor should be taken into consideration when evaluating the state interest in the denial of unemployment compensation. Rossman clarified that Black was terminated from his job for violating an employer's rule forbidding the use of drugs or alcohol by counselors who were former substance abusers, not for violating a criminal law. "The fact that there is an independent set of criminal laws which made his conduct coincidentally illegal is irrelevant, because he was not terminated for breaking the law." As such, the majority only considered the state's interest in protecting the integrity of the unemployment compensation fund when evaluating the denial of unemployment benefits. The illegality of peyote under the state's criminal law was deemed immaterial to the case at hand.

———

A key player in the next series of events in *Smith* and *Black* was Dave Frohnmayer, the popular state attorney general. Frohnmayer had been prominent in state politics for over a decade. The native Oregonian was raised in Medford, Oregon, by parents active in civic and social affairs who instilled in their children the importance of serving the community. In 1958 Frohnmayer left Oregon for Harvard University, where he earned a degree in

Government, followed by a Rhodes scholarship at Oxford University and a law degree from Boalt Law School in Berkeley. He worked for a short time in Washington, D.C., before returning to Oregon in 1971, where he settled down in South Eugene, married, and became a faculty member at the University of Oregon Law School. In 1974 the moderate Republican was elected to the legislature to represent one of the most liberal districts in the state. Frohnmayer quickly earned a reputation as a hardworking but cautious legislator who was well liked and respected by colleagues in both political parties. His work was heavily influenced by his legal education. Frohnmayer carefully monitored legislation to ensure that it did not violate the state constitution, and was affectionately nicknamed "the Professor" for his meticulous, scholarly speeches on the floor of the House.

Frohnmayer left the Oregon House to run for attorney general in 1980, and easily won reelection in 1984. A bid for governor seemed inevitable. As *Black* and *Smith* were moving through the Court of Appeals, Frohnmayer had contemplated running for the state's highest office in the 1986 election, but he backed out in spring 1985 to spend more time with his family. His reasons were personal rather than political. In 1984 the Frohnmayers learned that two of their daughters were diagnosed with Fanconi anemia, a rare, often fatal genetic illness with no known cure. After the family learned that a bone marrow transplant could slow the advancement of the illness, they initiated a national, and then international search for family relatives to find an exact match for a transplant. Frohnmayer dedicated his free time to this search, so a campaign for the governor's mansion would have to wait.

When *Black* and *Smith* were in the Court of Appeals, the attorney general's involvement in the cases was minimal. A great deal of his attention at the time was focused on the state's legal challenges with the Bhagwan Shree Rajneesh, who in 1981 fled India and settled in the small north-central Oregon town of Antelope, Oregon. Disciples of the Bhagwan flocked to the area, and by 1983 the religious sect had taken control of the city council and had incorporated the commune as Rajneeshpuram, an

Oregon city, in order to receive state funds. The attorney general was asked by the state legislature to investigate whether Rajneeshpuram was a real city or a religious commune. Frohnmayer then took the commune to court, and requested that the incorporation of the commune as a city be declared unconstitutional. Frohnmayer also took the Bhagwan and his followers to court under the state's Racketeer Influenced and Corrupt Organizations Act to respond to other problems with the religious sect involving voter fraud and a mass poisoning in a nearby town. Frohnmayer recalls that he probably only reviewed the state's briefs in the peyote cases and signed off on them because of his attention to the Bhagwan's case. However, he acknowledged that the state's tension with the Bhagwan Shree Rajneesh did have an "intellectual influence" on how the office handled *Smith* and *Black*. "It was a case study in the establishment of religion. It was a home-grown big-time theocracy, where the entire instruments of governance of a municipality fall into the hands of a religious group that was up to no good. Or at least in terms of the record of subsequent lawbreaking, was clearly over the line. And I think it was an object lesson in how far a theocracy can go, and that the values that underlie the establishment clause are of very great importance." As a result, Frohnmayer was very sensitive about how the state handled any cases where it might be accused of giving a religious group preferential treatment.

Most important to Frohnmayer, however, was the fact that *Smith* and *Black* involved peyote, an illegal substance in Oregon. From the time the cases were first heard by the Employment Appeals Board, the attorney general's office took the position that these were simple cases involving a drug proscribed by the state, and that to grant Black and Smith employment compensation would be rewarding them for behavior that was criminally unlawful to everyone else. Frohnmayer remarked, "We saw it almost completely as a drug case. We knew that there was a First Amendment issue related to it, because it was a religious practice, but it also seemed anomalous that someone would be able to use the First Amendment as a sword, not merely as a shield. That is to say, that belief and the action may well be protected against some form of criminal prosecution, but the notion that someone can affirmatively claim unemployment compensation, that is, to claim money from taxes that are coercively exacted from other people, for engaging in activity which for anyone else not of that religion would actually violate criminal law seemed almost non-sensical." The attorney general was concerned that an award of unemployment compensation would lead to religious challenges to other state laws proscribing illegal substances, which would complicate the state's enforcement of its drug laws.

The attorney general decided that the Court of Appeals was "simply wrong" and on January 9, 1986, filed a petition for judicial review of *Black v. Employment Division* and *Smith v. Employment Division* in the Oregon Supreme Court. The petition for review is essentially a request that the highest state court review or reconsider a decision from the lower court. It allows the losing party to set forth analysis as to why the case should be reconsidered, and if necessary, reversed. The state filed two petitions; the more extensive brief was filed in *Black* and a two-page petition in *Smith* directed the Court to *Black*.

In its petition for review, the state changed its strategy. Rather than arguing that it had a compelling enough interest in preserving the unemployment fund to justify the burden on the respondent's religious actions, the brief focused on the illegality of peyote. The state contended that because the ingestion of peyote was an illegal act, that the respondent's actions were not protected by the First Amendment because the respondent did not have a "protectable constitutional right to assert." At the very least, it insisted, the Court of Appeals should have properly considered the illegality of peyote when it evaluated the state's interest in denying unemployment compensation benefits. The state also argued that the Court of Appeals made an error when it failed to properly consider whether the respondent's conduct was actually motivated by religious principles. The brief described the peyote ritual as an optional part of the Native American Church ceremony, making this case different from previous unemployment cases such as *Sherbert*, where members of the Seventh-Day Adventist Church are explicitly prohibited from working on Saturday, their day of Sabbath. The brief also included two minor reasons why the Oregon Supreme Court should review the appellate court decision. First, because this was the "first non-criminal case in the United States where the religious conduct asserted to be protected by the First Amendment is criminal," making "the constitutional question raised by this case one of first impression." And second, because the court needed to reconcile the conflict between *Black* and *Soto.* The state argued that "It is anomalous that claimant's religious practice could not keep him out of jail but could, at the same time, permit him to qualify for unemployment benefits." It urged the Oregon Supreme Court to review and reverse the lower court decision.

In Oregon, after an individual has petitioned the Supreme Court for judicial review, the respondent on review has the option to file a response to the petition. However, it is not necessary that they do so, and if they choose not to file a brief, the brief in the Court of Appeals is considered the response. In both *Black* and *Smith,* Morrison chose the latter option. He was comfortable with the First Amendment free exercise argument contained in the brief for the Court of Appeals, which he believed settled the question. But it was also an issue of resources. Oregon Legal Services has limited funding, and although it was committed to the case, a response brief would be expensive and repetitive.

———

The Oregon Supreme Court, like many of the highest state courts in the United States, has both mandatory and discretionary review that gives it control over its agenda and policy-making authority because it can select cases it would like to review, and avoid others. In cases of discretionary review, petitions are allowed if one less than a majority of the judges eligible to vote on the petition vote to allow it. The court itself considers what it believes is relevant to its decision whether to grant review, and it does not have to specify why it accepts or denies review in a case. On February 25, 1986, six weeks after Dave Frohnmayer asked the Oregon Supreme court to review the decisions in *Black* and *Smith,* the court notified the attorneys representing both parties that it had granted the petition. It also directed the attorneys representing both parties to answer several specific questions regarding whether the state's denial of unemployment benefits violated the state constitution, and if so, whether the U.S. Supreme Court's analysis in *Thomas* was appropriate for the evaluation of the state constitutional question as well. The court also asked for clarification of several minor issues concerning the state laws that governed the distribution of unemployment benefits and the criminal law regarding the legality of peyote.

The next month the attorneys for both parties submitted a memorandum answering these questions. The brief on behalf of the petitioners was submitted by Mountain, and signed by Frohnmayer and Bennett. It focused on the first question of the applicability of the Oregon Constitution to the dispute. Mountain argued that not only was the denial of benefits appropriate under the state constitution, but that it was in fact necessary to avoid an establishment clause violation. According to the solicitor general, the respondents were asking that they be "singled out for special treatment on account of their religious beliefs," which is unconstitutional under article I, section 5, which prohibits state sponsorship or establishment of religion. He also questioned whether the religious guarantees of the Oregon Constitution "were intended by the framers to require state exemption of religious practices (such as peyotism) from regulation by laws distinctly secular in purpose and patently secular in their effects, separate from any inhibition of religious exercise. Such a mandatory exemption would conflict with the principles of equality of pluralistic faiths." Mountain also used this opportunity to reiterate the state's earlier argument regarding the illegality of peyote.

Suanne Lovendahl, an attorney who had recently been hired by the Roseburg legal aid office, assisted Morrison with the response to the Court's memorandum. Lovendahl argued that if the state supreme court were to evaluate the religious liberty claim under the state constitution, that it must use the same balancing test required in federal free exercise challenges, the *Sher-*

bert compelling interest test. "When presented with a case factually indistinguishable from *Thomas,* and its precursor *Sherbert,* this Court is bound by the federal analysis, and the same results must obtain." She also discounted the relevance of the legality of peyote to the issue of the award of unemployment benefits, but in anticipation that the court might consider the illegality of the respondents' use of peyote, argued that the applicability of *Soto* was questionable given federal and state efforts to guarantee American Indian religious freedom. Lovendahl then repeated the arguments presented in the brief to the Court of Appeals, that the Oregon Supreme Court must limit its evaluation to the state's interest in maintaining the integrity of the unemployment trust fund, and that this interest, when weighed against the burden on the respondents' sincere exercise of their religion, was less than compelling. She asked that the decision by the Court of Appeals reversing the Employment Appeals Board decision denying the claimants' unemployment compensation be upheld.

————

On occasion, outside individuals and organizations become involved in cases pending before state and federal courts because the legal issue is of particular importance to their own interests. Interest group activity is found mostly at the federal level, but in recent years has been increasing in state courts as more litigants bring challenges under state constitutions. In the cases of *Black* and *Smith v. Employment Division,* the Oregon chapter of the American Civil Liberties Union had expressed interest in the case from the beginning. The ACLU's early involvement was informal; it did not become formally involved until the Oregon Supreme Court accepted the case for review. When this happened, the ACLU decided that it would be appropriate to submit an amicus curiae ("friend of the court") brief addressing the questions the Oregon Supreme Court posed on review. According to Dave Fidanque, the executive director of the state chapter, the ACLU believed the cases provided the state Supreme Court the opportunity to elaborate upon the level of religious protection under the state constitution. "In the early stages of the case we had high hopes that the Oregon Supreme Court might use the facts of this case to flesh out the religious freedom provisions of the Oregon Bill of Rights. This didn't seem unreasonable because the Court has been in the forefront of the judicial movement to decide cases on the basis of state constitutional provisions."

It was also a good strategy, given a trend that has been taking place in state courts across the country over the last several decades. Beginning in the 1970s, as the federal Supreme Court became more conservative on issues involving individual rights and liberties, more litigants turned to state courts for protection. This "new judicial federalism" emphasizes that state courts rely on the protections provided in state constitutions rather than the federal Constitution. The reliance on state constitutions presents state courts with the opportunity to interpret state constitutional rights and liberties independent of the U.S. Supreme Court's interpretation of analogous rights. There are two advantages to this development of state constitutional jurisprudence. First, according to its decision in *Michigan v. Long* (1983), the Supreme Court does not have the authority to review state court interpretations of civil liberties provisions that are based on state law, thereby shielding the results because there is no federal question for the high court to decide. Second, because the federal Constitution grants only minimal protection for individual rights and liberties, new judicial federalism allows states to extend judicial protection beyond these national guarantees.

There was an additional reason why the Oregon chapter of the ACLU thought this would be a good strategy in these two cases; the state of Oregon has been at the forefront of this movement. Indeed, one of the justices on the Oregon Supreme Court, Hans Linde, is considered "the architect of new judicial federalism." Linde first discussed this return to the states four decades ago when he was a law professor at the University of Oregon, and has published extensively on this subject. Given the growing conservatism of the U.S. Supreme Court and the uncertainty surrounding its interpretation of the religion clauses of the First Amendment, Fidanque called this opportunity "critical," not only for the results of this case, but for future cases as well.

The amicus curiae brief submitted on behalf of Smith and Black was written by David M. Gordon, a Springfield attorney affiliated with the civil rights organization. He stated that it was imperative that the court look to the state constitutional provisions protecting freedom of worship rather than rely on the federal Constitution. Gordon asked the Oregon Supreme Court to develop its own balancing test to evaluate whether the Oregon constitution was violated, rather than rely on the compelling government interest test used by the federal judiciary. The reason for doing so, he continued, was because it was necessary for the Oregon Court to aid in the development of the state constitution, which provides greater protection to individual rights than similar federal provisions. Gordon conceded that in the past, federal case law interpreting the federal Constitution provided guidance to state courts in their interpretation of similarly worded state constitutional provisions, but that this was no longer "jurisprudentially acceptable," given the conservatism in the Supreme Court.

Moreover, Gordon observed, the debates at the state's constitutional convention on ratification of the state religion clauses leads to the conclusion the framers "perceived the need for toleration of the broadest possible range of religious thought." He advised the court to adopt a more rigorous balancing test where religious conduct would be limited to instances that "constitute a clear and immediate danger to others." Applying this test, Gordon concluded that because the Employment Division was unable to illustrate such a danger to others, that the denial of unemployment benefits based on those religious acts violated the state constitution.

———

Several weeks before oral arguments in *Smith* and *Black*, there was a resolution in Smith's Title VII challenge against ADAPT. After weeks of negotiating, the EEOC and ADAPT settled the case to avoid a lawsuit in federal court. The consent decree, which was filed in U.S. District Court in Eugene on March 4, 1986, two years after Smith was terminated from ADAPT, favored the former employee. In exchange for no admission by ADAPT that there had been a Title VII violation, the facility agreed to not engage in "employment practices which deprive or tend to deprive any individual of employment opportunities or which discriminate against any individual with respect to compensation, terms, conditions, or privileges of employment on the basis of that individual's religion, in violation of Title VII." In response to future situations which might involve a conflict between the facility and the religious use of peyote, ADAPT promised to "revise or interpret hereafter by resolution all practices of ADAPT to eliminate any discipline against members of the Native American Church for the non-drug sacramental use of peyote during a bona fide ceremony of the Native American Church." The private rehabilitation facility also agreed to pay Smith back wages from the time he was fired, March 5, 1984, until December 1985.

In exchange for these commitments, the decree allowed ADAPT the latitude to impose "reasonable and job-related standards for hiring, measuring the performance of, and disciplining employees," as long as the standards did not discriminate against employees based on their religion. The decree also permitted the facility the right to institute rules proscribing employees from advocating the peyote ceremony or matters related to membership of the Native American Church unless those employees were specifically responding to an inquiry from a client. The decree was finalized on March 31, 1986, and Galen Black's complaint, which was almost identical in form, was finalized that day as well.

By changing its misconduct policies in a manner that ensured that other ADAPT employees would not be disciplined or face discrimination because of their religious beliefs, ADAPT would avoid a possible violation of Title VII. Although the facility did not admit that it had engaged in any religious discrimination against Smith that would warrant a suit under Title VII, the decree did ensure that any future ADAPT employees belonging to the Native American Church would not be penalized for practicing their religion. ADAPT also benefited from the decree because it allowed the rehabilitation facility to institute rules ensuring that employees would not advocate membership to the church as an approved treatment modality.

———

Oral arguments before the Oregon Supeme Court in *Smith v. Employment Division* and *Black v. Employment Division* were heard on April 1, 1986. James Mountain, Oregon's solicitor general, presented the case on behalf of the Employment Division and David Morrison argued on behalf of Alfred Smith and Galen Black. Oral arguments went well for both attorneys, who provided a summary review of the legal arguments contained in their legal briefs. The court's decisions were handed down three months later on June 24, 1986.

In two separate decisions, a majority of the Oregon Supreme Court affirmed, in part, the decision by the Court of Appeals that the denial of unemployment benefits to Smith and Black for using peyote as part of a religious ceremony was a violation of the free exercise clause of the First Amendment of the federal Constitution. In each case the court determined that the claimants ingested the sacrament in a bona fide religious ceremony, making it unnecessary to remand the cases back to the Employment Appeals Board for further consideration on this point. The court also considered, and rejected, the contention that the denial of benefits was a violation of the Oregon Constitution respecting freedom of worship and religious opinion. The Supreme Court used *Smith* to fully examine the constitutional issues.

Justice Robert Jones wrote the majority decision. He began with consideration of the state constitutional claim, which he rejected outright. "But here it was not the government that disqualified claimant from his job for ingesting peyote. And the rule denying unemployment benefits to one who loses his job for what an employer permissibly considers misconduct, conduct incompatible with doing the job, is itself a neutral rule." Therefore the court determined that *Smith* was not the appropriate vehicle to develop the state's religion clause jurisprudence.

His attention to the federal constitutional question was more detailed. Jones first stated that the free exercise clause of the First

Amendment requires that "the person claiming the free exercise right show the application of the law in question significantly burdens the free exercise of his religion. If the person shows this burden, the state then must demonstrate that the constraint on the religious activity is the least restrictive means of achieving a "compelling" state interest." Applying this test, Jones determined that the denial of Smith's unemployment benefits placed a significant burden on his ability to freely exercise his religion, and that the state's interest in uniformly applying the law and in preserving the financial integrity of the unemployment compensation fund were not compelling enough to deny compensation. The Oregon court ruled that the state's interest in *Smith* was indistinguishable from *Sherbert* and *Thomas*. It rejected the Employment Appeal Board's contention, and the state's argument, that the legality of peyote was a factor that should be considered. Jones noted, "The legality of ingesting peyote does not affect our analysis of the state's interest. The state's interest in denying unemployment benefits to a claimant discharged for religiously motivated misconduct must be found in the unemployment compensation statutes, not in the criminal statutes proscribing the use of peyote." Consequently, the Oregon Supreme Court did not discuss whether peyote possession was a felony in the state, whether the state had an interest in preventing drug use, or whether the Oregon criminal law provided an exemption for the religious use of peyote. Jones explained this omission because, according to the Employment Division's own rules, "The commission of an illegal act is not, in and of itself, grounds for disqualification from unemployment benefits. ORS 657.176(3) permits disqualification only if a claimant commits a felony in connection with work." Smith's conduct, the court ruled, did not fall into this category. It upheld the Court of Appeals decision overturning the Employment Appeals Board ruling, and awarded unemployment benefits to Smith. On the same day, in an opinion also written by Jones, the Oregon Supreme Court reached the same result in the companion case, *Black v. Employment Division*.

But the attorney general for the state of Oregon was not ready to give up. Several weeks after the Oregon Supreme Court handed down its decisions in *Smith* and *Black*, Frohnmayer asked the court to reconsider its decision. His focus, once again, was on the legality of peyote. The state's brief for reconsideration contended that the court had misinterpreted its position regarding the relevance of the criminal nature of Black and Smith's conduct to the question of whether they were entitled to unemployment compensation. Although the state conceded that the illegality of peyote was not directly relevant to whether they engaged in misconduct—the respondents were fired for misconduct for violating ADAPT's rule regarding use and misuse of any drugs or alcohol rather than for ingesting an illegal substance—it reasoned that the "criminal nature" of their conduct was relevant to whether they "can claim a constitutional right under the federal Free Exercise Clause to engage in that conduct." Frohnmayer's argument was that any activity that the state has proscribed in its criminal laws was not constitutionally protected. According to the state, because the respondents did not have a free exercise right to ingest peyote, it was not even necessary for the court to inquire whether there was a burden on their free exercise, or whether the state's interest was compelling, because "no right exists under the First Amendment to engage in that conduct." The state also argued that even if the court were to determine that Black and Smith's conduct was constitutionally protectable, that the criminality of the conduct must be taken into consideration when evaluating whether the law placed a burden on their religious freedom. Frohnmayer concluded that it was "just short of incredible" that the court determined that a denial of unemployment benefits burdened the respondents' religion when there were criminal laws that proscribed the drug.

The court has full authority to deny or allow reconsideration. Frohnmayer's attempt to persuade the court to reconsider the case was unsuccessful; on September 3, 1986, Edwin J. Peterson, the chief justice for the Oregon Supreme Court, handed down a one sentence opinion indicating that the court had considered the Employment Division's petition for reconsideration, and had denied it.

Morrison phoned Smith to tell him of the news. They had not been in frequent contact as the case was pending before Oregon's highest court, but Morrison knew Smith was eager for a resolution on the case. "I remember when I heard of the decision," recalls Smith. "I thought to myself, take that, Attorney General." Morrison also eventually contacted Galen Black, who was getting more difficult to track down as the case proceeded through the Oregon courts.

CHAPTER 6

An Appeal to the High Court

Dave Frohnmayer was disappointed when he learned the Oregon Supreme Court denied his request for reconsideration of *Employment Division v. Smith* and *Employment Division v. Black*. He was concerned the decisions would lead to further requests for religious exemptions from the state's criminal prohibitions against drugs. This, he believed, would hinder the state's ability to enforce the law and burden its criminal justice system. "We had this terrible precedent on the books in the Oregon Supreme Court, and so our feeling was that we could not live with that precedent because we had other drug cases coming up, and it would be impossible to distinguish them in a meaningful, principled way." The only option left was to appeal the case to the U.S. Supreme Court.

The process of appealing a case to the Supreme Court was familiar to the attorney general. At this point in his career he had already argued six cases before the Court, and won five of those cases. It was an extraordinary record of success, especially given the fact that few cases ever reach the U.S. Supreme Court. Frohnmayer's previous Supreme Court experience classifies him as a "repeat player" with the institutional and economic resources to have an advantage in the judicial process.

Frohnmayer's appeal to the Supreme Court was in the form of a petition for a writ of certiorari. Today, almost all cases come to the Supreme Court in this form, which is a request that the Court exercise its discretion to hear a case in the lower courts on the merits. When certiorari is granted, it is an order to the lower court to send up a record of the case so the Supreme Court can review the decision. Prior to 1925, almost 80 percent of all the cases on the Court's docket consisted of mandatory appeals. However, in part because the Court was unable to keep up with its rising workload, Congress passed the Judiciary Act of 1925, also known as the "Judges Bill," which replaced most mandatory reviews on appeal with discretionary review of petitions for a writ of certiorari. As the Court's workload continued to increase, Congress enacted additional legislation to give the Court even greater control over its docket. Most recently, in 1988 Congress passed Public Law 100-352, the "Act to Improve the Administration of Justice" which eliminated nearly all of the Court's remaining nondiscretionary appellate jurisdiction.

Currently, the Court has virtually complete discretion over the cases it will review; 99 percent of its docket comes from petitions for a writ of certiorari and the remaining 1 percent consists of cases that come to the Court directly on appeal and instances when the Court is acting as a court of original jurisdiction. Mandatory appeal to the Supreme Court is limited to a small number of cases decided by three-judge federal district courts that involve specific federal statutes, such as reapportionment and antitrust laws, civil rights acts, Presidential Election Campaign Fund acts, and voting rights acts. Congress may also occasionally provide for expedited Supreme Court review of cases it considers important, such as the legal challenge to the constitutionality of the Flag Protection Act of 1989. Rarer still is when a case is filed directly with the Supreme Court. These cases, outlined in Article III of the Constitution as cases of original jurisdiction when the Supreme Court acts as a court of first instance, occur in disputes "affecting Ambassadors, other public Ministers and Consuls and those in which a State shall be Party." The Court's control over its docket is significant because it gives the Court the power to set its own agenda. This facilitates the Court's role in judicial policymaking, empowering it to seek out or avoid certain issue areas.

Although many cases are taken to the Supreme Court each year, few are actually selected. Currently, the Court is asked to review over eight thousand petitions for writs of certiorari each year. In over 97 percent of the petitions it reviews, the Court declines to grant certiorari, which leaves the previous decision undisturbed. Only two hundred to three hundred cases are decided annually by the Court. At least half of these cases are disposed of summarily, when the Court bypasses oral arguments and issues a judgment based on the written briefs. These per curiam ("by the Court") opinions are generally uninformative and consist only of a short memoranda setting forth the issue, law, and decision. The remaining one hundred or so cases receive plenary review or "full dress treatment," which includes oral arguments and a written opinion. Even this number appears to be dwindling. Over the last several terms the Rehnquist Court has accepted less than ninety cases for full review. In 1999 the Court issued only seventy-four full opinions.

Writs of certiorari are granted in cases the Court considers are of sufficient public importance to merit its attention. Rule 10 in the Supreme Court rules of procedures indicates that writs "will be granted only for compelling reasons," but provides only limited information about which reasons are considered sufficiently compelling. The rule does indicate some important characteristics, such as conflicting legal interpretations among courts of appeals or between a lower court and the Supreme Court on a legal question; disagreement about the law in the nation; or if the case involves an important issue not yet decided by the Court, but it specifies that these reasons are "neither controlling nor fully measuring the Court's discretion."

Judicial scholars have spent considerable time examining which cases are granted certiorari in order to determine if a pattern exists in the cases selected by the Court. Some suggest that cases accepted for review often contain "cues" that make the cases stand out and act as shortcuts to help justices select petitions that are more "certworthy" than others. Cue theory studies reveal that important cues include when the federal government is a party to the dispute, when there is conflict in the federal courts among the circuits or with a decision of the Supreme Court, when an interest group is present as amicus curiae, either in favor or against granting certiorari, and when the prevailing ideology of the Court is at odds with the ideological direction of the lower court's decision.

Also important is when the case involves a specific issue area; between 1950 and 1970 civil liberties issues were an important cue, and currently federalism cases have a greater likelihood of being selected by the Court. These studies conclude that the presence of a cue significantly increases the probability that the case will be granted certiorari.

Certiorari is granted by the Court when four justices agree that the case has sufficient merit to warrant review. This is also called the "rule of four." The vote is taken after a lengthy process in which the petitions are screened by the Court. As the Court's workload has increased, the process of screening certiorari petitions has changed, and for the last three decades this responsibility has largely fallen to the justices' law clerks. Justices are assigned at least three and usually four clerks each year to assist them in the Court's business. Each justice has his or her own criteria for selecting a clerk, but important considerations include academic background, previous clerking experience, and personal compatibility. The responsibilities of the clerks and relationship to the justice varies in each instance, but in all cases, clerks play an integral role reviewing petitions for certiorari. Today, most of the justices take part in a "cert pool" where the clerks divide up the petitions. The clerks then prepare a short memo describing the case, the legal questions presented, and recommendations on whether the case should be accepted for review. The memos are shared with the clerks of the other justices, who may add their own recommendation. Only one current member of the Court, Justice Stevens, has one of his law clerks examine each petition for a writ of certiorari.

After the justices have reviewed the memoranda, the chief justice makes an evaluation of the merits of each case. He then creates two lists; cases considered meritorious are placed on the "discuss list" where they will later be considered in conference. All other cases are placed on a "dead list" and the petition will be denied. The lists are then circulated to the other justices on the Court, who may or may not request that a case be added to the discuss list. At this point in the screening at least 70 percent of the petitions have been placed on the dead list. The remaining 30 percent of the petitions move on to the next step, the weekly judicial conference, when the full Court discusses whether the petition will be granted.

At the conference, the chief justice, or the justice who placed the case on the discuss list, will open the discussion of the case and then each of the Court members, in order of seniority, will speak on the merits of accepting or denying the writ. Often the justices do not discuss the matter of whether a case should be accepted as much as they announce their position on the merits of each case. One of the reasons there is not a great deal of deliberation is because the decision to deny a writ of certiorari in a case is usually unanimous. The Court also decides at the weekly conference whether it will give the case full or summary treatment. In order to receive full treatment, four justices must agree this is necessary.

Petitions for writs of certiorari have to be filed at least ninety days after final judgment in the state or federal appeals court. The petition must follow the guidelines provided in the "Rules of the Supreme Court," which are even more specific than the guidelines governing appeals to state supreme courts. The petition for a writ of certiorari must be brief, accurate, clear, and not exceed thirty pages in length. In the case of *Employment Division v. Smith* and *Employment Division v. Black* the task of preparing the writs fell upon the attorney general's office for the state of Oregon. Dave Frohnmayer was committed to appealing the decision to the Supreme Court. Now he had to prepare the writ in such a fashion that it would catch the eye of at least four of the justices.

On December 2, 1986, Frohnmayer petitioned the U.S. Supreme Court to grant a writ of certiorari in *Employment Division v. Smith*. A separate petition was filed in *Employment Division v. Black*. Both petitions were also signed by William F. Gary, the deputy attorney general, Virginia L. Linder, the solicitor general, Michael D. Reynolds, the assistant solicitor general, and Margaret E. Rabin, the assistant attorney general.

In the brief requesting review of the Oregon Supreme Court's decision in *Smith*, the state presented the central question, "Does the Free Exercise Clause compel a state to award unemployment benefits to a drug rehabilitation counselor who agrees to refrain from using illegal drugs as a condition of his employment and is fired for misconduct after illegally ingesting peyote as part of a religious ceremony?" By highlighting the fact that the use of peyote was illegal in the state, and that the employee, who incidentally happened to be a drug rehabilitation counselor, had been dismissed for using the substance in a religious ceremony, the state posed a tantalizing question to the Court. Two reasons were presented to justify why the writ should be granted; the case provided the Court the opportunity to clarify its inconsistent free exercise jurisprudence and the Oregon Supreme Court wrongly decided the case when it failed to consider the criminality of peyote in its evaluation of the state's interest.

The state first recommended that the Supreme Court "refine" or "reexamine" its free exercise jurisprudence. The brief called attention to the Court's inconsistency in *Braunfeld v. Brown*, where it did not use heightened scrutiny in its evaluation of the religious claim for an exemption to an otherwise neutral law, and decisions such as *Sherbert v. Verner* and *Thomas v. Review Board* where the Court used the more stringent compelling government interest balancing test. Even more important, the state argued, was the fact that the Supreme Court failed to provide lower courts with instructions on how to evaluate the state's interests against burdens on an individual's religious exercise. "This Court's opinions do not directly address the critical nuances of determining the strength of the state's interest and the degree of the burden, if any, on religious practices." The state suggested that the Court use this opportunity to provide "additional guidance in evaluating and comparing the competing interests which serve as cornerstones of first amendment free exercise clause analysis," lest "the professed doctrines of religious belief [become] superior to the law of the land and in effect . . . permit every citizen to become a law unto himself (*Reynolds*)."

The second part of the brief focused on why this direction from the Court was necessary. The state challenged the Oregon

{ *Religious Freedom and Indian Rights* }

Supreme Court's decision on the irrelevance of the criminality of peyote use and characterized Smith's use of peyote as an "unprotected" religious activity because the state proscribed this conduct in its penal laws. "When there is no lawful ability to engage in conduct even when the conduct is religiously motivated, there can be no free-exercise interest to assert." The state suggested that this limited the applicability of *Sherbert* and *Thomas* as controlling precedent because both cases involved legal activity. Furthermore, it reasoned, the state's denial of unemployment compensation did not place a cognizable burden on Smith's free exercise of religion. "Loss of unemployment benefits simply cannot be said to be a significant burden on an individual's freedom to engage in conduct that is separately punishable by ten years in prison."

The petition concluded that the Employment Division was justified in denying the respondents' unemployment compensation benefits because it had "an interest in discouraging all employees, regardless of their personal motives, from engaging in any form of misconduct." According to the state, this interest was compelling and withholding unemployment benefits "a narrowly drawn means of achieving that interest." It urged the Court to accept the case for review so it could clarify its free exercise jurisprudence and direct the Oregon State Supreme Court to take the criminality of peyote into consideration in its evaluation of the state interest in denying unemployment compensation to Smith.

———

At the same time the state was preparing its brief on behalf of the Employment Division, Galen Black and Al Smith suffered a minor setback when their primary attorney from Oregon Legal Services, David Morrison, removed himself as counsel. Morrison recently left OLS to open a private practice, and although he stayed on as a consultant when the cases went to the Oregon Supreme Court, he realized he did not have the time to continue representing Smith and Black. It was a difficult decision for the former legal aid attorney. "I was torn about whether or not to hold on to the case, or to let go of it. I called one of my former law professors who had done a lot of work in the federal appellate courts, and she said, 'Are you prepared to spend six months of your life doing nothing but working on this case, preparing for oral argument before the Supreme Court?' And I had just opened my private practice, and I couldn't do it. But it was very hard to let go." However, Oregon Legal Services was committed to representing Smith and Black, and so the responsibility of responding to the state's certiorari petition fell to Suanne Lovendahl, another attorney at the Roseburg legal aid office. Lovendahl had assisted Morrison in the case before the Oregon Supreme Court, but this was her first brief in opposition to a petition for a writ of certiorari to the U.S. Supreme Court. At this point, outside groups became more interested in this case. The Native American Rights Fund, which had been monitoring the case, contacted Oregon Legal Services to offer its assistance. However, Lovendahl did not accept the offer; she preferred to work alone and was sensitive to criticism about her work. She was also extremely concerned that outside counsel might take over the case, leaving her with little control over its direction. Each factor influenced her decision to turn away assistance from the Indian rights organization.

Respondents have thirty days after the petitioner's writ of certiorari is filed to prepare a brief in opposition to the writ. The purpose of such a brief is to give the respondent the opportunity to present an argument about why the writ should be denied and to clarify any misstatements of fact or law presented by the petitioner. However, it is not mandatory that such briefs be filed except in capital cases or when ordered by the Court.

Lovendahl chose to prepare the brief. She hoped she could dissuade the Court from accepting the case for review. Given the fact that few cases are selected by the Court, the odds were certainly in her favor. On January 5, 1987, Lovendahl filed separate petitions opposing the writ of certiorari in *Smith* and *Black*. Each brief presented one factual correction and two arguments that specifically addressed why the Court should deny the petition for certiorari.

In her response brief, Lovendahl directed the Court's attention to the respondents' reason for ingesting the sacrament, and how the state's denial of unemployment compensation burdened Smith and Black's free exercise rights under the Constitution. In her question before the Court she asked "Whether a Native American Church member, who was discharged from his employment as a drug and alcohol rehabilitation counselor because his sacramental use of peyote in a bona fide Native American Church ceremony conflicted with the employer's total drug and alcohol abstinence treatment philosophy, is entitled to unemployment compensation under the Free Exercise Clause?" Lovendahl purposefully steered the question away from the issue of the criminality of peyote under state law, not wanting the Court to factor this into the state's interest in denying unemployment compensation. She did note, however, that the illegality of peyote was not a factor in the Douglas County Alcohol and Drug Abuse Prevention Treatment facility's decision to terminate Smith or Black. Rather, she clarified, they were terminated for violating a company policy regarding the use of drugs or alcohol by employees.

Lovendahl presented two reasons why the Court should deny the state's petitions. First, she observed that review was unnecessary because the federal question, whether the denial of unemployment compensation violated the free exercise clause, was settled when the Oregon Supreme Court ruled that the denial of unemployment benefits posed a substantial burden on the respondent's religious rights that was not outweighed by the state's interest in protecting the unemployment compensation fund. She established that the Oregon Court properly relied on U.S. Supreme Court precedent in *Sherbert* and *Thomas* when it decided the cases, and charged that the petitioner was not objecting to the Court's free exercise jurisprudence because it was unclear, but rather because the state was unhappy with the decision. The attorney general, she suggested, wanted to allow the Employment Division to deny unemployment compensation as a "civil penalty for criminal conduct."

Second, Lovendahl argued that the state's attention to the legality of the religious conduct would only "cloud" the free exercise question before the Court. She stated that because the respondents were not charged with a criminal offense, nor was it likely that they would be, that it was inappropriate for the state to "challenge the legality of respondent's religious practices by means of Employment Division law." Moreover, she added, it would be highly irregular for Smith and Black to "be deemed 'guilty' and penalized by a federal court when the courts in the state that purports to make practice of his religion a crime have declined to impose a penalty." Lovendahl also suggested that the state law prohibiting possession of peyote was outdated and most likely unconstitutional because it did not allow an exemption for members of the Native American Church, like the federal government and over half of the states in the Union. By downplaying the relevance of the legality of peyote to the case and by emphasizing that the federal constitutional question was properly decided by the state supreme court, Lovendahl was certain the Court would not find it necessary to review the case.

———

After the clerk of the Court received the petitions for certiorari and petitions in opposition to the writ in *Smith* and *Black*, the paperwork was distributed on January 7, 1987, and Chief Justice Rehnquist scheduled the review of the petitions for January 23, 1987. In the interim, the petitions were reviewed by the justices' law clerks, who passed on their recommendations. One of Justice Thurgood Marshall's law clerks, Margaret Raymond, wrote such a summary memorandum shortly after reviewing the petitions. The short memo recapped the case history and legal questions presented and ended with her suggestion that Marshall deny certiorari. Raymond wrote, "I have a feeling there will be a lot of interest in reversing this case; my recommendation would be to hope no one sees it and deny."

At its conference meeting, the Court decided to delay voting on the certiorari requests and "hold" the petitions until the Court resolved a pending free exercise case, *Hobbie v. Unemployment Appeals Commission*. The case was factually similar to *Sherbert v. Verner*. It involved a denial of unemployment compensation to a Seventh-Day Adventist who was fired for misconduct for refusing to work on Saturday, the day of her Sabbath. The state unemployment compensation law prohibited the payment of benefits to anyone discharged as a result of misconduct connected with work. The opinion of the Court had been assigned to Brennan, who was circulating a draft at the time. Therefore, the chief justice asked him to write a memorandum to the conference, which addressed whether *Hobbie* would have any bearing on the Court's decision to grant review to *Smith* and *Black*. Brennan's memo, which was circulated to the Court on February 27, concluded, "In my view, Hobbie sheds no light on this case. Hobbie was discharged for refusal to work Saturdays, and Smith and Black were discharged for ingestion of peyote. A simple application of Hobbie here would produce exactly the same result reached by the Oregon Supreme Court so there is no reason to grant, vacate, and remand." Brennan did note that there was a difference between *Smith* and *Hobbie* "in that the conduct for which Black and Smith were fired is proscribed under state law," but he added that because an illegal act under Oregon state law did not automatically disqualify an individual from unemployment compensation benefits, that the illegality of the respondents' conduct would not affect the outcome of the case. In fact, he observed, "denying Smith and Black benefits on account of their conduct, when their conduct alone would not result in disqualification under state law, singles out those whose religious practices happen to be unlawful for special unfavorable treatment," which implied that a decision overturning the Oregon Supreme Court would improperly target the petitioners and therefore violate the free exercise clause of the First Amendment.

The next week the petitions for certiorari were redistributed to the Court at the March 9, 1987, conference, and the Supreme Court granted Frohnmayer's petitions for a writ of certiorari in *Smith* and *Black*. Chief Justice Rehnquist, Justice White, and Justice Scalia voted to grant certiorari in the two cases, and Justices Brennan, Marshall, Powell, Stevens, and O'Connor voted to deny review. Justice Blackmun, who voted fifth, cast a vote to "Join 3," which is a strategy used by a justice when he or she believes the case presents an important question worthy of review but has not yet decided to either grant or deny certiorari. A "Join 3" vote provides the necessary fourth vote for certiorari if three other members agree to review the case. *Employment Division v. Smith* and *Employment Division v. Black* had barely met the threshold of four votes needed for review by the U.S. Supreme Court.

The Court consolidated the two cases and decided *Smith* would be granted plenary review. As is the tradition, the junior justice on the Court, at this time, Antonin Scalia, reported this decision to the clerk of the Court, who then notified both attorneys.

After a writ of certiorari has been granted by the Court, the petitioner has forty-five days to file a brief on the merits of the case. Such briefs include the questions presented for review; a list of the parties to the proceeding whose judgment is under review; a table of contents and a table of cited authorities; citations of the action at the lower courts and administrative agencies; a statement of the basis for jurisdiction of the Supreme Court; appropriately cited constitutional provisions, treaties, statutes, ordinances, and regulations involved in the case; a concise statement of the case and material facts; a summary of the main arguments that clearly exhibits the points of fact and law and properly cites the authorities relied upon; and a conclusion that states the relief sought by the petitioner. Briefs are prepared to persuade the Court to look at the facts and the legal arguments in a manner favorable to the party. They must be prepared according to the specifications laid out in the Rules of the Supreme Court, and cannot exceed fifty pages in length. Any deviation from these rules is "not favored," and is not allowed without formal approval of the Court. Consequently, when the attorney general needed additional time to file the brief on the merits, he had to file two such requests, which were granted by the clerk of the Court.

On May 29, 1987, Dave Frohnmayer, Deputy Attorney General William F. Gary, Assistant Attorney General Christine Chute, state Solicitor General Virginia L. Linder, and Assistant Solicitor General Michael D. Reynolds submitted their brief on the merits. The question presented to the Court was similar to the question posed in the petition for the writ of certiorari: "Whether a Native American Church member, who was discharged from his employment as a drug and alcohol rehabilitation counselor because his sacramental use of peyote in a bona fide Native American Church ceremony conflicted with the employer's total drug and alcohol abstinence treatment philosophy, is entitled to unemployment compensation under the Free Exercise Clause?" Three reasons were provided to justify the Employment Division's denial of unemployment compensation to Smith and Black.

First, the state repeated the argument listed in the certiorari petition; that the respondents engaged in conduct that was not protected by the First Amendment because it was proscribed by a state criminal law. An exemption to the criminal law was unwarranted, it argued, because it had a compelling interest in controlling the use of dangerous drugs, even the use of drugs that may be religiously motivated. Peyote was characterized as posing a "severe danger to human health and well-being," and the state suggested that its health and safety interest was so great in this instance that it required a "blanket prohibition on peyote use." The state also argued that an exemption was unwarranted because it would lead to requests for exemptions for other psychedelic drugs, such as marijuana, LSD, hashish, and heroin. Multiple exemptions, it contended, would "cripple" law enforcement and violate the "principle of neutrality" demanded by the establishment clause. "State criminal law would become a patchwork of prohibition, covering some people for some drugs, and other people for other drugs."

The state reasoned that the Oregon Supreme Court erred when it limited its consideration of the government interest justifying the denial of unemployment compensation benefits to the unemployment compensation statute. Although this was the same manner in which the U.S. Supreme Court evaluated the government interest in its previous unemployment compensation decisions such as *Sherbert, Thomas,* and *Hobbie v. Unemployment Appeals Commission of Florida*—which had just been handed down—the state suggested that there was no reason the assessment of the state interest should be limited to the unemployment compensation statutes when the behavior at issue was criminal.

The state then linked its discussion about the legitimacy of the state criminal law prohibiting peyote possession to the state's denial of unemployment compensation. It reasoned that even if the religious use of peyote were exempt from criminal prohibition, "the state should not have to reward that conduct with unemployment benefits." An award of unemployment compensation benefits was described as going beyond the "reasonable accommodation" of Smith's religious rights, and "confer[ing] a special benefit on religion under circumstances that intervene with compelling state interests." The state believed it should not be required to "subsidize" the use of controlled substances through a grant of unemployment benefits. Instead, it had "an interest in not encouraging, appearing to sanction or otherwise sponsoring an activity that violates its otherwise valid criminal law policies."

As a final point, the state suggested that the respondents should not be awarded unemployment benefits for "misconduct that actively and directly undermines the employer's interests." Smith and Black's behavior was described as an overt action that "threatened directly to undermine the employer's very purpose—its efforts to rehabilitate drug-dependent clients." To award this misconduct by a grant of unemployment compensation, the state predicted, would "undermine public respect for and confidence in the unemployment compensation laws," thus threatening the "integrity of the statutory scheme." This reason was compelling, the brief concluded, and independent of the state's other arguments regarding the criminality of peyote use in the state.

After the petitioner's brief was filed, Suanne Lovendahl had thirty days to prepare her brief on behalf of Smith and Black. Lovendahl continued to work on her own in Roseburg, turning away offers of assistance from other legal aid lawyers and attorneys at the Native American Rights Fund. After receiving an extension of time, Lovendahl filed her brief on July 29, 1987. It directed the Court to the state supreme court ruling. She asked, "Did the Oregon Supreme Court correctly hold that the state's interest in the financial stability of its unemployment insurance fund—the only interest the Oregon Court found to be pertinent under state law—was insufficient to outweigh the free exercise rights of two employees who were discharged for religiously motivated conduct that conflicted with a condition of their employment?" The legal services lawyer made three points in support of the decision to uphold the award of unemployment benefits to Black and Smith and countered the petitioner's main arguments.

First, Lovendahl likened *Smith* to the Court's previous unemployment compensation decisions. She explained that, as in these other cases, the respondents faced "an irreconcilable conflict between their religious practices and the conditions of their employment, and adhered to their beliefs at the cost of their jobs." In each of the precedent cases, she reminded the Court, it found that the state's interest in the integrity of the unemployment insurance fund was not sufficiently compelling to outweigh the burden on the individual's free exercise of religion. The Oregon Supreme Court, Lovendahl concluded, made the correct ruling.

Second, she repeated the argument in the certiorari petition that the state court properly ruled that the legality of peyote was not relevant to the assessment of eligibility for unemployment benefits and that the respondents were not charged or found guilty of any crime. She added that the state's failure to exempt sacramental use of peyote from its criminal laws violated the free exercise clause of the Constitution.

Third, Lovendahl responded to the state's concern that an award of benefits would make the state appear to sponsor illegal activities. On the contrary, she responded, to deny benefits in this case would be evidence of "hostility toward and discrimination against religion." The purpose of Oregon's unemployment compensation statutes, she described, is "to provide a means for living for the involuntarily unemployed, not to effectuate the state's interest in enforcement of its criminal code." According to the legal aid lawyer, it would be inappropriate for the courts to withhold funds in order to illustrate the state's displeasure with an individual's activity. Lovendahl cited several state court decisions to support her position that the Oregon courts had upheld the award of unemployment benefits to people whose misconduct was not connected to job performance, and in some instances was even illegal. The purpose of the unemployment statutes, she explained, was to allow the Employment Division the latitude to evaluate the behavior that led to the discharge for misconduct and factor it into the decision to award unemployment benefits. In this instance, she reasoned, the respondents were exercising a constitutional right, and were forced to choose between practicing religion and working—a difficult choice in any circumstance—and the Employment Appeals Board made the wrong decision to deny unemployment benefits based on this behavior. The Oregon Appeals Court and Supreme Court corrected this error, Lovendahl concluded, and the decision should stand.

———

Often, cases selected for review by the Supreme Court are of interest to individuals and groups outside the immediate parties to the case. Indeed, one of the reasons the Court grants certiorari is because the case is deemed sufficiently important to merit the Court's attention, so chances are high that others will follow the proceedings. Political interest groups, which are restricted from lobbying the Court directly, are able to participate in the litigation process in two ways. They can initiate and sponsor a test case or submit arguments to the Court through an amicus curiae, or "friend of the court" brief. Both strategies are attempts to influence the outcome of judicial decisions. The submission of an amicus curiae brief is the more common strategy. Legal briefs can be filed in support or opposition to the petition for a writ of certiorari, or if the case is accepted for review, on the merits of the case. Groups use this technique to bring information to the Court or to emphasize a different perspective. This strategy is also used to alert the Court of the broader ramifications of the questions presented in a case. Briefs are partisan documents designed to persuade the Court to rule in a manner favorable to the group's position.

Some groups regularly file amicus curiae briefs or sponsor test cases. And some cases, such as those involving religious liberty, will have at least one amicus brief filed in every case that reaches the U.S. Supreme Court. When interest group activity in the courts began in the 1930s and 1940s, groups from the left, such as the NAACP and ACLU, were very involved in the litigation process. In the area of religious liberty, the Jehovah's Witnesses were incredibly active and successful. These groups sought refuge in the courts because they were politically disadvantaged in traditional majoritarian forums. Other groups from the left, such as women's rights, public interest, and environmental groups, successfully duplicated this strategy. Then, beginning in the 1970s, conservative interest group activity increased dramatically. Now, groups such as the Chamber of Commerce, the American Conservative Union, the Mountain States Legal Foundation, and the National Right to Life Committee regularly participate in the courts. Today, interest groups from each end of the political spectrum use the courts to seek changes in the law or defend gains made in the other arenas.

On the same day Lovendahl filed her brief on the merits to the U.S. Supreme Court, several amicus briefs were filed on behalf of the respondents. The briefs were written by interest groups that had followed *Smith* since the state of Oregon petitioned the U.S. Supreme Court for review. Each group believed the case was sufficiently important that it allocate the time and resources necessary to participate in the case. The amicus briefs emphasized a different reason the Supreme Court should uphold the decision by the Oregon Supreme Court that the state's denial of unemployment compensation benefits was a violation of the free exercise clause to the First Amendment. One brief, written by Walter R. Echo-hawk and Steven C. Moore, senior staff attorneys for the Native American Rights Fund, was filed on behalf of the Native American Church of North America and the Native American Church of Navajoland. Although the church was not a party to the case, it believed it was important that it submit evidence defending peyote use, which plays a central role in its religious ceremonies. The brief focused on the history of peyotism among the indigenous people of Mexico and the United States and "the positive therapeutic and rehabilitative effects" of the sacrament by church members. The amici were particularly concerned "about the claims proffered by the State of Oregon in this case concerning peyote use by Church members," and characterized as "patently offensive" the state's "efforts to engender unwarranted emotional hysteria over controlled peyote ingestion in legitimate Native American Church ceremonies."

A second brief was submitted by Amy Adelson, Lois C. Waldman, and Marc D. Stern on behalf of the American Jewish Congress, a leading religious liberty organization committed to the preservation of religious freedom for all Americans, particularly the rights of minority groups. The brief presented an exhaustive review of previous free exercise decisions, and, applying the balancing test required by *Sherbert*, explained how the state burdened the respondent's religious exercise and failed to convincingly prove that its interest would be impaired by an exemption to members of the Native American Church.

The American Civil Liberties Union filed a third brief, written by John A. Powell, David B. Goldstein, Charles A. Horsky, David H. Remes, Charles G. Geyh, and Martin J. McKeown. The group argued that certiorari was improvidently granted because the Oregon Supreme Court held that as a matter of state law, the proscription on peyote was not relevant to the determination of whether the respondents were entitled to unemployment benefits, which left no substantive federal question to the U.S. Supreme Court. The brief urged that the state court judgment be affirmed because the case was controlled by the Court's previous free exercise decisions in the unemployment context, including *Hobbie*.

———

After all the briefs were filed, the clerk of the Court circulated copies to the justices, and on October 9, 1987, set the case for argument on December 8. In the interim, other motions may be made, and both parties, if desired, have the option to file a reply brief. In the case of *Smith*, the ACLU made two motions during this time. One was a request that it be allowed to participate in oral arguments and the second was a request that the cases be divided. The Court denied both motions. It rarely allows outside parties to participate in oral arguments, and its decision to consolidate the cases illustrates that it did not view the minor differences in the facts as significant enough to evaluate the cases separately.

One week before oral arguments, the state filed a reply brief to clarify the Employment Division's position in the case. It noted that the case was not about whether the state could constitutionally prosecute the respondents for their conduct, or whether the state's unemployment benefits program discriminates against members of the Native American Church. Rather, the state responded that the question before the Court concerned whether the Employment Division was obligated to provide Black and Smith special benefits because of their religion. The state's primary argument was that the respondents could not assert a free exercise interest in circumstances when they could not lawfully engage in such conduct. It suggested that it had the authority to impose "the lesser burden of disqualification from receipt of unemployment benefits" in situations where the state can punish and proscribe such conduct. The state insisted that its unemployment compensation program be administered neutrally, as required by the state and federal constitutions. "Instead of equalizing claimants' position with other citizens who might receive benefits for engaging in the same conduct for compelling personal reasons, an award of benefits would specially favor claimants. In contrast to *Sherbert*, *Thomas*, and *Hobbie*, here no state citizen, other than arguably those with religious beliefs like claimants', lawfully can engage in this conduct."

The state also defended the criminal law prohibiting peyote as constitutional, because it believed a special exemption for members of the Native American Church would violate the state constitution's requirement demanding neutrality toward religion. And although the state conceded that peyote plays a central role in the religious ceremonies of the NAC, and that it is only potentially dangerous for members of the church, it defended the government's prohibition against its use because the government should not be forced to "compromise its health and safety interest with such exemptions from dangerous drug laws."

With all the briefs filed and the date of oral arguments set, the attorneys for both sides prepared for their appearance before the

Court. There is a difference of opinion on the importance of oral arguments in the outcome of a case. In the past the Court has complained about the notoriously poor quality of the attorneys appearing at bar, and in 1993 the clerk of the Court began sending lawyers scheduled to appear a booklet that conferred advice on presenting before the Court. Suggestions include not interrupting a justice, listening to the justice when spoken to, and answering questions directly. At the very least, oral arguments provide attorneys an opportunity to clarify their position and correct misunderstandings, so careful preparation is very important. Frohnmayer, who had extensive experience before the Court, nevertheless prepared intently for his sixth Supreme Court appearance. His colleagues at the attorney general's office organized moot courts where Frohnmayer practiced his oral presentation and was grilled by attorneys representing justices on the Supreme Court. Then, several days before the Supreme Court was scheduled to hear the case, Frohnmayer, busy with other cases, asked his deputy attorney general, William Gary, to represent the Employment Division in Court. Gary quickly primed himself for Court, also participating in drills and mock sessions. It would be his first appearance before the U.S. Supreme Court.

Back in Roseburg, Lovendahl prepared for her first Court appearance, but did so on her own. At this point in her career, she had limited appellate experience. She had never before worked on a federal appellate case and had worked on only two state appellate cases. Nevertheless, she refused outside assistance. Lovendahl reviewed her notes on the case and her prepared statements for oral arguments. Attorneys at the Native American Rights Fund again offered to aid her in her preparations and even set up moot courts for Lovendahl, but she never showed up for the practice sessions.

CHAPTER 7

Employment Division v. Smith I:
Back to Oregon

The Supreme Court that would decide *Employment Division v. Smith* was a Court in transition. In June 1986 Chief Justice Warren Burger announced he would step down from the Court to run the Commission on the Bicentennial of the Constitution, giving Ronald Reagan the opportunity to nominate a chief justice. The president selected William H. Rehnquist, a sitting justice first appointed to the bench by Richard Nixon in 1971. Antonin Scalia, a judge Reagan appointed to the Court of Appeals for the District of Columbia Circuit in 1982, was nominated to fill Rehnquist's seat. When contemplating who should serve on the Supreme Court, presidents consider several criteria, including merit and ethics, policy preferences, political reward, and a candidate's strategic effect on future political support. Reagan, a chief executive intent on leaving a judicial legacy, considered a prospective nominee's policy orientation—his or her legal and political philosophy and how it might influence consideration of issues such as abortion and affirmative action—the most important criterion. Both Rehnquist and Scalia were judicial and political conservatives with track records consistent with the ideological Reagan administration, and had been outspoken critics of the liberal social policies of the Warren Court and the Burger Court's inability to halt this trend. Reagan was confident his nominees would not hesitate to reverse course and allow his influence to continue long after he had left office.

Nominating a justice is only half the battle, however. Presidential selections are subject to Senate confirmation, and approximately 20 percent of Supreme Court nominees fail to win Senate approval. In recent years the process has become even more politicized; whereas only one nominee was defeated between 1900 and 1967, four nominees were either rejected by the Senate or forced to withdraw between 1968 and 1986. Senate consideration begins with hearings by the Senate Judiciary Committee, where members question the candidate and consider testimony from individuals and interest group representatives who may appear in support or opposition. The committee then makes a recommendation to the full Senate, which later debates and votes on the nomination. The Senate, like the president, also considers several factors when reviewing the suitability of a potential justice, and the nominee's political ideology and policy preferences are important criteria for the legislative branch as well. Senate confirmation is also influenced by external circumstances, including whether the Senate is controlled by the same party in the presidency, which almost doubles the chance of the nominee's success, whether the president is a lame duck, which makes approval less likely, and the level of participation from outside pressure groups, which organize in favor or in opposition to the candidate and can affect the tenor of the proceedings. Also important is the ideological balance of the Court. The more closely divided the Court, the more critical the nomination, which increases the probability of a contentious Senate confirmation hearing.

The Rehnquist nomination was vigorously opposed by Democrats in the Senate, who viewed him as an extremist. Rehnquist's actions on the Court did little to change this impression. He was a conservative jurist who stood far to the right of the other members of the Court. Rehnquist did not seem to mind this label as an outsider, and often authored solo dissenting and concurring opinions, earning him the nickname "The Lone Ranger." In an effort to influence the Senate confirmation hearing, Democrats charged the sitting justice with a variety of ethics violations, such as intimidating minority voters in the 1960s and purchasing property with racially restrictive covenants. But above all, Senate Democrats opposed Rehnquist for his conservative judicial ideology. Nevertheless, he survived a politically charged Senate Judiciary Committee hearing and was confirmed by a sixty-five to thirty-five vote in September 1986. Conservative Southern Democrats joined Republicans to elevate Rehnquist to the chief justiceship. A Senate weary of the political atmosphere of the Rehnquist confirmation battle unanimously confirmed Antonin Scalia later that month.

However, even with the elevation of Scalia, Reagan's judicial selections did not significantly alter the balance of power on the Court. Joining Rehnquist and Scalia on the right were Sandra Day O'Connor, Reagan's 1980 judicial appointment, and Byron White, a 1962 Kennedy appointee. O'Connor and White were fairly consistent conservative voices on the Court, although each had displayed streaks of independence on various issues. O'Connor's conservatism was reflected mostly in cases concerning federalism, where she regularly voted in favor of states' rights, and in cases involving criminal defendants' rights. White shared O'Conner's conservatism on criminal procedure, but differed sharply on the issue of federalism, usually voting in favor of national power over the states. White was also conservative on civil rights and liberties issues, often voting in opposition to affirmative action and in favor of restrictions on free speech and abortion.

Reagan was given another opportunity to put his personal stamp on the Court eleven months after Scalia's confirmation when Lewis Powell announced his resignation. Powell, a conservative Democrat appointed by Nixon, had often cast the deciding vote with the conservatives on the closely divided Burger Court, but he was also moderate on social policy issues such as abortion and affirmative action, and occasionally voted with the more liberal justices. Because Powell provided the crucial fifth vote on many important issues, his replacement could swing the Court solidly to the right.

Reagan's first choice was Robert Bork, a conservative judge on the Federal Court of Appeals for the District of Columbia. Bork was a prolific author who had written dozens of articles reflective of his judicial philosophy, which was usually at odds with the decisions of the Warren Court. However, the nomination was doomed from the start, and Bork's extreme conservatism and a confluence of external events played a significant role in his Senate defeat. A newly Democratic Senate (fifty-four to forty-six), a lame-duck president weakened by the Iran-Contra scandal and other events, and the extensive involvement of pressure groups led to what is regarded as the most bitter confirmation battle in modern history. Democrats, concerned that the ideological balance of the Court was at stake, attacked the nomination, and the Leadership Conference on Civil Rights, a coalition of almost two hundred interest groups, coordinated a large-scale effort to reject the nomination. The conference organized rallies, sent mass mailings, and even purchased ads in major newspapers in an attempt to sway public opinion. Conservative pressure groups responded in kind, but were unable to combat the momentum against Bork. The final straw was the candidate's appearance before the Senate Judiciary Committee, where he unconvincingly tried to distance himself from his conservative views. The committee voted nine to five in opposition to the nominee, and Bork later failed to win confirmation by a fifty-eight to forty-two floor vote, with conservative Democrats and several Republicans handing him the defeat.

Reagan's second nominee, Douglas Ginsberg, a young conservative judge on the same circuit as Bork, met a swifter fate. Republicans in the Senate asked him to withdraw after learning of ethical lapses and his admission that he smoked marijuana two decades previously. Reagan's third nominee, Anthony M. Kennedy, a judge on the Ninth Circuit Court of Appeals, was finally successful. Although his record suggested that he might be as conservative as Bork and Ginsberg, he was a low-profile candidate that did not face the confirmation challenges of the two previous nominees. He was easily confirmed on February 3, 1988, in a unanimous Senate vote.

Although Powell was still seated on the Court when it heard oral arguments in *Employment Division of Oregon v. Smith*, he would be off the Court when it considered the case, and Kennedy would not be participating in the deliberations. Therefore, the Court was evenly divided on both ends of the ideological spectrum. On the right was Chief Justice Rehnquist, joined by Justices Scalia, O'Connor, and White, and on the left were Justices Brennan, Marshall, Blackmun, and Stevens. Brennan, the senior associate justice, was its leading liberal judicial activist. Appointed by Dwight D. Eisenhower, who later considered him as one of his worst mistakes, Brennan was a strong advocate for protection of civil rights and liberties and wrote many of the landmark decisions of the Warren Court. Brennan believed the Court should play an active role in helping those who are less fortunate in society and to correct social injustices. This judicial philosophy was shared by Marshall, appointed to the bench by Lyndon Johnson, who had an even more liberal voting record. Blackmun, who was elevated to the Court by Richard Nixon, who pursued the southerner after his two previous nominees failed to win confirmation, was frequently a voting partner of Brennan and Marshall. Although Blackmun joined the Court as a conservative, particularly in criminal procedure cases, by the mid-1970s he was consistently voting liberally on civil rights and liberties issues. Stevens, Gerald Ford's only appointment to the Court, was more difficult to classify on an ideological scale; a centrist on civil rights and liberties issues, he started to lean more toward the left as the Court started shifting to the right.

Since justices do not always consistently vote as a "conservative" or "liberal," however, a more accurate measurement of how the parties in *Employment Division v. Smith* would fare before the Court could be found in a review of the Court's free exercise decisions. The lawyers at the attorney general's office and Suanne Lovendahl at Oregon Legal Services therefore canvassed these decisions to roughly gauge their chances of prevailing in *Smith*.

———

The Court's interpretation of the free exercise clause had gone through an evolution during the Burger Court years, and it was likely that these changes would continue under Rehnquist. One of Burger's first free exercise decisions, *Wisconsin v. Yoder*, where the chief justice applied the compelling government interest test to evaluate the constitutionality of a neutral, generally applicable compulsory school attendance law, was the high-water mark for the protection of religious exercise. Only Justice Douglas dissented from the decision. Powell and Rehnquist had recently joined the Court and did not participate in the deliberation of the case. Burger also wrote *Thomas v. Review Board*, another significant free exercise decision similar to *Sherbert v. Verner*, where the Court used strict scrutiny analysis to justify an exemption to the state's unemployment compensation law. The lone dissenting vote in this case was cast by Rehnquist, who argued that the free exercise clause did not require exemptions to neutral, generally applicable laws. Based on *Thomas*, it was obvious that Rehnquist was hostile to the use of the compelling government interest test to evaluate laws not specifically intended to restrict religious liberties.

Interestingly, conference memos from Thurgood Marshall's private papers reveal that by 1981 Burger was also expressing reservations about the Court's free exercise jurisprudence. In a memo to Blackmun regarding Rehnquist's dissent in *Thomas*, the chief justice admitted that he also had "concerns" with *Sherbert*, which he believed was difficult to reconcile with some of the Court's establishment clause cases where the Court was unwilling to give preferential treatment to religion. He noted that "it would indeed be nice to clarify and give greater guidance to other courts," but added that "to try to do so would, in my view, muddy an already difficult area and likely produce greater division here." Unwilling to overturn *Sherbert*, Burger used *Thomas* to uphold the 1963 decision.

As noted in Chapter 3, the Burger Court continued to apply the high level of scrutiny initiated in *Sherbert* to free exercise challenges. However, the Court often found the government's interests sufficiently compelling to outweigh the free exercise challenge in cases such as *U.S. v. Lee* and *Bob Jones University v. United States*. These cases also reveal that there were signs that other justices might be uncomfortable with the Court's free exercise jurisprudence. For instance, in a concurring opinion in *Lee*, Stevens expressed concern about the appropriateness of the Court's use of strict scrutiny analysis in free exercise cases. He believed the test was overly stringent and placed a high burden on government to justify the constitutionality of its laws. This burden, he suggested, "should be shouldered by the religious claimant who must demonstrate that there is a unique reason for allowing him a special exemption from a valid law of general applicability."

Then, beginning in 1986, during the transition between Burger and Rehnquist, the Supreme Court began to stray from its consistent application of the compelling government interest test to free exercise cases. In *Goldman v. Weinberger* Rehnquist was able to successfully persuade a majority of the Court that the fact situation, which involved an Orthodox Jew's free exercise challenge to an Air Force regulation that prevented him from wearing a yarmulke, was of such a "special circumstance" that the *Sherbert* standard should not be applied. Rehnquist then used the highly deferential rationality review to rule that the Air Force regulation was constitutional. Stevens wrote a concurring opinion, joined by White and Powell, agreeing that the military should be provided deference given its unique circumstances. However, he went even further in his concurrence to argue that rationality review would be the best standard to evaluate all religious claims to neutral, generally applicable laws. Stevens expressed concern that accommodation of religious liberty requests under strict scrutiny analysis might lead to establishment clause violations, and suggested that use of rationality review would allow "uniform treatment for the members of all religious faiths." Also important in *Goldman* was the fact that Blackmun, O'Connor, and Brennan, joined by Marshall, wrote three separate dissents to the majority opinion that strongly criticized the Court for making an exception to the compelling government interest test, which they believed was the appropriate balancing test for the evaluation of all free exercise challenges.

Later that year, a badly divided Court decided *Bowen v. Roy*, a case involving a free exercise challenge by members of the Abenaki Indian tribe who were receiving government aid from the state of Pennsylvania. The respondents sued the state to prevent it from requiring and utilizing a Social Security number as a condition of receiving benefits. They contended that the requirement was a violation of the exercise of their religion because they could not control the state's use of the number, and, according to their faith, "Control over one's life is essential to spiritual purity and indispensable to becoming a holy person." Eight members of the Court rejected the free exercise challenge in a decision written by Burger, who determined that the family had not adequately proven that their religious exercise was burdened and that the free exercise clause does not "afford an individual a right to dictate the conduct of the Government's internal procedures." Significantly, Burger introduced a change in the Court's manner of evaluating the "burden" requirement at the first tier of the *Sherbert* standard. In order to meet the threshold requirement of a burden on religion, Burger stated, the contested government regulation must actually coerce an individual to act "contrary to his or her religious beliefs." Refusal to accommodate an individual, he noted, did not necessarily mean that they suffered a burden on their religious exercise. "It may indeed confront some applicants for benefits with choices, but in no sense does it affirmatively compel appellees, by threat of sanctions, to refrain from religiously motivated conduct or to engage in conduct that they find objectionable for religious reasons." Without the establishment of a burden, the Court avoided the application of the other two parts of the *Sherbert* standard. Also, in a controversial move joined only by Rehnquist and Powell, Burger suggested that in cases where the government action in question was not directed toward a particular religion, that the Court use the more deferential rationality review to determine whether the government action was legitimate. This proposal was strongly criticized in a separate concurring opinion by O'Connor, joined by Brennan and Marshall, who insisted that the Court consistently apply the *Sherbert* compelling government interest test to all free exercise challenges.

As the Burger Court ended in 1986, three members of the Court, Burger, Powell, and Rehnquist, were ready to reject application of the *Sherbert* balancing test to free exercise challenges to neutral, generally applicable laws that burdened one's religion. Burger was leaving the Court, to be followed soon thereafter by Powell, and it remained to be seen whether the outgoing chief justice's suggestion to discard this higher level of scrutiny would find support in the Rehnquist Court. In the two cases decided during Rehnquist's first term as Chief Justice, it appeared as if a majority would continue to apply the compelling government interest test to free exercise challenges. In *Hobbie v. Unemployment Appeals Commission* seven members of the Court, including Scalia, joined Brennan's majority opinion that the denial of unemployment compensation placed a significant burden on the respondent's exercise of religion, which was not outweighed by the state's interest in protecting the unemployment compensation fund. Rehnquist was the only dissenter. He wrote a one-sentence opinion, stating, "I adhere to the views I stated in dissent in *Thomas v. Review Board*. Accordingly, I affirm." Notably, Stevens and Powell wrote separate concurring opinions in *Hobbie*, choosing not to join Rehnquist's dissent.

The new Chief Justice, however, was able to craft a five-to-four majority in a second free exercise case decided that term that deviated from the *Sherbert* standard. The case, *O'Lone v. Estate of Shabazz*, concerned a free exercise challenge to a prison regulation that prevented inmates of the Islamic faith from being excused from their Friday work schedule to attend Jumu'ah, a central religious ceremony. Rehnquist's decision resembled his majority opinion in *Goldman*. He assigned the prison case to the "special circumstances" category owing to the special needs of the prison system and the need to defer to the expertise and judgment of prison administrators. Using the lower rationality review, Rehnquist rejected the free exercise challenge. The decision was joined by Powell, White, O'Connor, and Scalia. Brennan wrote a dissent, joined by Marshall, Blackmun, and interestingly, Stevens, which, among other things, criticized the majority for once again making an exception to the compelling government interest test.

By the end of the 1987 term Rehnquist found a majority for two exceptions to the Court's use of a high level of scrutiny in free exercise cases. However, he also made it clear that the circumstances were "special" and warranted the more deferential level of review. As a result, *O'Lone* and *Goldman* were not necessarily proof that the Court had discarded the compelling government interest test, but rather that a majority of the Court had differentiated these cases from the previous rule.

Based on these precedent cases, attorneys representing both parties in *Smith* evaluated their chances of succeeding before the Court. At the time the case was argued, only one member of the current Court, Rehnquist, had consistently argued that the compelling government interest test be discarded and replaced with the lower, more deferential rationality review. Powell shared this view, but he would not be on the Court when it handed down *Smith*. Stevens had expressed reservations with this high level of scrutiny in concurring opinions in *Lee* and *Goldman*, but he also wrote a concurring opinion in *Hobbie* to uphold a free exercise challenge to the denial of unemployment compensation rather than join Rehnquist's dissent, which called for the elimination of the *Sherbert* balancing test, and joined Brennan's dissent in *O'Lone*. White's record was also inconsistent. He joined Stevens's concurring opinion in *Goldman*, which was critical of the compelling government interest test, but also joined the majority opinion in *Hobbie*, which used that test in the evaluation of a free exercise challenge to a denial of unemployment compensation. Scalia had only participated in two decisions, and also sent mixed signals, joining the majority in *O'Lone* and *Hobbie*. The other justices, Brennan, Marshall, Blackmun, and O'Connor, were committed to the use of a high level of scrutiny in free exercise cases, including challenges to neutral, generally applicable laws. The four usually voted in favor of the free exercise claimant, although O'Connor was less willing than the three more liberal justices to grant religious requests for exemptions.

These precedent cases revealed that a majority of the Court endorsed the use of a high level of scrutiny in free exercise challenges. In order to prevail, attorneys for the Employment Division had to demonstrate that the government's interest in denying Smith and Black unemployment compensation was compelling enough to outweigh the burden placed on their free exercise of religion. Lovendahl would have to prove that this interest was less than compelling and that Smith and Black should be awarded unemployment compensation benefits because their religious activity, which led to their dismissal, was protected by the free exercise clause of the First Amendment. A conservative estimate of the sitting justices split the vote down the middle, with Rehnquist, White, and Scalia voting in favor of the petitioner, and Brennan, Marshall, and Blackmun voting in favor of the respondents. O'Connor and Stevens would probably split between the two camps, and Kennedy would not participate. The case could go either way.

The Court's review of *Smith* took place during the second month of its 1987–1988 term. Since 1917 the Supreme Court commences its annual session on the first Monday in October until the end of the term, which is usually in late June or early July when the Court has finished its business. The term is divided into two-week sittings where the Court meets in open session and two-week recesses when the justices work behind closed doors, considering cases and writing opinions. During sittings, oral arguments are held on Mondays, Tuesdays, and Wednesdays from ten in the morning until noon, and from one until three. Four cases are usually heard each day, so approximately twenty to twenty-four cases are heard during each two-week period. Since 1970 oral arguments have been strictly limited to one hour, divided equally between the attorneys. Oral arguments in the U.S. Supreme Court do not resemble a trial—there are no witnesses or a jury—and they often have an ad hoc appearance because the attorneys are frequently interrupted by questions from the justices. Most justices come to oral arguments equipped with "bench memos" prepared by their law clerks that summarize the facts and the legal questions in each case and often include questions to ask the attorneys. Justices may also use this time to communicate to their colleagues, because oral arguments are one of the few times the Court meets together to consider a case.

Smith was the second case heard on December 8, 1987. Bill Gary, the deputy attorney general, represented the petitioners, the Employment Division, and Suanne Lovendahl presented on behalf of the respondents, Al Smith and Galen Black. The focus of Gary's presentation was his contention that the Oregon Supreme Court erred when it limited its consideration of the state interest solely to the unemployment compensation statute. He stated that the Oregon court believed it was "bound" by the "wooden application of the *Sherbert* rule" to look only at the interest in the unemployment compensation statute, and that the state court's analysis was therefore "hopelessly infected by a misreading of this Court's decision in *Sherbert*." Gary argued that because the conduct at issue, the ingestion of peyote, was "prohibited as a matter of criminal law . . . then these claimants had no free exercise right to engage in the conduct, and *Sherbert* simply doesn't apply." The criminality of this underlying conduct, Gary stated, made it appropriate for the Court to also look at the interests served by the state prohibition against peyote possession, such as protecting public health and safety, when evaluating the denial of unemployment compensation. The assistant attorney general concluded that these interests were compelling enough to justify the denial of unemployment compensation benefits to Smith and Black.

Lovendahl disagreed sharply with the assistant attorney general's suggestion to extend consideration of the state's interest to its need to control illegal drugs. She stated that when the Court evaluated the constitutionality of the state's denial of unemployment compensation, then, as in the precedent cases of *Sherbert*, *Thomas*, and *Hobbie*, it was only necessary to "look at the statute at issue that is imposing the burden in the unemployment context scheme," which was limited to maintaining the financial integrity of the unemployment fund. The state cannot, she stated, "bootstrap another statute" to add to its consideration of the state interest.

When Justice Stevens asked Lovendahl whether "there is a free exercise clause right to engage in criminal conduct?" Lovendahl replied that although she did not believe it was necessary to answer this question, she understood that the act of ingesting peyote was constitutionally protected because the respondents participated in the ceremony "in response to a dictate of their religion." She noted that the state's most disturbing suggestion was that they can "extinguish a free exercise guarantee simply by labeling conduct as criminal," but even so, under Oregon law, she clarified that the Employment Division had paid benefits to those who engaged in a criminal act.

Most of the oral arguments focused on the attorneys' differing perspectives regarding how the Court should balance the state's interest in this case. In addition, there was some discussion regarding whether the Oregon Supreme Court ruled on the criminality of Black and Smith's use of peyote, or whether the respondents were granted an exemption to the state peyote prohibition because of their religion. It was not until the last minute of oral arguments that Lovendahl was able to offer any analysis about the importance of the peyote ritual to the members of the Native American Church and its role as an "extremely important culturally-specific treatment plan" to help Native American people "overcome the problems of drug addiction and alcohol abuse."

During the sittings when the Court is hearing oral arguments, it holds judicial conferences on Wednesday afternoons and all day Friday. It is during this time that the Court considers the cases it heard earlier in the week. Justices prepare for conference by reviewing the list of cases to be discussed, which is provided by the chief justice prior to the meeting. During the meeting the justices then make a preliminary decision on the cases held earlier that week and discuss the cases that will be argued the following week. Other judicial matters, such as review of certiorari petitions, are also conducted during this time. During these conferences, the Court's internal deliberations are secret. Since 1910 only the justices have been present, and their personal notes are the only record of the meetings. When asked about how the Court conducts its business, however, most justices are candid about the process, so we have a general idea of what takes place in a conference meeting. When justices open up their private papers after leaving the Court, these papers often provide valuable information about the Court's business.

Three days after oral arguments in *Employment Division v. Smith*, the Court considered the case at its Friday conference. The chief justice, who presides over the conference, has a great deal of influence in directing the discussion of the cases being considered on the merits. He introduces each case, summarizes the facts and legal issues, and is the first to offer his opinion of the correct ruling. The other justices follow suit in descending order of seniority. Because time is limited, members speak only briefly and are dissuaded from interrupting or questioning one another. Often, justices state their opinion rather than attempt to persuade, so there is very little collaboration or collective decision making in conference. Justice Scalia has stated, "To call our discussion of a case a conference is really something of a misnomer. It's much more a statement of the views of the nine justices." Furthermore, at this point most of the justices have already made a decision on the cases being discussed, so there is little opportunity to lobby for votes. Chief Justice Rehnquist has noted that "It is the exception rather than the rule that minds are changed in conference."

Rehnquist began the *Smith* discussion. He first reviewed the facts of the case and the Oregon Supreme Court's decision to award Smith and Black unemployment compensation because the state's denial of benefits placed a substantial burden on their religion that was not outweighed by a compelling interest in the preservation of the unemployment compensation fund. Then Rehnquist offered his opinion. His comments focused on the main issue raised by the attorneys for the state: the legality of peyote in Oregon. However, he was unable to determine from the lower court record whether the state allowed an exemption for the sacramental use of peyote from its criminal law proscribing possession of the substance. As a result, Rehnquist voted to vacate the Oregon Supreme Court decision and remand the case back to the Oregon Court to determine whether the religious use of peyote was "lawful or not under state law."

Brennan spoke next. He reiterated his comments printed in his memorandum in February, that the case was indistinguishable from *Hobbie*, and that the legality of peyote was irrelevant to the evaluation of the state's interest in denying unemployment benefits, especially because according to state law, the "commission of an illegal act is not, in and of itself, grounds for disqualification from unemployment benefits." Brennan agreed with the Oregon court that the only relevant state interest in the case was financial, which was not compelling enough to overcome the burden on Smith and Black's free exercise rights. He voted to affirm the Oregon Supreme Court decision. Brennan was followed by White, who voted to reverse and remand the Oregon Supreme Court decision outright. Marshall and Blackmun presented their opinions next; both agreed with Brennan that the Court affirm the Oregon Supreme Court decision. Then, in order of seniority, Stevens, O'Connor, and Scalia aired their views on the case. Each was persuaded by Chief Justice Rehnquist's suggestion that the legality of peyote was relevant to the resolution of the case, and that the case should be vacated and remanded back to the Oregon Supreme Court for a decision on this issue. After the discussion, Rehnquist tabulated the original vote on the merits; there were four votes to vacate the state court decision and remand the case back for discussion on whether religious use of peyote was proscribed by state law, three votes in favor of affirming the state court decision, and one vote to reverse and remand the case. The Court followed this process for the other cases scheduled, and adjourned.

After the conference, Brennan returned to his chambers and jotted a quick note to Marshall and Blackmun, "We three are in dissent. I'll take it on." Over the weekend, Rehnquist reviewed the list of cases the Court had considered over the past two weeks and decided which justice would be assigned to write the opinions of the Court. The chief justice takes a number of considerations into account when dividing up the opinion writing responsibilities, including equality of workload, the selection of a justice in the ideological middle, and issue specialization. Often, he will assign some of the more important cases to himself. If the chief justice is not in the majority, the assignment of the case writing responsibility is made by the senior justice in the majority. On Monday Rehnquist circulated his list of opinion assignments. *Employment Division v. Smith* had been assigned to Stevens.

Each justice on the Court differs in his or her approach to writing opinions, but all rely to some degree on their law clerks, who frequently write the initial draft after consultation with the justice. The justice usually recounts his or her views and summarizes the conference discussion to give the clerk an idea of the Court's deliberations, and offers suggestions on the content of the opinion. After a draft is completed, the justice makes revisions and then circulates the draft opinion to the other members of the Court, who provide feedback to the author. There will likely be multiple drafts of the opinion as the justice writing the draft tries to maintain a majority. Chief Justice Rehnquist has noted that "the willingness to accommodate on the part of the author of the opinion is often directly proportional to the number of votes supporting the majority result at conference." This is also the time when justices may opt to write a concurring or dissenting opinion. Because the Court has been closely divided over the last several years, the opinion writing phase is crucial. The defection of one justice could turn a majority opinion into a dissenting opinion. Judicial decision making is unique; there is no logrolling or pressure from outside groups. The key to a good decision is a strong argument and an opinion that is crafted in a manner that preserves a majority vote.

Justice Stevens circulated the first draft in *Employment Division v. Smith* on February 20, 1987. The first part of the opinion included a detailed review of the facts of the case and the Oregon Supreme Court's consideration of the federal constitutional question, particularly its decision that the legality of peyote was irrelevant to the distribution of unemployment benefits because according to state law, an illegal act did automatically disqualify one from receiving unemployment benefits. Then, in the second part of the decision, Stevens declared that the legality of peyote use by members of the Native American Church *was* indeed relevant to the consideration of whether the Employment Division violated the free exercise clause of the First Amendment. He noted, "For if a State has prohibited through its criminal laws certain kinds of religiously motivated conduct without violating the First Amendment, it certainly follows that it may impose the lesser burden of denying unemployment compensation benefits to persons who engage in that conduct." Stevens agreed that the unemployment precedent cases cited by the respondents did

{ *Religious Freedom and Indian Rights* }

concern similar situations where an employee was required to choose between fidelity to his or her religious beliefs or acceptance of unemployment benefits, and that the Court in each case ruled in favor of the religious claimant, but he explained that the factual situations were not absolutely identical, and that "the results we reached . . . might well have been different if the employees had been discharged for engaging in criminal conduct."

Of paramount concern to the justice was whether the respondents engaged in a criminal act. Citing *Hobbie*, Stevens stated that the protection that the First Amendment provides to "legitimate claims to the free exercise of religion," does not extend to conduct "that a State has validly proscribed." It was the same argument made by the state of Oregon in its briefs to the Court. He was unable to determine whether the religious use of peyote was legal in Oregon, however, because the question was not directly addressed by the Oregon Supreme Court. Consequently, he chose not to discuss whether Smith and Black's First Amendment free exercise rights were violated, stating that this discussion was "premature" owing to the uncertainty regarding the legality of the religious use of peyote. "It may ultimately be necessary to answer that federal question in this case, but it is inappropriate to do so without first receiving further guidance concerning the status of the practice as a matter of Oregon law." Stevens added that "a substantial number" of jurisdictions did exempt the sacramental use of peyote, and included a footnote that reviewed several state court decisions, such as *People v. Woody* and *Whitehorn v. State*, where the courts carved out an exemption for the sacramental use of peyote, and several state and federal court rulings where similar religious requests for use of marijuana and LSD had been rejected.

Stevens therefore vacated the Oregon state court judgment and remanded the case to the state to decide the legality of the sacramental use of peyote. He also provided a hint as to how the Court might confront the federal constitutional question if it reviewed the case a second time. In the last paragraph of his opinion he observed, "If the Oregon Supreme Court's holding rests on the unstated premise that respondents' conduct is entitled to the same measure of federal constitutional protection regardless of its criminality, that holding is erroneous. If, on the other hand, it rests on the unstated premise that the conduct is not unlawful in Oregon, the explanation of that premise would almost certainly preclude any further review in this Court."

Two days later Brennan sent a note to Stevens indicating that he would be circulating a dissent in the case, and Marshall followed a day later with a note that he would "await the dissent." Then, on February 24, White, who initially voted to reverse and remand the Oregon Supreme Court decision, sent Stevens a memo stating he would join his majority opinion. The next day Rehnquist also joined the majority. A second draft of the opinion, which included minor changes to a footnote, soon followed.

Two weeks later Brennan sent out the initial draft of his dissenting opinion. The first part of his opinion reviewed the Court's previous free exercise decisions in the unemployment compensation context in order to highlight the similarities between *Smith* and *Sherbert*, *Thomas*, and *Hobbie*. The only difference between the cases, Brennan observed, was that "the Employment Division has asserted in court a 'compelling state interest . . . in the proscription of illegal drugs.'" He then suggested that the state had not "sought to advance" this interest when it enacted its unemployment compensation statute, and emphasized that the state supreme court "authoritatively disavowed it." He remarked, "the Oregon Supreme Court could scarcely have been clearer. The state court understood that the Employment Division may not overcome the burden on religion by invoking a theoretically plausible interest that in fact the state legislature had no intention of furthering when it enacted the unemployment compensation statute." Brennan determined that the only interest that should be considered in this case was the interest in protecting the unemployment compensation fund, not the interest in proscribing illegal drugs, because the state of Oregon was not trying to enforce a criminal law prohibiting peyote possession by denying Smith and Black unemployment compensation.

Brennan did not favor remanding the case back to the Oregon court to deliberate an issue it had already ruled was irrelevant to the disposition of the case. He ended his opinion with a subtle reprimand to the majority:

> A slot on this Court's calendar is both precious and costly. Inevitably, each Term this Court discovers only after painstaking briefing and oral argument that some cases do not squarely present the issues that the Court sought to resolve. . . . Today's foray into the realm of the hypothetical will surely cost us the respect of the State Supreme Court whose words we misconstrue. That price is particularly exorbitant where, as here, the state court is most likely to respond to our efforts by merely reiterating what it has already stated with unmistakable clarity.

On March 14 Marshall sent Brennan a memo indicating that he would join the dissent, and two weeks later O'Connor joined Stevens's majority opinion. After Brennan circulated the second draft of his dissent, which included minor changes, Blackmun joined the opinion. The last justice to comment on the circulating drafts was Scalia, who sent a lengthy memo to Stevens suggesting two necessary changes before he would join the majority opinion of the Court. Scalia asked Stevens to remove the footnote that reviewed the state court decisions exempting the religious use of peyote from criminal laws because he believed it "too strongly hints to the Oregon Supreme Court that it should find such use lawful as a matter of state law because of the federal constitutional concerns," and to omit the last sentence of the opinion, which stated that if Oregon determined that the ingestion of peyote was not unlawful, "the explanation of that premise would almost certainly preclude any further review in this Court." Scalia was troubled that such a statement suggested that the federal First Amendment question was settled and not open to review by the Supreme Court.

After he received Scalia's memo, Stevens phoned him to discuss the case, and several days later wrote a response addressing the junior justice's concerns. He agreed to omit the footnote in question and then offered suggestions as to the rewording of the last sentence in the opinion. One suggestion, that he end the opinion with the phrase, "If, on the other hand, it rests on the unstated premise that the conduct is not unlawful in Oregon, the explanation of that premise would make it more difficult to distinguish this case from our holdings in *Sherbert, Thomas* and *Hobbie*," was acceptable to Scalia, who joined the opinion on April 19, 1988.

———

Back in Oregon, the attorneys and parties to the case anxiously awaited the Court's decision. Although by most estimates it takes the Court several months to decide a case, the Court does not announce its opinions according to any schedule. Decisions are usually announced on Tuesdays and Wednesdays during the first part of the term, and every day during the latter part of the term. Because it was late in the term, the attorneys awaited word from the high court each day. Both sides believed they had an equal chance of prevailing. Then, on April 21, 1988, there was a development that collapsed the confidence of Smith's supporters. That afternoon the Supreme Court announced its decision in *Lyng v. Northwest Indian Cemetery Protective Association*. The case concerned a challenge by three American Indian tribes to the building of a seventy-five-mile U.S. Forest Service road that would link two small California towns and provide a route for the harvesting and selling of timber. A six-mile section of the road passed through the Chimney Rock section of the Six Rivers National Forest, land that is considered sacred by tribal members. The tribes argued that the land on the proposed site, known as "high country," was central to their religious ceremonies and that the construction of the road would significantly interfere with the free exercise of their religion. The state responded that the road was necessary to link the towns together, increase the accessibility to timber harvest, and improve the local economy.

O'Connor wrote the majority opinion, joined by Rehnquist, White, Stevens, and Scalia. She first evaluated whether the government action placed a burden on the tribes' free exercise of religion. In order to assess the burden, she cited the new threshold requirement announced in *Bowen*—that the government action must "coerce" an individual to act contrary to his or her religious beliefs to constitute a burden on religion, thus differentiating government interference with religious beliefs from government coercion. O'Connor concluded that although "the challenged Government action would interfere significantly with private persons' ability to pursue spiritual fulfillment according to their own religious beliefs . . . the affected individuals would [not] be coerced by the Government's action into violating their religious beliefs; nor would either governmental action penalize religious activity by denying any person an equal share of the rights, benefits, and privileges enjoyed by other citizens." Because the burden requirement was not fulfilled, she explained that it was inappropriate for the Court to apply the compelling government interest test to evaluate the constitutionality of the government action. O'Connor also reiterated the Court's majority holding in *Lee*, that the government is not compelled by the Constitution to alter its affairs according to the religious views of the people. "The government cannot operate efficiently, if it had to satisfy everyone's religious beliefs-desires . . . the First Amendment must apply to all citizens alike, and it can give none of them a veto over public programs that do not prohibit the free exercise of religion. The Constitution does not, and courts cannot, offer to reconcile the various competing demands on government, many of them rooted in sincere religious belief, that inevitably arise in so diverse a society as ours."

Brennan wrote a scathing dissent to the opinion, joined by Marshall and Blackmun. The focus of his dissent was O'Connor's decision to strictly enforce the burden threshold, which made it impossible to invoke the higher level of scrutiny provided in the *Sherbert* compelling government interest test. Brennan observed, "Today, the Court holds that a federal land-use decision that promises to destroy an entire religion does not burden the practice of that faith in a manner recognized by the Free Exercise Clause." He suggested that the Court measure a burden on religion by assessing how the government action affected one's free exercise of religion, rather than the intention of the government in passing a particular piece of legislation. Brennan reasoned that such an approach would allow the proper balancing of the government interest with the burden on the Native Americans' free exercise of religion, and would reveal that the ruling "sacrifices a religion at least as old as the nation itself, along with the spiritual well-being of its approximately five thousand adherents, so that the Forest Service can build a six-mile segment of road that two lower courts found had only the most marginal and speculative utility, both to the Government itself and to the private lumber interests that might conceivably use it."

Court watchers saw *Lyng* as a harbinger that the Rehnquist Court had turned its back on protection for the free exercise of religion. Some asserted that the Court used the higher burden requirement as an excuse to discriminate against an unpopular religion and continue its track record against the rights of American Indians. Although O'Connor technically followed the *Sherbert* precedent by first assessing the nature of the burden on religion before applying the compelling government interest test, the "coercion test" was characterized as dangerous because it allowed the Court to avoid any real consideration of the importance of the government interest.

More immediately, Smith and his attorneys felt a sense of foreboding after learning of *Lyng*. If a majority of the Court did not believe that a six-mile road through sacred Indian country placed a burden on three Indian tribes' exercise of religion, how would it feel about the denial of unemployment benefits to alcohol and drug treatment counselors who were terminated from their job for engaging in misconduct for ingesting peyote, a Schedule I drug under state law, as an exercise of their religion?

———

Smith and Black would not have to wait long to find out. The Supreme Court handed down its decision in *Employment Division v. Smith* one week later, on April 27, 1988. Unfortunately, what both parties found out was that the Court needed additional information to rule on the First Amendment challenge and remanded the case back to Oregon. The decision did reveal, however, that both the attorney general's office and Suanne

Lovendahl had found an audience for their arguments, and that the state had the edge in the case. Although the larger free exercise question would be put off until another day, this initial decision by the Court illustrated that at the very least, the fact that Smith and Black may have engaged in illegal activity was going to be a factor in the Court's ultimate decision.

CHAPTER 8

A Difference in Perspective

After *Employment Division of Oregon v. Smith* was remanded back
to the Oregon Supreme Court, Bernie Thurber, the litigation
specialist for the state office of Oregon Legal Services, reviewed
OLS's legal strategy. Because the question on remand asked the
attorneys to specifically address the legality of the sacramental
use of peyote in the state, it became more of an Indian rights case
and Thurber thought it would be wise to bring in an Indian law
specialist who could discuss the centrality of the peyote ritual to
members of the Native American Church. He reached for the
phone and called Craig Dorsay, executive director of the Native
American Program at Oregon Legal Services (NAPOLS). Dorsay had litigation experience on Indian issues and was well connected with others in the Indian legal community who could
assist him with the case. Thurber knew Dorsay would be an excellent resource for Suanne Lovendahl, who had taken over the
case from David Morrison.

Craig Dorsay never intended to become an Indian law specialist. A wildlife biology major from the University of Michigan,
his original goal was to attend the University of Oregon Law
School and eventually practice natural resource law. His interest
in Indian law grew out of a course he took from Professor
Charles Wilkenson, a former Native American Rights Fund attorney who started teaching at the university in 1975. The two
became close friends and Dorsay's interest in Indian issues grew,
whereas his desire to go to law school did not, so he took a leave
of absence for a year and a half. During this time he worked in
the field doing Indian advocacy work, including a clerkship at the
Native American Rights Fund, where he first met John Echo-

hawk, NARF's executive director, and his cousin, Walter Echo-hawk, a senior staff attorney at the center.

After his experience at NARF Dorsay returned to law school in 1978 to finish his degree. His senior year he worked with Wilkenson and other academics and professionals at NARF on revisions to the Cohen Law Treatise, a project that updated Felix Cohen's seminal 1941 work, *Handbook on Indian Law*. Dorsay continued working on the treatise as one of the coordinating editors after graduation, and was later hired as a staff attorney at Oregon Legal Services in 1981. Like Morrison, Dorsay wanted to work in the area of public interest law, and at the time OLS was the primary avenue for this type of work. He specialized in Indian law cases, including work involving recognized tribes in the state. Dorsay also pursued cases under the recently passed federal Indian Child Welfare Act.

Dorsay left Oregon Legal Services in 1983 to work on the Navajo Reservation, which had recently opened an in-house Department of Justice. As the assistant attorney general in charge of Human Services, Dorsay handled over two hundred active cases in at least twenty-eight different states. Most of his work involved cases under the Indian Child Welfare Act, and he soon became nationally known for his advocacy. Dorsay found the work rewarding, but it involved a great deal of travel and he eventually left the reservation in 1985 to return to the Pacific Northwest. He settled in Portland and continued to work on child welfare and juvenile defense cases for the Navajo on a contract basis. He was also employed as general counsel for the Coos tribe and taught Indian law courses at the University of Oregon and Lewis and Clark's Northwestern School of Law. In 1987 Dorsay was hired as NAPOLS's executive director, a job he held on a part-time basis while he continued his work in private practice. He was soon able to triple the size of the office by bringing in contract work from tribes in the area.

Dorsay had been at NAPOLS only a short time when Thurber contacted him about *Smith*. He had not followed the case as it worked its way through the Oregon courts because in its early stages the emphasis was on the denial of unemployment compensation. "The law in Oregon was pretty clear about how you couldn't be fired or denied unemployment benefits for drug use or other misconduct done outside of work. There were no real Indian issues involved except for the fact that Al was an Indian and he had participated in an Indian religious ceremony." However, when the Supreme Court sent the case back on remand to discuss the legality of peyote, it changed from a civil case to a criminal case, and, stated Dorsay, "That triggered the Indian aspect of it. So you now had a direct assault on the Native American Church."

Dorsay and Thurber knew the case would have far-reaching implications in the state and possibly the nation, and were very interested in participating in Oregon Legal Services' representation of Smith and Black before the Oregon Supreme Court. However, they ran into trouble trying to coordinate their legal strategy with Lovendahl. Dorsay recalls some of the challenges he and Thurber had with the Roseburg legal aid attorney. "She was very private, and didn't share anything. I remember that Suanne was working on her brief and Bernie finally pried a copy of the draft brief from her, and we spent days working on revisions, and writing some Indian aspects of it, and helping her posture the case, and then faxed the changes to her, and she told us she had already filed her brief."

The brief Lovendahl filed was in response to the question specifically posed by the U.S. Supreme Court on remand. It duplicated many of the arguments that appeared in previous filings, but also included notice that ADAPT had entered into the consent decree with the EEOC and had agreed to accommodate any future employees belonging to the Native American Church. This additional information, she noted, "warrant[ed] a reexamination of the finding that [respondents] were terminated for 'misconduct' within the meaning of the Employment Division law." On the specific question before the state court regarding the legality of peyote, Lovendahl argued that the court should not answer this question, which would be "advisory" because the respondents had not been arrested for peyote use. She then suggested that if the respondents were charged with a violation of the law, that they should be granted an exemption based on the fact that other state courts and the U.S. government protected the religious use of peyote as required by the First Amendment.

The state's brief on behalf of the Employment Division also repeated much of the information contained in its earlier briefs. It established that possession of peyote was a crime in Oregon, and that there was not an exception for members of the church. The state concluded that because Black and Smith's use of the substance was illegal, that the conduct was not protected by the federal Constitution and that the state had a compelling interest in regulating the use of dangerous drugs that overrode the burden on the respondents' religious exercise. It asked the court to reverse its earlier decision and reinstate the Employment Appeals Board's order disallowing unemployment compensation.

After the Oregon Supreme Court received the briefs from both parties on September 1, 1988, it moved quickly to consider *Smith*. Oral arguments were scheduled one week later, and on September 8, 1988, Lovendahl and William Gary, the deputy attorney general, each presented their case before the court. Lovendahl's unwillingness to accept assistance from Thurber and Dorsay continued. She never informed the other OLS attorneys that she argued the case before the state supreme court.

So Bernie and I heard about the argument before the Oregon Supreme Court on the radio," said Dorsay. "I was flabbergasted. But she just didn't want us there and she couldn't stand to have anyone look at her work product. It's not exactly the way you want to work as cocounsel. So we had limited involvement in the work on remand from the Oregon Court. Which is unfortunate, because we would have argued the case differently and hopefully avoided having the case go back to the U.S. Supreme Court.

The Oregon Supreme Court handed down its per curiam decision five weeks later on October 18, 1988. It declined to answer the U.S. Supreme Court's question regarding the legality of the respondent's use of peyote, stating that it was not evaluating a criminal case. However, the court did concede that "the Oregon statute against possession of controlled substances, which includes peyote, makes no exception for the sacramental use of peyote." The decision could have ended there, but the court went on to add that "outright prohibition of good faith religious use of peyote by adult members of the Native American Church would violate the First Amendment directly and as interpreted by Congress." The decision referred to the fact that twenty-three states had some level of protection for the religious use of peyote and that the Native American Church enjoyed a religious exemption to federal controlled substances laws. It also cited the 1978 American Indian Religious Freedom Act where Congress declared that it was U.S. policy to "protect and preserve for American Indians their inherent right of freedom to believe, express and exercise the traditional religions . . . including, but not limited to access to sites, use and possession of sacred objects, and the freedom to worship through ceremonials and traditional rites." The Oregon Supreme Court concluded, "we hold on remand that the First Amendment prevents enforcement of prohibitions against possession or use of peyote for religious purposes in the Native American Church," and sent the case back to the Employment Appeals Board to award Smith and Black unemployment compensation benefits.

When Dorsay found out about the Oregon Supreme Court decision, he was obviously pleased, but he also thought it had decided the case in a manner that assured the U.S. Supreme Court would once again review the decision. "The story I heard was that there was a fight between the courts. The Oregon Supreme Court couldn't resist and went on and said, you ignorant people at the U.S. Supreme Court, you have applied the test wrong, and this is what it really is, and you are allowed to use peyote and not be penalized for it under federal Constitution."

Frohnmayer also believed the Oregon Supreme Court over-reached.

I was surprised because it seemed almost to have flaunted the question that was posed for review. And I'm not sure they had to go back and answer the First Amendment free exercise argument. I think in casual conversation since, that some of the justices believed they were compelled to answer the free exercise argument. But that is not what they were asked. They were asked on remand to say whether [the religious use of peyote] was criminal or not, and they could have said yes or no, but they went on gratuitously to raise a couple of federal statutes that were clearly not applicable, and which no one went to the court to defend, and so it appeared to be gratuitous. The Court seemed to be taking its cues from Justice Brennan's dissent. It was saying that the free exercise clause applies, and was applying Brennan-type reasoning, when Brennan was a dissenter.

After the Oregon Supreme Court ruling, Frohnmayer faced the difficult decision of whether he should appeal *Smith* a second time to the U.S. Supreme Court. He was aware that his decision to pursue the case might be perceived as hostile to the Native American community. He saw this case as less about American Indian rights, however, and more about law enforcement and how a decision allowing the religious use of illegal drugs would lead to future requests for exemptions to drug laws. The state's case against Alan C. Venet, the ordained minister of the Universal Industrial Church of New World Comforter, weighed heavily in Frohnmayer's mind. In July 1987 Venet had been arrested for possession of marijuana, which he was growing on his rural property. He argued that marijuana was a sacrament of his church and defended his actions as necessary for the exercise of his religion. Venet had lost at the state trial court, but he was appealing the decision to the Oregon Court of Appeals. Frohnmayer was concerned *Smith* would make it more difficult for the state to prevail against *Venet* and similar cases.

Frohnmayer also faced other problems associated with the *Smith* case. On April 15, 1987, Smith and representatives from the Native American Program at Oregon Legal Services had requested that the Oregon Board of Pharmacy adopt a rule exempting peyote from the state drug laws. Smith testified at a hearing on September 25, 1987, and after the hearing the board agreed to allow a religious exemption for peyote. The rule would essentially allow the religious use of peyote in the state, regardless of the outcome of *Smith*.

Frohnmayer was stunned. The board had not consulted with him about the rule change. He informed the board that its action potentially violated the establishment clause of the First Amendment of the state and federal constitutions by giving preference to one religion over another and recommended that they withdraw the rule. The board held an emergency meeting on October 7, 1987, when it reversed their previous action, and the rule was formally repealed several months later.

Frohnmayer found it difficult to persuade the public that *Smith* would have ramifications beyond the immediate decision. "There was a part of us that said, we wish it had been anything but a Native American and peyote, because there are other drugs in other religions that are more seriously implicated." There was only limited discussion in the attorney general's office about whether to take the case up a second time because of the negative public reaction. Frohnmayer claimed, "Our job is to represent principle, and if the principle is the issue of drug use, even religiously inspired drug use, and if it compromised our position in other drug and religion cases, as was the case, then even though we knew that this was politically unpopular, we felt it was important to proceed ahead and to define the state's interest in those broader ways." Some of the criticism took the attorney general by surprise because he believed his office had been successful in developing positive relations with Indian tribes in the state. "And it was really sort of ironic because ours was one of the offices that had done the most of the Western states to reach out to Indian tribes, and I chaired a Committee of the Western Attorneys General on state tribal relations, trying to improve relations from the traditionally almost racist attitude of some states toward Native Americans."

Even in light of the criticism, Frohnmayer still believed he was doing the right thing by continuing with the case. "Would it have been a better move to not appeal the case? I didn't make any of my appellate decisions on political grounds. Ever. That was the tradition of our office." His own political standing was not an issue. Frohnmayer had easily won the Republican primary election for his third term as attorney general and prevailed as a write-in candidate for the Democratic primary as well. The popular attorney general then went on to win the general election against a Libertarian Party candidate with 965,000 votes—setting a record for the most votes received in a statewide race.

———

There were problems at Oregon Legal Services as well. After the state Supreme Court decision, Thurber and Dorsay deliberated with others in the office about how legal counsel for Smith would handle any future action in the case. Dorsay expressed concern over how he had been shut out before the Oregon Supreme Court and how this may have disadvantaged the case. To avoid these challenges in the future, Suanne Lovendahl was given directives on OLS's protocol for handling *Smith*, which included the requirement that Dorsay participate fully in the preparation of the case and that he "sign off" on all briefs before they were submitted. In the end, Lovendahl chose to withdraw from the case. It had changed significantly since she took over as lead counsel, and coordination with Dorsay would be difficult from her office in Roseburg. "After that," said Dorsay, "she disappeared completely. I was surprised by that. I wanted to meet with her and discuss what happened at oral arguments, and what to expect before the Court. We may have had one conversation, but she was not very helpful." It was now Dorsay's case, and the part-time NAPOLS executive director had a lot of preparation before him.

———

Dave Frohnmayer filed his second petition for a writ of certiorari on January 17, 1989. His new deputy attorney general, James E. Mountain, Solicitor General Virginia L. Linder, and the new assistant solicitor general, Michael D. Reynolds, also appeared on the brief. The state argued that it was necessary for the Supreme

Court to grant the writ in order to "review the Oregon Court's weakly analyzed conclusion that the First Amendment protects religious peyote ingestion." It also criticized the state supreme court for relying on arguments made in other state and federal courts, "thus substitut[ing] a survey of 'conventional wisdom' for constitutional analysis," and for not acknowledging the state's interest in regulating the use of dangerous drugs in order to protect the public interest. Frohnmayer was certain the U.S. Supreme Court would grant certiorari a second time. Its decision to review *Smith* in the first instance signaled the Court's interest in the dispute and the fact that it remanded the case back to the Oregon Supreme Court to address the legality of peyote was a sign it believed the question was relevant to resolution of the case.

Craig Dorsay filed his brief in opposition to the petition for writ of certiorari one month later. He made six brief arguments about why the writ should be denied: first, the state court had denied the relevance of the criminality of peyote as a matter of state law, therefore making it improper for the Supreme Court to do so; second, the Supreme Court's decision would be advisory because the respondents had never been arrested or prosecuted for peyote possession; third, the ruling would be of limited precedential importance because most states with significant Indian populations already had exemptions for the religious use of peyote; fourth, because there were no decisions in conflict with the Oregon Supreme Court ruling, the case presented a unique fact situation that would not likely be repeated; fifth, the state court's opinion was consistent with the Supreme Court's previous free exercise opinions in a similar context, making review unnecessary; and sixth, the respondents would never be convicted in state court for possession of peyote even if the state were to institute criminal proceedings, because the statute of limitations had passed. Dorsay's strategy was to persuade the Supreme Court that the case was of limited importance and had been properly decided by Oregon's highest court, thus making it unnecessary and perhaps even inappropriate for the Supreme Court to review the case a second time.

The attempt was unsuccessful. The briefs were distributed to the Court shortly after they were filed, and on March 20, 1988,

Chief Justice Rehnquist, joined by Justices Stevens, O'Connor, and Scalia, voted to grant certiorari; Justice White, who voted third, cast a vote to "Join 3." Justices Brennan, Marshall, Blackmun, and Kennedy voted to deny. There were five votes in favor of certiorari, and four against. This time it was Justice Kennedy, the Court's newest member, who informed the clerk of the Court's decision to review *Employment Division v. Smith* a second time.

Back in Oregon, the attorney general's office began preparations for its second appearance before the Supreme Court. The state's strategy followed the cue from the Court regarding the importance of the legality of peyote in Oregon. The case had changed significantly since it began in the state system. Frohnmayer observed, "One has to bear in mind what happened between *Smith I* and *Smith II*. The United States Supreme Court, on its own volition, changed this from an unemployment compensation case to a criminal case. Which is paradoxical, because there was never a criminal prosecution, nor the threat of one." The state postured its case around the fact that peyote possession was illegal in Oregon. The Court must, it claimed in its brief, "decide whether, and under what circumstances, the Free Exercise Clause protects religious drug use from the reach of generally applicable and religiously neutral drug regulations." To evaluate this question, the state recommended the Court use the same balancing test it employed over the last several decades when it evaluated religious requests for exemptions to state or federal laws; the state's interests must be balanced against the individual's religious interest, and "religious conduct must give way to regulations that serve public interests of compelling importance."

There was no reason the state needed to consider any other strategy. One week after the Court granted certiorari in *Smith II*, it handed down its ruling in *Frazee v. Illinois Department of Employment Security*, another religious challenge to a denial of unemployment compensation. The case concerned an individual who refused to accept a temporary job because it would have required him to work on Sundays—a violation of his personal religious belief that he not work on "the Lord's day." The state unemployment board determined that he had declined "an offer of suitable work without good cause," which made him ineligible for benefits. The unanimous decision by White was similar to the Court's previous unemployment compensation rulings; he determined that the respondent suffered a burden on his religious exercise because he was forced to choose between fidelity to his religious beliefs and employment, and he concluded that the state's interest was not sufficiently compelling to outweigh his request for a religious exemption to the law. It was the Court's fourth unemployment case in nine years. Considering the few cases the Court decides each year, it appeared unusually preoccupied with religious challenges to unemployment compensation.

The state's brief on behalf of the Employment Division covered familiar ground. It established the dangers of drug use in America and the need for the state to protect the health, safety, and welfare of the public by regulating dangerous drugs, including peyote.

> Few problems confronting society today are as devastating in their consequences, as unmanageable in their proportions, and as immediate in their danger as that of drug use and abuse. The nation's drug crisis pervades every fact of our citizens' lives. It is present in our cities, our streets, our work places, our schools and our homes. Illicit drug use also crosses all social boundaries: age, economic class, gender, profession, national origin, religious and political affiliation, geographic location.

Because of this danger, the state argued, it was necessary that there be a comprehensive and uniform set of regulations addressing this drug epidemic.

The state's second argument focused on whether the government should accommodate religious drug use by making exemptions to its neutral criminal laws. "In actual practice," it claimed, "this Court has found no room for 'accommodating' religion-by-religion exemptions from neutral laws of general applicability when those laws directly serve health, safety or public order interest." The brief included examples such as *Reynolds*, where the

Court determined that polygamy was dangerous to the social order, and *Lee*, where it decided that multiple exemption requests to the federal tax code would undermine government regulations. The state also suggested that one reason the Court avoided granting religious exemptions from facially neutral laws was because of potential conflicts with the establishment clause. Accommodation of the respondents, it argued, would open the door to requests for future exemptions which could "weaken the entire fabric of the nation's controlled substances laws" and potentially violate the Constitution's demand for nonpreferential treatment of religion. "In matters of religion, the Constitution does not permit cracking the door open in such a way as to permit one government-favored religion to pass through, and to deny passage to all others. Under settled Free Exercise and Establishment Clause principles, government cannot show partiality to any one religious group or promote one religion over another." The state urged the Court to respect the state and federal constitutions' demand for religious neutrality and find the government interest in public health compelling enough to reject the respondent's request for an exemption to the law.

Frohnmayer had confidence in his case. The state had properly used the *Sherbert* balancing test previously applied by the Supreme Court, and the attorney general believed the brief effectively highlighted the state's compelling interest in controlling drug use. "The Court had not only decided *Sherbert*, but then came *Thomas*, then came *Hobbie*, then came *Frazee*, and we said to ourselves, it is a loser to go in the face of *Sherbert*, and so you have to win arguing on *Sherbert*'s grounds. And so we said there is a compelling interest, and I think there was."

Craig Dorsay prepared the brief on behalf of Smith and Black. He was assisted by NAPOLS staff members Michael Mason, Lea Ann Easton, and Andrew Miller. He also ran the brief past attorneys Walter Echo-hawk and Steve Moore from the Native American Rights Fund, who had been working with Dorsay since he took over the case. "I knew all of the attorneys at NARF and I considered their involvement an asset. I ran briefs past Moore and Bunkie [Walter Echo-hawk] and we discussed strategy. We knew early on that it would be a difficult case." The NARF attorneys were pleased to assist Dorsay. They had repeatedly volunteered to help Lovendahl, but she purposely avoided all outside assistance during her preparation before the Supreme Court.

Dorsay's brief first emphasized that the Oregon court had ruled on two occasions that the criminality of the religious use of peyote was "irrelevant as a matter of state law to Oregon's unemployment scheme," and thus should not be considered in an evaluation of whether the respondents were entitled to benefits. Because the Oregon Supreme Court had not officially ruled on the criminality of the religious use of peyote, which would have been "advisory" because there was no criminal case before it, Dorsay suggested that it was inappropriate for the Supreme Court to order the state court to consider "the state's interest in proscribing the use of dangerous drugs" when it explicitly declined to do so. Such action, he observed, would allow the Supreme Court to "overrule the Oregon Supreme Court on a matter of state law" because the unemployment compensation statute did not provide for the consideration of the state's interest in controlling drug use. Therefore, he noted, the question of the legality of the religious use of peyote was not "ripe" or ready for consideration by the U.S. Supreme Court.

Second, Dorsay contended that the respondents were entitled to unemployment benefits based on the Supreme Court's previous decisions in *Sherbert* and its progeny. Even if peyote use were criminal, he added, "it should not alter the result." He likened *Smith* to the situation in *Wisconsin v. Yoder*, where the respondents were "charged, tried and convicted" for violating a state criminal compulsory attendance law. In *Yoder*, Dorsay reasoned, the Court applied the *Sherbert* compelling government interest test to consider the state's specific interest served by the attendance law rather than the state's more general interest in law enforcement. In *Smith*, he stated, the Supreme Court must evaluate the state interest in the financial integrity of the unemployment compensation statute rather than the state's general interest in proscribing drug use.

In the third part of the brief Dorsay evaluated the state's interest in proscribing the religious use of peyote. He called the state's fears "speculative" and criticized it for its attempt "to lump the highly regulated and limited religious use of peyote by the Native American Church with other drugs that are used almost exclusively for improper purpose." Moreover, he responded, there were no law enforcement problems in the twenty-three states that permitted the religious use of the sacrament, and there was no illegal trafficking of peyote. The petitioners' assertions, he concluded, "are purely imaginary."

Dorsay added three minor points: that the free exercise clause required accommodation for Smith and Black's religious use of the sacrament in order to ensure that Native American Church members were able to practice their religion in a manner equal to other faiths; that the writ should be dismissed as improvidently granted because the respondents were not being criminally prosecuted and the state was precluded from charging the respondents with violating the state's drug laws at this late date; and that accommodation would not violate the establishment clause because similar past religious exemptions were constitutional and an exemption in this instance would be consistent with the federal government's stated intent to protect the practices of the Native American Church.

At the same time Dorsay was preparing his brief on the merits, his staff was working with NARF attorneys to coordinate amicus curiae briefs submitted by the American Civil Liberties Union, American Jewish Congress, Native American Rights Fund, and the Council on Religious Freedom. The amici either supplemented or elaborated on the arguments made in Dorsay's brief. There were no amicus briefs offered on behalf of the state.

The attorney general filed a short response brief on August 21, 1989, that reiterated the state's contention that *Smith* differed from previous unemployment compensation cases because of the illegality of the underlying conduct. The brief also questioned the respondent's conclusion that the religious use of peyote was safe. It characterized the Native American Church's use of peyote as "controversial" and relevant to only 10 to 20 percent of church members, and described the evidence regarding the safety of peyote as "fragmentary."

As the attorneys for both parties prepared their legal briefs and oral presentations before the Supreme Court, representatives from the Native American Rights Fund became more directly involved in the case. The two NARF attorneys who would play a central role in this second journey to the Court were John Echohawk, NARF's founder and executive director since it began in 1977, and Steve Moore, a senior staff attorney.

NARF had initially participated as amicus for the respondents on *Smith*'s first trip to the Supreme Court. However, it did not significantly increase its involvement until after the second Oregon Supreme Court decision when it appeared likely the case would go to the U.S. Supreme Court a second time. At this point the elected leadership of the Native American Church of North America asked NARF to represent the church's interests and increase its participation in the proceedings. Although the church was not a party to the case, it believed it had a right to be involved because its manner of worship was on trial, and a Supreme Court decision on the sacramental use of peyote would have national implications. At its annual convention in Wyoming in the summer of 1988 the church leadership unanimously agreed to empower NARF to work on its behalf and to see what it could do, according to Moore, "to change the course of the legal proceedings." It was the church's position that Echohawk and Moore try to get the parties to come to an agreement to dismiss the case and avoid having it return to the Supreme Court.

The NARF attorneys agreed with this strategy. One factor that led to this conclusion was the Court's recent decision in *Lyng v. Northwest Cemetery Association.* "We had been seeing some troubling signs in decisions from the Supreme Court, and things really began to turn in the mid-8os for Native Americans in the Court," said Moore. "The tea leaves were pretty clear, especially after *Lyng*. I think we took the attitude in advising our clients that we've got to make an effort to get this case out of the hands of the Supreme Court. There's a train wreck coming here." According to the rules of the Supreme Court, if the parties agree to dismiss the case, then it is removed from the Court's docket.

The situation was complicated, however, by the fact that there was tension between the Native American Church's national leadership and Smith. Although Smith had been regularly attending meetings of the church in Oregon, there was only a small group of peyotists in the state, and the Oregon church chapter was not formally recognized by the national organization. "It was a pretty loose affiliation of peyotists in Oregon," stated Moore. "I remember talking to the national leadership and saying, you know you've got this chapter in Oregon, and they were like, What? And there's this guy named Al Smith, and he has this case going, and they were like, Al who? I don't think the chapter in Oregon was organized under the state laws of Oregon. The chapter, if you call it that, was not officially sanctioned." Although *Smith* had been of little concern to the national leadership when it was in the state court system, the Supreme Court's question on remand regarding religious exemptions from state drug laws would set a national precedent on the issue. In the church's opinion, this was much more than a case about a single litigant's appeal for unemployment compensation from the state of Oregon. "I think the most frustrating aspect for the national church was that they were not a party, and the very essence of their belief system was on trial here," said Moore. "They wanted to bring that message to the parties in a way that would carry some moral force and weight to it."

NARF's involvement would be frustrating for Smith, as well. When he was first terminated from his job in 1983 he had requested assistance from the Indian rights organization, but was told that NARF protected tribes rather than individuals, and that it was not interested in the case. "I went to the big guys first," said Smith, "but they turned me away." Up to this point in the proceedings he had been represented by Oregon Legal Services and the Native American Program at Oregon Legal Services. The Eugene branch of the American Civil Liberties Union provided direction early in the process. Smith's moral support was local as well. His legal effort was supported and encouraged by his Roadman, Stanley Smart, and members of the local church who wanted a resolution on the legality of peyote in the state of

Oregon. Smith had no ties to the Native American Church's national organization, and had no contact with attorneys at the Native American Rights Fund until several weeks before oral arguments in Washington, D.C.

What happened next remains a point of contention between the NARF attorneys and Smith, his family, and his lawyer, Craig Dorsay. John Echohawk insists that Smith invited NARF to come to Oregon and try to negotiate with Frohnmayer to stop the litigation. "We went there at his invitation. Otherwise, we would not have gone. We would have no authority to do anything. He invited us up there, and we were proceeding with his permission, at his behest. Because he understood that if he lost the case, which was likely, that it was going to be on his head. And he didn't want to get left holding the bag and be responsible for a Supreme Court loss." Smith, on the other hand, contends that he never invited NARF to intervene in the case. "I wasn't involved with them in any way. There was no request that they come to Eugene. The one time I asked for help, they turned me away. They really came out of nowhere. It was a surprise." Dorsay agrees, stating that it was extremely unlikely that Al would call NARF. "I was in constant contact with Al and I would have known." Also significant, adds Dorsay, was the fact that Echohawk and Moore never discussed their intention to negotiate a settlement between Frohnmayer and Smith with him, even when he visited NARF headquarters to participate in a moot court on October 2, 1989, five weeks before oral arguments.

———

Echohawk and Moore arrived in Eugene in October. Their strategy was to gather a coalition of church and community leaders from the Pacific Northwest to appeal to Smith and Frohnmayer to come to a resolution and avoid having the case go to the Court. Before their arrival in Eugene, Moore had contacted his friend John Magnunson, a reverend for the Church Council of Greater Seattle, to assist him in bringing the leaders together. In 1987 Magnunson had helped coordinate a similar coalition of church leaders representing the mainline Protestant and

Catholic denominations in the Pacific Northwest to support Indian religious freedom. The coalition issued a "Public Declaration" to the tribal councils and traditional spiritual leaders of the Indian and Eskimo peoples of the Pacific Northwest apologizing "on behalf of our churches for their long-standing participation in the destruction of traditional Native American spiritual practices." The declaration was prompted by the Supreme Court's record of anti-Indian decisions over the past decade. It stated, "We have frequently been unconscious and insensitive and have not come to your aid when you have been victimized by unjust Federal policies and practices," and pledged to "support you in the righting of previous wrongs." After the declaration was issued, Moore and Magnunson became friends and the NARF attorney kept him abreast of developments in *Smith*.

Moore also contacted Roy Haber, a civil liberties attorney in Eugene who specializes in religious prison issues, for his assistance. Moore knew Haber professionally, and Haber volunteered to help out the NARF attorneys. Haber was familiar with the local political landscape and knew a number of religious and civic leaders in the community. He also considered himself a "friendly acquaintance" of Smith and states that he had "talked with Al over the years about this case." Although Haber was not on NARF's staff at the time, he acted as counsel to NARF in its attempt to facilitate a settlement agreement between Smith and Frohnmayer. However, Haber had an adversarial relationship with Frohnmayer, having battled him in court on several occasions, so he worked quietly behind the scenes.

Two events were arranged to introduce the religious and community leaders to the parties in the case. First, Haber hosted a dinner party at his home in Eugene for the leaders and Smith and his wife, Jane Farrell. John Echohawk and Moore flew in from Boulder for the dinner and met Smith for the first time in person. "It was a dinner meeting for Al to get the support of the mainstream religious leaders of the Northwest," explained Haber. "It was a lovely dinner. We all sat around that table before, during and after the dinner was complete, talking things out, and it was a beautiful night. . . . You had some of the most wonderful leaders of the church there, wanting to help." Both Haber and Echohawk remark that Smith was thankful for NARF's efforts to bring the church leaders together. Echohawk notes, "That dinner at Roy's was the first time I met Al and I remember him thanking me profusely for coming up to help him get out of this case because he didn't want it on his head."

Smith and Farrell have a different recollection of the purpose of the event. They believed the evening was planned as a show of support for Smith. It was also the first time they became aware of the significance of the case and the number of people involved. "When they came out here," Smith noted, "I was really wide-eyed. I had no idea what was happening. No idea what was going on." He remembers that he did not get any pressure about the case at the dinner and saw the meeting more as an opportunity to get acquainted with the religious and community leaders. "They were wining and dining me. I was almost ignorant about what they were doing. Haber approached me like we were buddy buddy, and he had a lot of energy. He acted like he was my best friend. I really didn't know or understand what was happening." Smith recollects that "there was not heavy talk about whether I should settle the case or not." Farrell adds, "it was a dinner party, not business."

The second event was a meeting between the church and community leaders and Frohnmayer. The NARF attorneys knew in advance that it would be difficult to convince the attorney general to drop his appeal to the Supreme Court. Haber characterizes the attorney general as a "bright guy" who had a "myopic view" of the criminal justice system, which limited his manner of looking at the case.

Dave was unable to take the steps from his own religious beliefs and really understand that there were others with other religious beliefs, and that they were entitled to be protected under our laws. No amount of legal argument on Dave was working. The courts in Oregon had spoken very clearly on the subject, the decisions were correct, the underlying jurisprudence was correct. . . . He also knew what kind of Supreme Court we had at the time, and the social and political proclivities of the judges of that Supreme Court—that they would support a very strict, backward view of the criminal laws. He made a political decision that he wanted to win at all odds.

Moreover, an earlier attempt at a settlement by individuals at NAPOLS after the case came back from the Oregon Supreme Court had failed.

The NARF attorneys believed that the church leaders could successfully appeal to Frohnmayer about the need to protect Indian religious freedom and keep the case out of the hands of the Supreme Court. Moore stated, "We knew that Frohnmayer was a religious man, and we thought, if there is any way that Dave Frohnmayer can be persuaded to give this a second thought, it is going to be through influential leaders in Oregon. We thought that because Frohnmayer is an establishment kind of guy, if we could get church and civic leaders to come to a meeting or contact him privately, then they could deliver the message that the Native American Church did not want its religion to be on trial."

The meeting with Frohnmayer was NARF's first formal contact with the attorney general about *Smith*. There had been an earlier, informal discussion about the case several months earlier when Frohnmayer and his deputy attorney general, Bill Gary, visited NARF on other business, but the conversation was limited. Frohnmayer only remembers that Walter Echo-hawk gave him a book about the peyote religion and told him, "You should really read this book and drop this case." And, stated Frohnmayer, "He didn't say it jokingly, but he didn't say it in a heavy-handed way. And while he doesn't remember it, it is my memory that we were invited to a peyote ceremony at the time. For fairly obvious reasons, I declined the invitation."

The meeting with Echohawk and Moore, representing the Native American Church, and the religious and community leaders was held at the downtown Hilton hotel in Eugene several weeks before oral arguments. Moore stated, "We went to Dave and said, we want an unconditional agreement from you and your office to withdraw this appeal. It's immoral. There is no reason to take the Native American Church down in this context." Frohnmayer recalls that he used this meeting to explain why the state was taking the case to court. His emphasis was that a *Smith* precedent would lead to other religious challenges to the state's criminal laws proscribing drugs. The leaders, which included Paul Olum, the president of the University of Oregon and Frohnmayer's friend, asked him to reconsider his point of view. Frohnmayer observed, "I don't know if you would call that political pressure, or look at them as significant leaders in the public whose views I respected. But clearly, there were many among them that wanted the case to go away."

Moore thought the position of the mainstream churches seemed to "catch [Frohnmayer] a little off guard." However, the meeting was successful in getting Frohnmayer to at least consider an alternative resolution to the case. Moore believes that "the weight, the moral weight of the people that were in his face that day bowled him over, and he had no choice, I think, at that point, to say, 'I will talk.'"

The meeting was followed by letters to Frohnmayer reiterating the concerns of the religious leaders. Oregon Ecumenical Ministries, an interdenominational religious lobbying group, sent a letter in early October expressing its concern about his decision to pursue the case. "We are hard pressed to understand why you are so determined to press this case forward to the U.S. Supreme Court," it stated. The clergy leaders were unpersuaded by Frohnmayer's concern that *Smith* would lead to other religious challenges to the state's drug laws. "We would like to express confidence in the American system of justice in being able to ferret out valid religious traditions from sham ones." This was followed by a letter from the Pacific Northwest religious leaders, who wrote, "Our position is that your efforts to prosecute a Klamath Indian, Mr. Al Smith, (and as a consequence, the entire practicing religion of the Native American Church in the United States), are misguided and ill-founded. We join with the clergy in Oregon, who recently wrote you, in the opinion that you have selected the wrong religion and the wrong set of factual circumstances to make a public statement about the 'cult of worship of drugs.'" The letter urged Frohnmayer "to respect the religious freedom of the Native American Church" and "withdraw the case from the Supreme Court docket." It concluded with a pledge of solidarity to the Native American Church and affirmed its right "to practice its traditions as it has for centuries."

Pressure on Frohnmayer regarding his actions in *Smith* came from other quarters as well. By this time Frohnmayer was receiving a great deal of negative publicity about his dogged desire to take the case to the Court a second time. It could not have come at a worse time. On October 10, 1989, he had declared that he would be seeking the Republican nomination for the 1990 gubernatorial race against the incumbent Democrat, Neil Goldschmidt. "And the irony here, because as the case was pending, I was a candidate for governor, and people argued that I was doing this as part of a war on drugs stance for political advantage, and nothing could have been further from the truth. I think it was a public relations loser. From day one. I knew it was absolutely no win . . . and the coverage was very pro–Al Smith."

After the meeting at the Hilton, Echohawk, Moore, and a smaller group of religious and community leaders spent several days in late October trying to persuade Frohnmayer to consider settling a case he clearly believed he would win before the Supreme Court. The attorney general found himself in a difficult position because he believed the state's reputation was on the line, in part because his office had invested so much time and energy in the case, and he was unsure about how the Supreme Court would react to a decision to pull out of a case it obviously wanted to reconsider.

In fact, we took some professional risks in doing this. The Court had obviously decided that this case was important enough to take it a second time, and our state's credibility was on the line, and if we were to yank the case right out from under them, a) would they even let us do it, and b) what are they going to think of the state that does something like that? So I was receiving a lot of advice from within my office that said we were going to lose a lot of credibility if we settled the case at this point.

Nevertheless, Frohnmayer believed the case might be resolved in a manner that could serve the interests of both Smith and the state, so he agreed to speak with John Echohawk and Moore about the possibility of settling the case.

During this period of time when they were meeting with Frohnmayer to discuss the case, Echohawk and Moore maintain that they kept Dorsay and Smith apprised of the discussions taking place. However, Dorsay contends that he was unaware of many of the discussions with Frohnmayer, and that he was kept in the dark about the content of these conversations. Dorsay states, "I was very surprised with the level of NARF's involvement. I had no idea what they were doing, which did not please me." He recalls instances where he literally drove down to Eugene and "barged in on the meetings" that were taking place. "Once or twice I heard they were meeting and drove down on my own to Salem. I understood their position, but didn't like some of the underhanded tactics they were using." Dorsay was alarmed that the negotiations were accelerating without his participation and was unhappy because he had not been included in all of the discussions at the attorney general's office. He was Smith's attorney and Oregon Legal Services had stood behind Smith since the case began in 1984. "When I found out that they had been contacting Frohnmayer independently and directly, when they were not a party to the case, that's when I got a little upset. I think Steve and John were trying to strike a side deal without even letting me know. I didn't even know what was going on, and I was struggling to keep up with their conversation. I was calling them, asking them what was going on, and they were not keeping me informed."

Another person who felt out of the loop was Al Smith. "I had no idea they were meeting with Frohnmayer," stated Smith. "I was not involved in anything, and I was always the last to know." He only learned of the level of NARF's involvement through his attorney. "I recall thinking, where have you been for all of these years? This case had been stewing for six years. Where have you been?" Farrell agrees. "There was a feeling when they arrived in Eugene that the timing was not good. The timing did not feel right. It was bizarre. We had our plane tickets to Washington, D.C., and then all of a sudden, NARF is involved. NARF is telling us we need to stop the case because the Native American Church was afraid of the case moving forward."

———

Two weeks before the Court had scheduled the case for oral argument, there was a flurry of activity in the *Smith* case. Frohnmayer finally agreed to discuss a substantive settlement agreement with the NARF attorneys to have the case removed from the Supreme Court docket. On October 24 Echohawk and Moore had a meeting with Frohnmayer at the Department of Justice in Salem, Oregon, to discuss the terms of the settlement agreement. Frohnmayer stated, "They wanted to settle. And John and I had enough of a professional and personal relationship based upon the work we had been trying to do on tribal sovereignty issues over the last year and a half, that we were able to talk it through. Steve Moore was no help, but Echohawk was a real savvy, wise, and honest negotiator."

There were several hours of discussion about the case. Frohnmayer recalls that Echohawk took the lead in the negotiations and because of his friendship with the NARF founder and his negotiating style, spoke mostly with him. Around eight or nine in the evening, once the discussion got to the point where Frohnmayer began placing conditions on his agreement to withdraw the case from the Supreme Court docket, Dorsay was called, and he drove to Salem to join the conversation. At this point, according to Moore, "The negotiations halted until Craig could get down here and then we could talk substantively about those conditions . . . it became more of a bilateral negotiation, and Dorsay was involved in every aspect of that."

Frohnmayer took the position that the state could only withdraw the case if the Oregon Supreme Court decision in favor of the award of unemployment benefits to Smith and Black could be vacated in some way. This would address the state's concern of a *Smith* precedent, which the attorney general believed would lead to other requests for religiously based exemptions to the state's criminal laws. "[It] would have gotten rid of the case," observes Frohnmayer, "and leave to another day a decision about drugs and the constitution." Moore and Echohawk, whose goal was to keep the case out of the hands of the Court, would then get the result the church wanted, whereas Dorsay would have the responsibility of working with Smith on any further legal action. Frohnmayer describes the conversation as "a very intense and emotional time."

Smith did not play a direct role in this discussion about the terms of the settlement with the state. That evening after he arrived in Eugene, Dorsay phoned Smith to let him know of some of Frohnmayer's conditions before the state would withdraw the appeal, but the legal aid attorney and Smith did not have a detailed conversation about settling the case at that point. Dorsay recalls that by this time Smith was feeling "very uncomfortable" about how events were transpiring.

The tentative agreement that resulted from the late-night meeting mandated that Black and Smith "repay the unemployment compensation they had received to date," that they "file statements with the United States Supreme Court withdrawing their federal constitutional claims," and ask the Court to "vacate the Oregon court's judgment and remand to the Oregon court for entry of a new order." After the case was sent back to the Oregon Supreme Court, the agreement noted that "the parties would stipulate before the Oregon Supreme Court that the appropriate disposition of the case would be reversal of the Oregon Court of Appeals and remand to the Employment Division for entry of an order denying benefits." There were several additional minor conditions; that Smith and Black "pay the costs assessed by the Supreme Court for dismissal," and "repay the State for any 'nonrefundable travel expenses' incurred as a result of the cancellation of oral argument." However, the "State would seek no other costs from them," and "neither party would ask for attorney fees from the other."

In exchange, the attorney general's office agreed to "notify the Court supporting vacatur and remand."

Dorsay was frustrated. Although he believes that it was probably the best deal they could get from the state at that time, he did not see how Smith benefited from the settlement. He also sensed that NARF's involvement would cease after the case was dismissed, once again leaving Oregon Legal Services alone to fight for justice for Smith. NARF did pledge to help Smith and Black raise funds to help pay for the unemployment compensation, but did not commit to any further participation in the case. Dorsay tentatively signed the agreement to move the process forward, but told Echohawk and Moore and Frohnmayer that his signature was contingent upon a decision from Smith to settle the case. "I knew Al was uncomfortable, so I said, this is something I had to run by Al."

As he was leaving the Department of Justice around two or three o'clock the morning of October 25, Dorsay conveyed his frustration with the NARF attorneys, who had no party status, about their efforts to settle the case. He was displeased with NARF's involvement several weeks before the case went to the Supreme Court and that Echohawk and Moore had essentially presented him with a finalized deal. He recalls having a spirited discussion with Moore about why he believed some of NARF's actions were inappropriate. "I had a shouting match with Steve and told him that I thought what he was doing was unprofessional and unethical. I am not quick to lose my temper, but I had had it at that stage."

The next day Dorsay went over the terms of the settlement with Smith and his family. Dorsay told Smith, "Look, this is what is happening. You have to decide if it is too much for you, or if you need to do what the church tells you to do. It is not up to me to decide that." He believed it was Smith's decision, and did not want his personal feeling about the case to interfere with his choice. Instead, Dorsay encouraged Smith to speak to people with a variety of different viewpoints to help him make up his mind about whether he should go forward with the case. "Part of the reason I wanted him to talk to other people was because I wanted to be clear that it wasn't my decision—I obviously wanted to go—every lawyer wants to go to the Supreme Court, but I was expressly attempting not to give him advice that would be colored by my own desires or personal feelings." The legal aid lawyer recalls that Smith asked several questions about how a decision to drop the case would affect Oregonians who were members of the Native American Church. "We talked a lot, obviously, and he was really troubled. Al and I discussed what it would mean to have the case dismissed in the state of Oregon, and how that would leave the members of the local branch without any protection to practice their religion. At the time Al was feeling that he might be betraying the people of Oregon. He really wanted to do what the Church wanted . . . but I think they betrayed his trust by engaging in these antics. And I'm sure I told him, you aren't getting much of a deal here."

Smith had mixed emotions about whether he should officially sign off on the settlement agreement. He didn't want to hurt the church, which had helped him spiritually, but he also didn't want to hurt American Indians in Oregon. Moreover, those closest to him, including Stanley Smart and members of the local church branch, were encouraging him to continue with the case. If the Oregon Supreme Court decision was vacated, there would be no protection in the state for the religious use of peyote. Smith found himself under extraordinary pressure. To make matters worse, for the last several months Smith and Farrell had been receiving dozens of phone calls at their home from Native American Church members who were pleading that he drop the case. Dorsay was well aware of the pressure being placed on his client. "Keep in mind, Al is going back and forth. He was being told by NARF that the Church wanted to settle, but his medicine man, the Peyote Chief, Stanley Smart was saying, no you are right, you should continue with the case. He was getting conflicting advice—no you have to do it, even though we understand you may lose . . . we need to clarify this issue, so we can't cut and run."

Smith and Farrell also clearly felt uncomfortable with NARF's involvement in the case. They were aware that Echohawk and Moore were only acting on behalf of their clients, the Native American Church, but they did not understand why NARF had only become involved at the "eleventh hour" and they were uncomfortable with NARF's approach. "It was happening behind closed doors," said Farrell, "It was very secretive. We did not know the full extent of the negotiations until we saw the settlement agreement." Moreover, adds Smith, "NARF's involvement at this point in the game was not to be on my side."

In the end, Smith was presented with a settlement agreement that he had no involvement in designing. "I started to feel bothered about all of the pressure from this," said Smith. "They came in as representatives of the Native American Church. They were there to do what they could to get things going their way." Farrell believes NARF was essentially asking Smith to take a dive in his battle with the state. She stated, "They were meeting with Frohnmayer and trying to find a way to get out—to fold the cards while excluding Al from the process. It didn't feel right. They represent Native American rights, but somehow, an individual's religious rights were not deserving of being represented? How do you overlook the individual's rights as a Native person? It was hurtful. And I think that was the difference in perspective in what was before everybody in the case."

Farrell and Smith spoke at length about the agreement and each expressed their concern that Smith's rights were not being adequately protected by the settlement agreement. Jane wrote down her thoughts on the back of their copy of the settlement agreement. Emotions were running high in the Smith family.

Craig says to be on gard [*sic*] for possible character bashing. Steve Moore has already commented to Craig—Al was just a flake, not a real member, just hangs out w/white women, not traditional. this hits below the belt—all trust is gone. How can Al take advice from these men who have shown themselves this way. . . . The effort began as an appeal to clergy for "moral support for Mr. Smith" and to urge [Frohnmayer] not to appeal decision of Oregon Supreme Court. . . . Al's case was negotiated away to nothing. NARF's stand was a heavy pressure on Al to give up whatever he had to "save the church"— threatened him with full responsibility of "killing the church because he was too pigheaded to back out. . . . They are willing to sign away everything that was gained here in Oregon— the SC decisions granting NAC protection, they want Al to admit his wrongdoing in going to church, admit his peyote ingestion was criminal, pay back $$, (NARF will) and withdraw his constitutional right to practice his religion in this case. Is this not the same persecution NARF has pleaded to end? Is this moral support for Smith? How can one deny an individual his freedoms, and justice in order to save those freedoms for this larger community?

That evening Smith found himself unable to sleep.

They sent me home with the settlement and with the decision. Jane is asleep, it's late at night, and I don't know what to do. I felt that if I signed it, then I am admitting that I am guilty. If I don't sign it, I'm likely to get the Church in trouble all over the country. They were saying, if you don't sign, Al, you're liable to wipe out all Church privileges. And I'm thinking, what am I getting into, anyway? Am I causing that much trouble for native people, for the Native American Church? I didn't know what to do. But it got to the point that I had to make a decision. I figured, I hadn't really done anything wrong. I wasn't guilty. I was just going to church.

He was awake most of the evening. On more than one occasion his thoughts turned to Edison Chiloquin, the lone Klamath Indian who refused to sell his land after the federal Termination Act in the mid-1950s. Chiloquin was the lone holdout, and his seventy-two-acre plot was the only Indian-controlled land left of the Klamath Reservation. The Klamath tribe had been the only Indian tribe to receive money as part of a termination agreement, and for years the other tribes criticized the Klamaths for being "sell-outs." Smith didn't want to sell out fellow natives in Oregon by signing an agreement that would vacate the Oregon Supreme Court decision that gave Native American Church members the right to worship in the state.

In the end, it wasn't the advice of the church, or his peyote Road Chief, or the state of Oregon that helped Smith make up his mind about whether he would proceed with the case. It was his children. His son, Lalek Levi, was only a year old. Kaila was seven. "And so it was early in the morning, and I'm still pondering, and what made me change my mind were my kids, Kaila and Lalek. They were still little, and I knew they would grow up, they would get older, they were going to be teenagers, and there are going to be people that are going to say, Smith? Farrell-Smith? Was Al Smith your father? Wasn't he that sellout . . . and my kids are going to hang their heads in shame, and be ashamed of their father. That was my thinking. I said to myself, I'm not going to do that to my kids."

The next day Smith called Dorsay and told him he could not accept the settlement agreement to dismiss the case. He wanted to go to court. Dorsay phoned NARF to let Echohawk and Moore know they were headed to Washington, D.C. They were stunned. They had left the state thinking they had a signed settlement. In fact, Echohawk had told Frohnmayer that he "would not leave Oregon until [he] agreed to withdraw the case and we signed the deal." After the NARF attorneys learned of Smith's decision, there was a final effort to get Smith to reconsider his decision. The next day Haber went to see Smith where he was working as an attendant at a Goodwill Industries trailer parked outside a grocery store. "So I went to the Goodwill truck because we wanted to save the deal and wanted Al to make sure he understood what was going on," stated Haber. "We needed to find out what the problem with the deal was." Haber also suggested that Smith phone John Echohawk to get his perspective on the case, and watched the Goodwill trailer while Smith made the call.

After Haber left, Smith called Dorsay. He told him, "This guy Haber is harassing me. He just showed up without any notice and he is berating me to drop this case." Smith reiterated his decision to go to court. Earlier that day Dorsay had received a call from Haber, who told him that it was Smith who initiated the contact with NARF and wanted to talk. According to Dorsay, "and I remember this very clearly," Smith had not asked for a visit from Haber and was resentful the pressure from NARF had not ceased. Dorsay stated, "I think the contact was inappropriate."

Back in Boulder, Echohawk and Moore were shocked by the

sudden turn of events. They had left Eugene with a signed settlement agreement, and now they were headed to court. "The deal was done," said Moore. "And Al undid the deal." John Echohawk was frank about his feelings about Smith's decision. "Al just wasted our time and effort. That's what happened. He changed his mind. [At the beginning] he said, we want out of this case, and then he said, we changed our mind and I don't want out of the case now. That's all that happened. . . . It was a waste of our time and energy . . . and it really kinda makes me mad, that he put us through this, and he changed his mind. Because it was a gargantuan effort. An uphill effort that people thought was impossible. But we got it done and Al changed his mind."

Dorsay defends Smith's decision to go to court. "They presented Al with a done deal and told him, you have to sign. I don't think they had any respect for Al." He believes Echohawk and Moore's impression that Smith reneged on the deal comes from "their memory of Al making statements about wanting to be a good soldier. Wanting to be a good member of the church, and Al knowing the church wanted the case to be dismissed. He really wanted to support the church, but in the end it was clear that the attorney general wanted to put more conditions on the deal, and each condition left a worse taste in his mouth. And then he finally said, well, this isn't going to work."

CHAPTER 9

Employment Division v. Smith II:
The Court Comes Full Circle

In the final week before going to the Court a second time, Craig Dorsay and Dave Frohnmayer prepared for what each hoped would be the final word in *Employment Division v. Smith*. Dorsay reached out to Walter Echo-hawk and Steve Moore, the Native American Rights Fund's senior staff attorneys, for assistance. The NARF attorneys arranged six mock trials in Denver and Washington, D.C., to help Dorsay refine his oral presentation. According to the director of the Native American Program of Oregon Legal Services, once the decision was made to go to the Supreme Court, everyone "put on their war paint" and prepared for battle. "You spend hours," he said, "researching every conceivable point that might come up. You know what the questions will be about, and you need to be prepared." Although Dorsay had never argued before the U.S. Supreme Court, he felt comfortable with oral presentations, and was looking forward to the opportunity to engage in a dialogue with the justices about the case. He understood he would only have a short time to present his case and win at least five votes in his favor. His strategy was to target the swing votes of O'Connor and Stevens. He knew Scalia, Rehnquist, and White were "lost causes from the beginning," and that it was likely Kennedy would join his conservative colleagues. He could count on Brennan, Marshall, and Blackmun voting in favor of exempting Smith and Black from the state criminal law proscribing peyote possession.

Frohnmayer was also rehearsing his oral presentation and participating in moot courts. The attorney general was widely regarded for his meticulous preparation before Supreme Court appearances and he knew what to expect based on his previous six visits to the Court. He was confident about the state's case. "I think everybody knew," he said, "that the state would win." Frohnmayer had a similar strategy to Dorsay. He essentially ignored Brennan and Marshall, who "had never voted for the state in all of my appearances," and focused on five of the remaining seven justices. The attorney general was certain Rehnquist, White, Scalia, and Kennedy would vote in favor of the state, and that it was likely that he would lose Blackmun, so he, too, looked to the swing votes of O'Connor and Stevens.

Several days before oral arguments, the attorneys arrived in Washington, D.C. Accompanying Dorsay were Al Smith, his wife Jane Farrell, and their two children, Kaila and Lalek. Oregon Legal Services had raised the funds to bring Smith and his family to hear oral arguments. The family joined up with some of Farrell's relatives from the East Coast who came to offer moral support. Also in Washington were dozens of Native American Church leaders and members who arrived to watch their religion on trial.

On November 6, 1989, Al Smith woke up with his family. It was his seventieth birthday, but his attention was elsewhere. His right to freely exercise his religion was about to be scrutinized for a second time by the Supreme Court. He understood the significance of the moment, but did not personally feel any pressure about the case. The pressure, Smith believed, was on the Court. Before leaving Eugene he told a reporter covering the case, "I'll be watching and listening to the U.S. Supreme Court, to see how they dance. It'll be interesting to see how they wriggle out of this one. They're the ones on trial."

That morning the attorneys entered the Supreme Court building and waited for their case to be called. *Employment Division v. Smith* was the second case that morning. Dorsay tried to relax. He understood it was going to be an uphill battle because many Court observers predicted the state would prevail. He estimates that he personally put in at least fifteen hundred hours preparing the case, and knew he had done all he could to be ready for this moment. Interestingly, when asked over ten years later what he recalls from his visit to the Supreme Court, the first thing that comes to Dorsay's mind is the scene that greeted him when he entered the Supreme Court building. Dozens of Native American Church members had gathered inside and outside the building. "You go to the Supreme Court, and they have their security protections, and you have to walk through metal detectors, and there were all these Indian people there, especially Navajos, who are strong in the Church. And the Navajos traditionally wear their jewelry as their wealth—they wear it on them, and they had to take off this jewelry in order to go through the metal detectors. And there were heaps of priceless jewelry stacking up as these Indians were taking off more and more, even their belts, their boots and articles of clothing. So you could see this mound of priceless Indian jewelry as they were trying to get through the damn metal detectors." The presence of the church leaders was a remarkable contrast to the formality of the Marble Palace.

At eleven o'clock Dorsay took his place at the respondent's table with Walter Echo-hawk and Steve Moore. Although they would not present before the Court, the NARF attorneys were there as a sign of solidarity for Dorsay and Smith. David Frohnmayer stood at the lectern, ready to start his presentation. It was the same spot he had spoken from on his previous six trips to the Court. A repeat player, a bright and self-assured attorney, and an attorney general who firmly believed that an exemption for the religious use of peyote would lead to further requests for religiously inspired drug use, potentially unraveling the state's ability to enforce the law, Frohnmayer believed his position was best for the state of Oregon.

Frohnmayer spoke first. He emphasized the state's three compelling interests: protecting the "health and safety interests of its citizens," providing a uniform "regulatory scheme as a whole, so that law enforcement does not face a patchwork of exemptions of other drugs on a drug-by-drug, religion-by-religion, believer-by-believer basis," and the need to meet the state "constitution's heightened requirements of neutrality in our jurisdiction, [which] requires it to avoid giving the preference of one church over another." In his description of the state's need to protect public health, the attorney general characterized peyote "as a powerful and unpredictable hallucinogen," that is "very risky" and that induces "psychotic reactions in a small number of users." The illegality of the substance, Frohnmayer stated, must be taken into consideration by the Court when it evaluates the state's interest. Furthermore, he added, it differentiated this case from previous unemployment compensation cases, all of which involved legal activity. In his second and third argument about the need for the uniform application of the law, and the need for the state to maintain neutrality in its treatment of religions, Frohnmayer stressed the difficulty the state faced distinguishing other religious challenges to the state's proscriptions against drugs. "And our point is that if we cannot accommodate [these challenges] on equal grounds, then the requirement of accommodation must fail."

The attorney general suggested that the only way the state could meet these compelling interests was in the neutral application of its drug laws. When Scalia pressed him about whether this "flat rule position" would "permit a state to outlaw totally the use of alcohol, including wine, in religious ceremonies?" Frohnmayer responded that the issue of sacramental wine was a different question because of the "limited potential danger of the ingestion of sacramental wine in small quantities," compared to peyote, which is used specifically for its "hallucinogenic properties" and is "unquestionably a very dangerous substance for everyone else." Frohnmayer ended his presentation with a response to a statement by White about how the drug counselors had violated the employer's rules, which would justify the state's denial of unemployment compensation. He concluded, "Yes, Justice White, it's so intuitively obvious that drug counselors ought not to be partaking of the substances which they are asking others to refrain from."

Dorsay used the attorney general's reply to Scalia's question about sacramental wine to begin his presentation. Frohnmayer's answer about the safety of alcohol compared to peyote struck a nerve with Dorsay, who was familiar with how millions of Indian people have been negatively affected by alcohol, including his client, Al Smith, who struggled with the disease for over three decades. Furthermore, the dangers of alcohol were well documented compared to the evidence regarding sacramental peyote use in the ceremonies of the church. He deviated from his prepared notes and began his presentation. He stated,

> I think if you looked at this situation and Indian people were in charge of the United States right now, or in charge of government, and you look at the devastating impact that alcohol has had on Indian people and Indian tribes through the history of the United States, you might find that alcohol was the Schedule I substance, and peyote was not listed at all. And we are getting here to the heart of an ethnocentric view, I think, of what constitutes religion in the United States. And I think that needs to be looked at very hard before determining what is a dangerous substance and what is not.

Dorsay then directly countered the state's conclusions about the harmful effects of peyote. "There is no documented evidence that the use of peyote in these carefully circumscribed ceremonials has any harm to the individual, to society at large, or to the state's law enforcement efforts." The safety of its use by members of the Native American Church, he indicated, is evident in the fact that Congress and a number of states have "acted to exempt the use of peyote."

Dorsay's presentation focused on his contention that *Smith* was indistinguishable from *Sherbert* and the other unemployment compensation cases because the Oregon Supreme Court had concluded as a matter of state law that the criminality of the conduct was irrelevant to the award of unemployment compensation. Even if it were relevant, he observed, the state had not met its burden of proving that peyote was harmful when used in Native American Church ceremonies, and that it had a compelling interest in denying the respondent's request for an exemption to the criminal law proscribing peyote.

The only moment of levity in the proceedings took place about halfway into Dorsay's presentation when O'Connor asked him to distinguish the religious use of peyote from "marijuana use by a church that uses that as part of its religious sacrament?" Dorsay responded, "Well, see, I think we can get into a lot of examples, and I don't want to go down that road too far because we don't . . ." O'Connor interrupted, "I'll bet you don't," to the sound of laughter in the courtroom. Dorsay tried to recover by highlighting the differences between the two substances, including the fact that marijuana is used recreationally and that there is a large amount of illegal trafficking in the drug that contributes to law enforcement problems, but the damage had been done. Recalling the exchange, Frohnmayer said, "We knew we had won the case at that point."

There was also an uncomfortable moment during Dorsay's presentation when Scalia was discussing neutral and generally applicable laws and stated that "a law against human sacrifice would, you know, would affect only the Aztecs," as a comparison to the state law prohibiting peyote and its effect on members of the Native American Church. Dorsay tried to change the subject with a suggestion that the Court consider how a neutral law proscribing the handling of poisonous snakes would allow the state to meet its burden of proving it had a compelling interest in regulating that conduct. "I don't think there is any dispute about the harm that rattlesnakes can cause—" when Scalia shot back, "I don't think there is any dispute about the harm that peyote can cause." Dorsay ended his presentation with an explanation of the importance of the peyote ritual in the religious ceremonies of the Native American Church.

After oral arguments, Smith, his family, and the NARF attorneys joined members of the Native American Church for a brief religious ceremony in a park near the U.S. Supreme Court building. Church leaders burned cedar, prayed, and sang songs, but did not ingest peyote.

It was the first time Smith had seen members of the Native American Church since several of them arrived in Eugene to persuade Smith to settle the case. Steve Moore noted, "I do remember that the feelings were still running pretty cold between Al and the church leaders. He just looked uncomfortable that day being around the church leadership." Smith recalls feeling left out. "I remember the president of the church, Emmerson Jackson, elbowed me out of the way at the press conference." He still believed, however, that he had done the right thing to protect his religious freedom and the religious rights of Oregonians belonging to the church.

After the ceremony, the attorneys met and evaluated their presentations before the Court. Dorsay recalls, "I thought we did better than we expected," and Moore was very complimentary about Dorsay's work. "I thought Craig did a really good job. I thought he went toe to toe with Scalia. We had spent a lot of time working on the series of issues that Scalia attacked him on, and he was well-prepared." Frohnmayer was even more confident about his showing. "The wind was at our back. I think the oral argument went our way the whole time." He believed it was a good strategy to focus on the "slippery-slope" argument, which he concedes is a difficult argument to make. "But this is a classic case where the slippery slope argument really works. And, the two mantras to which the argument deliberately, not insidiously, but deliberately returned, was that drugs are bad, and this is a slippery slope. And you can't distinguish among drugs, and you can't, in a principled way, distinguish between or amongst religions. And it was clear that the Court was sympathetic to that view."

They would know for certain in a few months.

———

Three days after oral arguments the Court met in conference to deliberate and vote on the merits of the case. Rehnquist, White, Stevens, O'Connor, Scalia, and Kennedy voted to reverse the decision of the Oregon Supreme Court, and Brennan, Marshall, and Blackmun voted to affirm. Frohnmayer had reached six of the justices on the Court. After the conference, Brennan typed a brief memo to Marshall and Blackmun, "We three are in dissent. . . . Will you, Harry, try it?" Blackmun replied later that day that he would be "glad to try my hand at the dissent in this case." On Monday Rehnquist assigned the opinion to Scalia, who would release the first draft on January 2, 1990. It wasn't the decision some Court members expected. Rather than follow

Frohnmayer and Dorsay's suggestion to evaluate the state's denial of unemployment compensation using the compelling government interest test first established in *Sherbert* and reaffirmed in *Yoder* and other free exercise cases, Scalia cast the decision in an entirely new light and rewrote the Supreme Court's free exercise jurisprudence in the process.

Scalia divided the opinion of the Court into two parts; in the first part he rationalized that according to his interpretation of the Court's free exercise jurisprudence, neutral, generally applicable laws had never been limited by the free exercise clause of the First Amendment. In the second part, he explained why challenges to these laws should not be subject to the high level of scrutiny articulated in *Sherbert*. At the end of this latter discussion Scalia demonstrated why the First Amendment's free exercise clause did not mandate that Smith and Black be provided an exemption to the Oregon state law prohibiting the possession of peyote.

Scalia began with the observation that while the free exercise clause absolutely protected freedom of religious beliefs, it did not protect all forms of religious conduct. The free exercise clause, he explained, only protects religious action when the state has acted in an intentional manner that is "specifically directed" at religiously inspired behavior. It does not safeguard individuals "from compliance with an otherwise valid law prohibiting conduct that the State is free to regulate." He described *Smith* as such a case. "Respondents in this the present case, however, seek to carry the meaning of 'prohibiting the free exercise [of religion]' one large step further. They contend that their religious motivation for using peyote places them beyond the reach of a criminal law that is not specifically directed at their religious practice, and that is concededly constitutional as applied to those who use the drug for other reasons." Scalia suggested that the Court had "never held that an individual's religious beliefs excuse him from compliance with an otherwise valid law prohibiting conduct that the State is free to regulate." He supported this claim with a reading of free exercise jurisprudence that revealed that the Court had consistently denied the proposition that the First Amendment protected religiously inspired lawbreaking, and cited Justice Felix Frankfurter's majority opinion in *Minersville School District Board of Education v. Gobitis* and several other free exercise decisions to illustrate how the Court previously rejected requests for religious exemptions to otherwise neutral, generally applicable laws.

Then, perhaps anticipating criticism, Scalia distinguished free exercise precedent that offered a contrary reading of the Court's free exercise jurisprudence. In particular, he explained that earlier decisions that authorized exemptions to neutral, generally applicable laws never concerned the free exercise clause alone, but rather, the free exercise clause in combination with other constitutional guarantees. Scalia characterized these as "hybrid rights" cases involving the free exercise clause in conjunction with other constitutional guarantees. For instance, he described *Cantwell v. Connecticut* as violating both the freedom of press and religion clauses of the First Amendment. And *Wisconsin v. Yoder* was defined as a hybrid rights case involving both freedom of religion and the freedom of parents to direct the education of their children under the Fourteenth Amendment. Scalia differentiated *Smith* from these hybrid rights cases, noting that in *Smith*, the respondents were challenging a neutral, generally applicable law only under the free exercise clause. The doctrine for cases that only raise a religious claim, he explained, is that the religious action is unprotected by the free exercise clause unless government targets religion or coerces an individual to act against their religious beliefs. "The rule to which we have adhered ever since *Reynolds* plainly controls."

Scalia then directly confronted whether it would be appropriate for the Court to analyze the respondents' claim for an exemption under the compelling government interest test announced in *Sherbert*. He explicitly refused to apply this heightened level of scrutiny to *Smith*, explaining that the test had only been used in the isolated context of unemployment compensation. *Sherbert*, *Thomas*, and *Hobbie*, Scalia argued, were unique situations where the Court applied this test to invalidate state unemployment compensation rulings that conditioned the availability of benefits on an applicant's willingness to work under conditions forbidden by his religion. Scalia described these cases as distinctly different from *Smith*, because in each instance the unemployment board had the option of providing an exemption to the application of the law, but declined to do so, thus illustrating hostility to religion, which made it appropriate for the Court to utilize a higher level of scrutiny when evaluating the constitutionality of the government action. In the few instances when the *Sherbert* standard had been employed outside of the unemployment compensation context, Scalia observed, the requirements of the test had been fulfilled, thus implying that the high level of scrutiny should not be used because an exemption would not be forthcoming. Not to mention, he added, that these previous free exercise decisions had "nothing to do with an across-the-board criminal prohibition on a particular form of conduct." Scalia then stated that in recent years the Court had been reluctant to use the compelling government interest test, which he took as a sign that the Court was moving toward abandoning the *Sherbert* standard altogether. He cited *Bowen v. Roy* and *Lyng v. Northwest Indian Cemetery Protective Assn.*, as well as the "special circumstances" cases of *Goldman v. Weinberger* and *O'Lone v. Estate of Shabazz* to support this observation.

By isolating the specific instances where the Court used the *Sherbert* balancing test, and explaining away any aberrations in his review of the Court's free exercise decisions, Scalia essentially argued that the higher level of scrutiny used in the unemployment context was the exception to the rule that religious challenges to neutral, generally applicable laws do not implicate the free exercise clause. He remarked, "It is a permissible reading of the text to say that if prohibiting the exercise of religion is not the object of the [law] but merely the incidental effect of a generally applicable and otherwise valid provision, the First Amendment has not been offended."

In the conclusion Scalia suggested that it would be unwise for the Court to apply a *Sherbert*-like balancing test to evaluate the constitutionality of religiously based challenges to generally applicable laws because the Court would be straying from constitutional norms. "To make an individual's obligation to obey such a law contingent upon the law's coincidence with his religious beliefs, except where the State's interest is 'compelling'—permitting him, by virtue of his beliefs, 'to become a law unto himself,'—contradicts both constitutional tradition and common sense." Furthermore, he added, this approach was potentially dangerous because it could make government unworkable. "Any society adopting such a system would be courting anarchy, but that danger increases in direct proportion to the society's diversity of religious beliefs, and its determination to coerce or suppress none of them." Scalia found this threat to be particularly salient in the United States. "Precisely because 'we are a cosmopolitan nation made up of people of almost every conceivable religious preference' . . . [and] . . . precisely because we value and protect that religious divergence, we cannot afford the luxury of deeming preemptively invalid, as applied to the religious objector, every regulation of conduct that does not protect an interest of the highest order." In order to demonstrate this potentially dangerous situation, he listed a number of laws that might be challenged should the courts continue to make exemptions to generally neutral laws: payment of taxes, health and safety regulations, drug laws, social welfare legislation, child labor, environmental protection, and laws providing for equality of the races.

Scalia did note that this interpretation of the free exercise clause of the First Amendment did not necessarily preclude protection for religious believers who might be forced to act against their beliefs in order to comply with the law. Religious proponents, he explained, could always resort to the democratic political process for the protection of their religious practices. In fact, he observed, many states "have made an exception to their drug laws for sacramental peyote use." Although he did acknowledge that appeals to the legislature would place minority religions at "a relative disadvantage," he concluded "that unavoidable consequence of democratic government must be preferred to a system in which each conscience is a law unto itself or in which judges weigh the social importance of all laws against the centrality of all religious beliefs."

Consequently, in his evaluation of the case before the Court, Scalia ruled that because the respondents had ingested a substance that was illegal under a valid, generally applicable criminal law, the state could, "consistent with the free exercise clause, deny respondents unemployment compensation when their dismissal results from use of the drug." He therefore reversed the Oregon Supreme Court decision and reaffirmed the Employment Division's denial of unemployment compensation to Smith and Black.

It was a short opinion—only fifteen pages long—but its significance was unmistakable. Scalia had reevaluated what many believed were decades of settled free exercise jurisprudence that required the application of the compelling government interest test to free exercise challenges to government action that substantially burdened one's religious exercise, regardless of whether the law was neutral and generally applicable, or targeted at religious activity. In fact, the opinion of the Court returned to the rule of law that prevailed under *Reynolds v. U.S.* (1878). Justice Scalia had hardly even acknowledged the evolution of free exercise jurisprudence over the last one hundred years.

———

The next day Brennan, Marshall, and Blackmun sent Scalia memos indicating that they would be dissenting from his decision. Just as quickly, Stevens sent a memo asking to join the opinion of the Court, followed by a similar memo from Rehnquist. One week later, White sent Scalia a memo stating, "If there are three others with you, I could make the fifth vote for the position stated in your circulating draft." That third vote came a week later when Kennedy indicated that he would be "pleased" to join the opinion. A mere two weeks after Scalia had sent out the initial draft opinion in *Smith*, there were five votes in favor of reversing the Oregon Supreme Court and establishing a new rule of law for free exercise challenges. Remarkably, none of the justices in the majority raised any questions about Scalia's reformation of free exercise jurisprudence or asked him to revise any parts of the opinion. When one considers the absence of any criticism, at least from the conference records, of the four justices who joined the majority opinion, they might question whether *Smith* was anything other than a routine free exercise case.

One month later, O'Connor's concurring opinion provided the first indication that Scalia's opinion was more than routine. Although she originally voted with the other justices to reverse the Oregon Supreme Court and deny the respondents' claim of unemployment compensation, she refused to join Scalia's opinion, which she stated "dramatically departs from well-settled First Amendment jurisprudence, appears unnecessary to resolve the question presented, and is incompatible with our Nation's fundamental commitment to individual religious liberty."

The bulk of O'Connor's opinion, which was longer than the opinion of the Court, was dedicated to her scathing criticism of Scalia's misguided interpretation of the Court's free exercise jurisprudence. "To reach this sweeping result . . . the Court must not only give a strained reading to the First Amendment itself, but must also disregard our consistent application of the free exercise doctrine to cases involving generally applicable regulations that burden religious conduct." She pointedly disagreed with Scalia's conclusion that generally applicable laws did not invoke the protection of the free exercise clause.

> But a law that prohibits certain conduct—conduct that happens to be an act of worship for someone—manifestly does prohibit that person's free exercise of his religion. A person who is barred from engaging in religiously motivated conduct is barred from freely exercising his religion. Moreover, that person is barred from freely exercising his religion regardless of whether the law prohibits the conduct only when engaged in for religious reasons, only by members of that religion, or by all persons. It is difficult to deny that a law that prohibits religiously motivated conduct, even if the law is generally applicable, does not at least implicate First Amendment concerns.

O'Connor characterized Scalia's distinction between laws that target a particular religion and those that are generally applicable, as arbitrary. The First Amendment itself, she stated, does not distinguish between these two types of laws, and "few States would be so naive as to enact a law directly prohibiting or burdening a religious practice as such."

O'Connor explained that in order for the Court to fairly distinguish between conduct that is constitutionally protected and that which is not, that it should always use the compelling government interest test announced in *Sherbert*. She observed that the high level of scrutiny ". . . effectuates the First Amendment's command that religious liberty is an independent liberty, that it occupies a preferred position, that the Court will not permit encroachments upon this liberty, whether direct or indirect, unless required by clear and compelling governmental interests."

O'Connor challenged Scalia's contention that application of the *Sherbert* standard had been limited to a few select cases. In fact, she noted, the Court invoked this high level of scrutiny either explicitly or implicitly in each of the religion cases since *Cantwell v. Connecticut*. "We have not," she stated, 'rejected' or 'declined to apply' the compelling interest test in our recent cases. Recent cases have instead affirmed that test as a fundamental part of our First Amendment doctrine." O'Connor dismissed Scalia's attempt to distinguish some of these as "hybrid" cases. "There is no denying that [the] cases expressly relied on the Free Exercise Clause, and that we have consistently regarded those cases as part of the mainstream of our free exercise jurisprudence." In response to his claim that all of the free exercise challenges outside of the unemployment compensation context were unsuccessful, she replied that in each case the constitutional claim was rejected only after the *Sherbert* standard had been invoked. Furthermore, she added, the Court's use of this high level of scrutiny to evaluate, and then reject free exercise challenges was proof that the standard worked well to balance government interests and free exercise rights. It was not, she retorted, a reason to discard the test, as suggested by Scalia. "That we rejected the free exercise claims in those cases hardly calls into question the applicability of First Amendment doctrine in the first place. Indeed, it is surely unusual to judge the vitality of a constitutional doctrine by looking at the win-loss record of the plaintiffs who happen to come before us." Although O'Connor agreed that the

Court had chosen not to utilize the compelling interest test in the two special circumstances cases of the military and prisons, she determined that these cases were "distinguishable because they arose in the narrow, specialized contexts in which the Court had not traditionally required the government to justify a burden on religious conduct by articulating a compelling interest."

The Court must be particularly vigilant in the protection of religious liberty, O'Connor explained, because it is a preferred freedom in America. She stated that Scalia's suggestion that religious observers resort to the political process for redress of their grievances to neutral, generally applicable laws was based on a fundamental misunderstanding of the purpose of the Constitution's First Amendment. "The First Amendment," O'Connor explained, "was enacted precisely to protect the rights of those whose religious practices are not shared by the majority and may be viewed with hostility." This special role, she noted, was recognized long ago by Justice Jackson in *West Virginia v. Barnette*, the decision, incidentally, that overturned *Gobitis*, cited by Scalia. "The very purpose of a Bill of Rights was to withdraw certain subjects from the vicissitudes of political controversy, to place them beyond the reach of majorities and officials and to establish them as legal principles to be applied by the courts."

After this detailed criticism of the majority opinion, O'Connor evaluated the question before the Court using "our established free exercise jurisprudence." She determined that the criminal prohibition against peyote did place a burden on Smith and Black's free exercise of religion, which triggered heightened scrutiny. She found the government's interest in prohibiting peyote compelling, and stated that the "uniform application of Oregon's criminal prohibition is essential to accomplish its overriding interest in preventing the physical harm caused by the use of a Schedule I controlled substance." An exemption for the respondents, she concluded, would "seriously impair" this interest. O'Connor therefore joined the majority judgment that the state of Oregon could legitimately deny the respondent's unemployment compensation claim because his dismissal was the result of misconduct from the illegal use of peyote.

O'Connor made some minor changes in the second draft of her opinion, which was circulated February 14, 1990. This was followed one month later by several additions to Scalia's decision of the Court. His second draft included several footnotes responding to O'Connor's concurring opinion, but there were no significant changes to the body of the decision. This same week Blackmun circulated his dissenting opinion, which Marshall and Brennan soon joined. Blackmun also strongly criticized Scalia for abandoning the *Sherbert* standard, and discarding a "settled and inviolate principle of this Court's First Amendment jurisprudence." The majority ruling, he noted, "effectuates a wholesale overturning of settled law concerning the religion clauses of our Constitution." Blackmun was equally concerned with Scalia's conclusion that it was not the Court's responsibility to protect minority religions. "I do not believe the Founders thought their dearly bought freedom from religious persecution a 'luxury,' but an essential element of liberty—and they could not have thought religious intolerance 'unavoidable' for they drafted the Religion Clauses precisely to avoid that intolerance." He also criticized the majority for addressing the question of the constitutionality of the state law prohibiting peyote possession in the first place, because the state court had not elected to address this issue, and it could still invalidate or ignore the Court on remand. In a footnote he observed, "It is surprising, to say the least, that this Court which so often prides itself about principles of judicial restraint and reduction of federal control over matters of state law would stretch its jurisdiction to the limit in order to reach, in this abstract setting, the constitutionality of Oregon's criminal prohibition of peyote use."

Blackmun agreed with O'Connor that the Court should employ the same standard it had been using since *Sherbert* to evaluate the situation in *Smith*, and that the only real question before the Court was whether exempting Smith and Black from the state's general prohibition against the use of peyote "will unduly interfere with fulfillment of that government interest." However, he disagreed with her conclusion that the state's interest in the uniform application of the law was compelling. Instead, he characterized this interest as "symbolic" because the state did not present clear evidence that it consistently enforced its drug laws against religious users of peyote, and its interest in protecting the health and safety of its citizens as "speculative" because there was no evidence religious peyote use caused harm. Moreover, Blackmun claimed, "Peyote simply is not a popular drug; its distribution for uses in religious rituals has nothing to do with the vast and violent traffic in illegal narcotics that plagues this country." He concluded that because the state had not proven that it had a compelling interest in denying the religious exemption, that the state of Oregon could not, consistent with the free exercise clause of the First Amendment, deny the respondents' unemployment benefits.

At the end of March O'Connor circulated the third and fourth drafts of her concurring opinion, which contained minor revisions, and Brennan, Marshall, and Blackmun sent O'Connor memos indicating that they would like to join the first two parts of her opinion criticizing the majority. The fifth, sixth, and seventh drafts of O'Connor's opinion followed soon thereafter; each contained limited editing and included several case citations. The last circulated opinion in *Employment Division v. Smith* was Justice Scalia's third and final draft on April 6, 1990. It included one change regarding a clarification of his definition of "hybrid rights" cases. That day Justice Kennedy also sent the last memo in the conference records on this case. Interestingly, the memo reflects the fact that Kennedy may have been contemplating a separate concurring opinion after reading O'Connor's and Blackmun's opinions. Had he done so, this may have given Scalia a total of only four votes for his analysis that the First Amendment free exercise clause only protects individuals burdened by government action that directly targets religious exercise. Instead, Kennedy sent a note to Scalia, stating, "After careful study of the opinions in this case, I have decided it is not necessary to write separately. I have already joined your opinion, and am still with you."

In the days before the widespread use of personal pagers, faxes, E-mail, and the World Wide Web, which has sites that post Supreme Court decisions within minutes after they are released, people learned about Supreme Court rulings through the media. For attorneys involved in a case, this contact usually came in the form of a news report or an unexpected question from a reporter about their reaction to a decision they had not read. Dorsay heard about the Court's decision in *Employment Division v. Smith* while he was working out at the gym by his office, and Frohnmayer learned of his success when Linda Greenhouse from the *New York Times* phoned him for his reaction.

Dorsay recalls stepping off the Stairmaster and staring at the television in the gym. He was disappointed about the loss, but the breadth of the ruling was not readily apparent from the news report. His thoughts turned instead to his client and friend, Al Smith. "The unfortunate part of this case, the worst thing, is that Al was somewhat vilified for what happened. Look at what you did." Later, when he read the decision, Dorsay learned of the significance of the ruling: that the Court used *Smith* to establish the rule that neutral, generally applicable laws that burdened religious freedom were not protected by the free exercise clause of the First Amendment. He thought to himself, "Was I there? It doesn't sound like anything I had any involvement with. I never anticipated this decision. We were counting the votes as if the Court would apply the *Sherbert* standard." Back in Eugene, Smith tried to remain upbeat. "Maybe a battle's lost," he said, "but the war's not over. I've lost battles before." Then, acknowledging the gravity of the decision, he added, "If the First Amendment doesn't protect me, how the hell's it going to protect you?"

Frohnmayer's reaction was similar. Although he expected to prevail, he was stunned at the breadth of the Court's ruling.

We had no clue that the Court would reconsider free exercise doctrine. We thought we had won on the *Sherbert v. Verner* test. We thought that if there were ever a compelling state interest, it would be one that you could find in a state's uniform enforcement of its drug laws, and the fact that Oregon had a compelling state interest in its own Constitution in religious neutrality, and our argument that the Oregon Supreme Court's second decision violated the establishment clause because it singled out the Native American Church, giving it preference over other church denominations.

Frohnmayer never suggested the Court abandon use of the compelling state interest test. "Did I think that *Sherbert* would be discarded? It had just been reaffirmed in *Frazee*, for heaven's sake. And that came as a total shock. We hadn't briefed it, we hadn't argued it, we hadn't been questioned about it, and we hadn't suggested it. And Scalia had found his fifth vote for a fundamental doctrinal revisitation. He resuscitated the *Reynolds* case from the dead, or at least we thought had been interred, anyway. He resuscitated the belief-action distinction, even in terms of the facial meaning of the free exercise clause, so we were really surprised at how sweeping this case was, and surprised that the Court had taken the occasion of a very straightforward case that they could have reversed on state interest grounds to revisit that test altogether."

———

Smith II stunned individuals in the religious and civil liberties communities. Many had expected, at worst, a decision denying the respondents' request for unemployment compensation because of the state's compelling interest in controlling drug use. Instead, the Court removed an entire category of laws from the protection of the free exercise clause. The decision, which had not received much media attention up to this point, was widely denounced in the popular press and in academic and legal journals. As William Bentley Ball, a well-known constitutional law scholar recognized, "What first appeared to be a trivial free exercise challenge to an unemployment compensation ruling has resulted in a constitutional fault of San Andreas proportions." The focus quickly moved from Smith's plight to what the decision meant for the future of religious liberty for all Americans.

The fact that *Smith* was a landmark development in free exercise jurisprudence was readily apparent from the reaction of leading law scholars. University of Chicago law professor Michael McConnell called the decision "undoubtedly the most important development in the law of religious freedom in decades," and University of Texas law professor Douglas Laycock, well known for his scholarship in this area, found it difficult to comprehend the Court's sudden departure from its earlier decisions. "The opinion appears to be inconsistent with the original intent, inconsistent with the constitutional text, inconsistent with doctrine under other constitutional clauses, and inconsistent with precedent. It strips the free exercise clause of independent meaning." Within a short period, several dozen scholarly articles were published harshly criticizing Scalia's reasoning and result. Few could hide their surprise at the Court's change in jurisprudence. A handful of scholars supported the decision, but they were in the distinct minority.

One reason for the overwhelmingly negative reaction to *Smith* was because many believed that the free exercise of religion, the "first freedom of the First Amendment," was a preferred freedom to be safeguarded with the same vigilance as other First Amendment liberties such as freedom of speech and of the press. Some openly questioned the majority's motivation for going out of its way to change the status of the free exercise clause. Criticism of *Smith* centered on three areas; the Court's use of precedent, its activism for going beyond the immediate case at hand, and the suggestion that the legislature rather than the courts should safeguard religious liberty.

Critics were most disturbed that Scalia seemed to purposely misread and misapply Supreme Court precedent to justify his decision to restrict the meaning of the free exercise clause. One scholar called it "troubling, bordering on the shocking." Others described it as "strained," "untrustworthy," "internally inconsistent," "fiction," and even "bizarre." Scalia not only selectively cited Supreme Court precedent to find cases that supported his ruling, in some instances he ignored relevant free exercise cases or cited cases that had no current precedential value. For example, he cited *Gobitis* as an authoritative rule that the free exercise clause did not excuse individuals from obeying otherwise valid laws, without mentioning the fact that *Gobitis* was overruled several years later in *West Virginia v. Barnette*.

Justice Scalia appeared to go to great lengths to manipulate free exercise decisions to suit his reasoning and the result in the case. In some instances he reinterpreted decisions that presented a contrary view. Scalia even went so far as to create a new "hybrid rights" category of cases to explain why in some instances the Court utilized the compelling government interest test in cases involving religious challenges to neutral, generally applicable laws. Although it is true that several of the cases cited by Scalia involved multiple First Amendment challenges, or, as in *Yoder*, the free exercise clause combined with a Fourteenth Amendment claim for parents to educate their children, this did not mean that the free exercise claim was ignored by the Court. In fact, a clear reading of each of these decisions reveals that the free exercise clause was considered in each case.

Scalia was also chastised for engaging in judicial activism, a term usually reserved for liberal members of the Court. Rather than limit the decision to the immediate case at hand, he clearly reached beyond the issue posed to the attorneys and overruled or differentiated decisions that previously controlled free exercise challenges. Because the Court's ruling was completely unexpected, those who argued the case never had the opportunity to debate the broad question of the applicability of the free exercise clause to challenges to neutral, generally applicable laws. Nor had the Court suggested in previous cases that it was considering a reevaluation of its free exercise jurisprudence. As late as 1990, the same term as *Smith*, the Court applied the *Sherbert* standard in *Jimmy Swaggart Ministries v. Board of Equalization of California* (1990). This higher level of scrutiny was also used in two free exercise cases the previous term; *Texas Monthly, Inc. v. Bullock* (1989) and *Hernandez v. Commissioner of IRS* (1989). Although the state did prevail in each decision because the free exercise claimants were unable to fulfill the threshold requirement that the government regulation placed a burden on the exercise of their religion, the fact remained that the petitioners lost their case only after the Court applied *Sherbert* to religious challenges to neutral, generally applicable laws outside of the unemployment compensation context.

Criticism also focused on Scalia's discussion regarding the inability of the courts to properly evaluate religious liberty cases and his suggestion that religious adherents appeal to the legislative process to request exemptions from neutral, generally applicable laws that burdened religious beliefs. It was ironic that Scalia was suggesting that the Court would be "courting anarchy" if it continued to evaluate free exercise claims using this level of scrutiny. The Court had, after all, been using the *Sherbert* standard to evaluate free exercise challenges for decades, and it had not resulted in anarchy. *Sherbert* even had a built-in mechanism for disallowing an exaggerated number of claims; many challenges would not be able to meet the threshold requirement that a government action burdened their religion. Even if the worst-case scenario was true and the courts were flooded with claims for free exercise exemptions, this was not a legitimate reason for the Court to turn its back on protection of a fundamental freedom.

Scalia's proposed solution, an appeal to state legislatures, sounded good in principle—legislatures have successfully protected civil rights and liberties; but closer consideration reveals its shortcomings. Obviously this avenue would disproportionately disadvantage the smaller, less politically powerful religious groups that did not have the resources to effectively manipulate the political process to protect religious liberty. These difficulties were recognized by Justice Scalia in his majority decision, but were dismissed as an "unavoidable consequence of democratic government." In addition to the logistical difficulties of fighting for exemptions in the legislative arena, Scalia's proposed solution fails to take into account *Smith*'s effect on how legislatures would view calls to protect religious freedom. Prior to *Smith* when legislatures considered requests for religious accommodation, they sometimes granted the request because they believed the behavior was protected by the free exercise clause. Legislators were previously motivated to create religious exemptions because they were concerned that the legislation may fail constitutional scrutiny if such exemptions were excluded. The Court's decision in *Smith*, on the other hand, tells legislators that they need only a rational reason to justify government regulations that may affect one's religious exercise.

There is also the possibility that the Court's new hands-off approach to religious challenges might have an even more insidious effect by allowing legislatures to actively—although not overtly—discriminate against minority religions. Under *Smith*, governments would find it easier to persecute smaller religions as occurred in the past, when majoritarian institutions either directly or indirectly forced unpopular minority religious groups to conform to majority opinion. Evidence of this possibility, of course, is provided in the country's past, replete with examples of hostility toward Catholics, Mormons, Jehovah's Witnesses, Quakers, and significantly, American Indians.

Overall, *Smith* took many by surprise. The unwillingness of a majority of the Court to shield religious liberty beyond what was already offered by the political process was inconsistent with the Court's previous free exercise jurisprudence and antithetical to the very purpose of the Bill of Rights.

———

After a long, seven-year battle, Al Smith and Galen Black's simple request for unemployment compensation received a definitive answer from the U.S. Supreme Court, which ruled that the Employment Division of the state of Oregon had rightfully denied their request for benefits because they were appropriately discharged from their job for ingesting a substance proscribed by state law. What few could have anticipated, least of all the respondents or the attorneys who argued the case, was the fact that five justices also took the Court back to the rule that it established when it decided its first free exercise case over one hundred years earlier.

But would this be the final word on the meaning of the free

exercise clause? Perhaps to those who believe the Court has the sole authority to debate the meaning of the Constitution and to protect civil rights and liberties. To this group, *Smith* might be construed as the Law of the Land, and the Court's final word on the subject until it decided to revisit its ruling. However, there was another possibility, consistent with the theory of coordinate construction of the Constitution. As described by congressional scholar Louis Fisher, other branches of government have a responsibility to engage in independent constitutional analysis, which could lead to action to protect rights under the Constitution. Would there be an appeal to the public and the other branches of government to protect religious liberty? Shortly after *Smith* was announced, critics were already looking for alternatives. Academics critical of *Smith* and members of the religious and civil liberties communities united to fight for religious liberty and to bring this fight to political institutions other than the Supreme Court.

Legal scholar Edward Gaffney argued that Americans should not rely exclusively on the Court for the protection of essential rights and liberties, but also appeal to the other branches of government to act aggressively to protect the principles embodied in the Constitution.

> When the judiciary gives a minimalist interpretation of the importance of religious liberty, it is time for the political branches of government to extend greater protection through legislation grounded in the values secured by the Bill of Rights. And when we, the People, encourage our representatives to safeguard the first of our civil liberties, religious freedom, we are doing the very thing that this bicentennial session demands of us: securing the "blessings of Liberty for ourselves and our Posterity" and promoting that "more perfect Union" that our Constitution was ordained to establish.

This legislative appeal, inspired by a rejection of *Smith*, began days after the Court's ruling.

CHAPTER 10

Many Rivers to Cross

The day after the Court's ruling in *Smith*, legal experts with American Jewish Congress started working with Craig Dorsay on drafting a petition for rehearing. The Supreme Court rarely grants such petitions—a majority of the Court must agree to re-hear a case, and the last time was in the 1960s—but *Smith* critics were hopeful the Court would reconsider the decision because it had not allowed briefing on the broader issue of whether the free exercise clause protected individuals from neutral, generally applicable laws that burdened their religion. By the time the petition was filed on May 10, 1990, it had been signed by dozens of religious and civil liberties groups belonging to the Coalition for the Free Exercise of Religion (CFER), an umbrella group united in response to *Smith*. It was an extraordinarily eclectic alliance representing both sides of the ideological spectrum, from organizations on the left such as the ACLU, the Baptist Joint Committee on Public Affairs, Americans United for Separation of Church and State, and AJ Congress, and organizations from the right, such as the National Association of Evangelicals, People for the American Way, the Christian Legal Society, and the Home School Legal Defense Association. The brief was also signed by fifty-five constitutional law scholars who joined the petition to illustrate how widely *Smith* was criticized in the academic community.

The petition for rehearing characterized *Smith* as a "major step away from settled law." It declared,

> The case briefed by the parties and the amici was, in retrospect, a different case from that decided by the Court. The is-

sues presented were directly focused, and narrowly tailored toward one concern, namely, whether the State of Oregon had a compelling state interest in regulating illegal drugs that overrode the Respondents' religious liberty interest in the sacramental use of peyote. The majority opinion eschewed discussion of the question briefed and decided the case on far-reaching grounds without the benefit of briefing or oral argument on the specific concerns raised de novo by the Court's opinion.

Attached to the petition was a recently published *Harvard Law Review* article, "The Origins and Historical Understanding of Free Exercise of Religion," by University of Chicago law professor Michael McConnell. It was a significant scholarly effort that traced the origins of the free exercise clause of the First Amendment. The article illustrated the historical roots of accommodation for the free exercise of religion, and coalition members believed it might persuade the Court to at least reconsider its revision of free exercise jurisprudence.

However, members of the coalition were also realistic about the odds that the Court would grant the petition, and were discussing an alternative strategy at the same time the brief was being written. The strategy concerned whether Congress could enact legislation to negate *Smith*, and this conversation was taking place among several key players in the coalition: Morton Halperin, director of the Washington office of the American Civil Liberties Union and chair of CFER; Dean Kelley, general counsel for the National Council of Churches; and Oliver Thomas and J. Brent Walker, general and associate counsel for the Baptist Joint Committee.

Several days after the Court's ruling, Halperin walked into Representative Steven Solarz's Washington, D.C., congressional office and handed him the *Employment Division v. Smith* slip decision. "You have to read this," he said. Halperin and Solarz had been friends for years. Both shared an interest in foreign policy and constitutional rights issues, and Halperin knew Solarz would be interested in a Supreme Court decision that had such far-reaching implications for religious freedom. Halperin is best known in Washington as an expert in foreign affairs. He previously served in several high-ranking posts in three presidential administrations, and has been associated with a number of think tanks in Washington since entering the public sector in 1966. Throughout his career Halperin had combined his policy expertise with a strong interest in, and respect for, civil rights and liberties. For the last seventeen years he worked as the director of the Center for National Security studies, and during the last eight years at that job served as director of the Washington office of the ACLU, which is responsible for the organization's national agenda.

Solarz also enjoyed a long tenure in public service. He was first elected to the New York State Assembly in 1968, where he served for six years before being selected to serve New York's 13th Congressional District. Solarz won reelection eight times, and distinguished himself in the House with his work on the Foreign Affairs Committee. He was chair of the Subcommittee on Africa and the Subcommittee on Asian and Pacific Affairs, and also served on the Budget, Joint Economic, Education and Labor, Post Office and Civil Service, and Merchant Marine and Fisheries Committees during his sixteen years in the House. Solarz was also a forceful advocate for religious freedom, and played an instrumental role in several campaigns to protect religious liberty, including Public Law 100-180, which was in direct response to William Rehnquist's *Goldman v. Weinberg* (1985) decision. The regulation allowed military personnel the wearing of "unobtrusive religious headgear." It was a controversial bill that was strongly opposed by the military for several years. When the bill was in Conference Committee, where members of the Judiciary Committee "mark up" draft bills, the Pentagon sent up a team of admirals and generals to lobby against the measure. "And one of the Generals told the conferees that the defeat of the Solarz yarmulke amendment was more important to the Pentagon than approval of the MX Missile." Solarz recalled, chuckling, "And I remember thinking at the time that that was the best argument I had heard yet against the MX Missile." After the bill was enacted in 1987 Solarz sent a letter to Justice William Brennan, who had urged Congress to pass legislation to overturn *Goldman* in his dissent to that opinion. Solarz included a gift of a yarmulke made out of camouflage fabric to celebrate the law. "I wrote that Congress had finally taken his advice—and I'm told he was so delighted to receive the yarmulke, that he put it on, and when he went home later that day, he had apparently forgotten to take it off, so he had to explain to his wife why he was wearing a camouflage yarmulke. I was later told that when Justice Brennan went to Israel to meet with the President, that he wore the yarmulke."

Halperin was familiar with Solarz's previous work on behalf of religious freedom. He knew Solarz was respected in the religious community for his legislative efforts, and that the congressman could aid the coalition in its response to *Smith*. Because only members of either house can introduce a bill to Congress, Solarz was a logical choice to sponsor the legislation. After briefly discussing *Smith*, they made arrangements to meet for dinner several weeks later to plan a strategy. In the interim, Halperin went to work. "I buried myself in the library for two weeks to explore possible legislative alternatives. I was looking for the best legal theory, the best avenue to address the problem created by the decision." He found an argument: section five of the Fourteenth Amendment, which grants Congress the "power to enforce, by appropriate legislation, the provisions of this article," could be used to secure the rights guaranteed by the Constitution. Congress had previously used its section five authority to enact federal antidiscrimination legislation such as the 1964 and 1990 Civil Rights Acts and the 1965 Voting Rights Act. Each law provides statutory protection for civil rights and liberties beyond what is required by the Supreme Court. Because the due process clause of the Fourteenth Amendment makes the free exercise clause, as well as other guarantees protected by the Bill of Rights, binding against encroachments by states, this section five authority empowers Congress to protect the free exercise of religion.

Halperin also discovered that the Supreme Court had recognized Congress's section five authority to remedy state violations of Fourteenth Amendment rights in the past. In *Katzenbach v.*

Morgan it sustained an amendment to the 1965 Voting Rights Act, which provided that states could not deny individuals who completed the sixth grade in an accredited Spanish language school in Puerto Rico the right to vote. Congress enacted the legislation to ensure nondiscrimination in voting, which would also help empower minority groups in the political arena. The amendment in question invalidated a New York state law that required English literacy as a prerequisite to voting rights—a law the Supreme Court sustained as legitimate under the equal protection clause of the Fourteenth Amendment. Justice William Brennan, writing the opinion of the Court, interpreted section five as an affirmative grant of discretionary power to Congress to determine "whether and what legislation is needed to secure the guarantes of the Fourteenth Amendment." He concluded that Congress had "specially informed legislative competence" to find discrimination in voting qualifications and that the Court should defer to congressional judgment in its attempt to remedy discrimination by states. Brennan also implied that Congress had independent authority under section five to define the "substantive scope" of rights protected by the Fourteenth Amendment.

It was this latter suggestion that gave some pause, including Justice John Marshall Harlan in his *Morgan* dissent. He argued that congressional authority under section five should be limited to remedial actions by Congress; in other words, to judicially "recognized state violations of federal constitutional standards." According to Harlan, it was up to the Court to determine whether a state action violated the Constitution, not Congress. In a decision handed down the next year, however, he conceded that the Court should provide deference to legislative conclusions reached by Congress because of the institution's superior fact-finding ability.

Subsequent decisions by the Court reaffirmed and even expanded congressional power to act in a remedial fashion under its section five authority, as well as congressional power to act in a similar fashion under the enforcement clauses of the Thirteenth and Fifteenth Amendments. For instance, in 1966 in *South Carolina v. Katzenbach* the Court upheld Congress' power to use "any rational means" to enforce the Fifteenth Amendment's ban on voting discrimination, and in 1980 in *Rome v. United States*, the Court broadened this enforcement power to permit Congress to use any "appropriate" methods to ban discriminatory practices, both intended and unintended. However, since *Morgan*, the Court has never directly established whether Congress has the substantive power to define the rights protected by the Fourteenth Amendment as suggested in Brennan's majority opinion, leaving little judicial guidance in this area. The Court came close to addressing this issue in 1970 in *Oregon v. Mitchell*, a case that addressed the constitutionality of a federal statute that granted citizens eighteen years or older the right to vote in state and federal elections. The Court was badly divided in this decision, sustaining the statute as it applied to federal elections, but striking it down with respect to state elections. A majority could not agree on the extent of Congress' power to define the substantive content of constitutional guarantees. In one of the more recent decisions concerning Congress' authority under the Civil War Amendments, *Mississippi University for Women v. Hogan* (1982) where the Court struck down a state statute that restricted men from a nursing school, a majority agreed that if Congress has the power to modify constitutional rights, this authority could be used to expand constitutional rights, although it could not be invoked to "restrict, abrogate, or dilute" these guarantees. The opinion by Justice Sandra Day O'Connor drew upon the footnote in Brennan's *Morgan* decision to justify this reasoning. However, despite these and several other decisions where the Court skirted the issue, the extent of Congress' substantive power under the enforcement guarantees of the Civil War Amendments was less than clear.

Nevertheless, with a series of Supreme Court cases validating some measure of congressional authority under section five of the Fourteenth Amendment to enforce constitutional rights, Halperin believed this was a viable avenue for Congress to justify federal legislation that protected religious liberty against encroachments from the states or the federal government. He prepared some notes and met Steven Solarz for dinner.

"I recall," said Solarz, "that the whole idea behind the Religious Freedom Restoration Act was hatched over that dinner." In the middle of the meal, Halperin said to him, "Steve, I have an opportunity that could make you a hero of the religious community." He told Solarz that a solution to *Smith* might be legislation to reinstate the compelling government interest test that was used for almost three decades after the Supreme Court's 1963 *Sherbert v. Verner* decision. To essentially "take the law back to where it was before *Smith*." Halperin suggested passage of a general law that mandated this high level of scrutiny if a neutral, generally applicable law placed a burden on an individual's free exercise of religion. Solarz was encouraged by the idea. "It seemed to be a sensible approach, and it made a lot of sense on principle."

Halperin told Solarz that he should further investigate Congress' authority under section five of the Fourteenth Amendment, and told him the coalition would be available to assist him in drafting legislation and lobbying other organized groups and members of Congress to support a legislative remedy to *Smith*. Solarz quickly agreed to act as chief sponsor of such a measure in the House.

The next day Solarz asked his legislative assistant, David Lachmann, who had worked for the congressman since 1989, to explore the feasibility of such a legislative attempt. Lachmann then reached out to individuals in the religious and civil rights communities for assistance in preparing the legislation. One of the many people he contacted was Nat Lewin, a prominent Washington attorney known for his work on religious liberty issues. Lewin is an experienced litigator; he argued twelve cases before the Supreme Court when he was an assistant to the solicitor general between 1963 and 1967, and fifteen additional cases since entering private practice. The cases ranged from representation of commercial interests and criminal cases to issues of constitutional law. Most notably, he represented S. Simcha Goldman in *Goldman v. Weinberg*. Lewin would later represent the Satmar Hasidic village of Kiryas Joel in *Bd. of Education of Kiryas Joel Village School District v. Grumet* (1994). Lewin was active in national and local Jewish community affairs, at one point serving as president in both the American Section of the International Association of Jewish Lawyers and Jurists and the Jewish Community Council of Greater Washington, and as founder and vice-president of the National Jewish Commission on Law and Public Affairs. At COLPA, Lewin prepared over fifty legal briefs on behalf of Jewish interests.

Lewin and Solarz previously worked together on several pieces of legislation to protect the rights of public and private employees to freely observe their religion. For example, Lewin drafted, and Solarz successfully lobbied Public Law 100-180 allowing religious headgear in the military. They also joined forces in 1972 to enact an amendment to the 1964 Civil Rights Act, which defines religion to include religious observance and requires private and government employers to make reasonable accommodations to allow employees to exercise their religious obligations. Lewin's skill and experience in drafting religious liberty legislation and overseeing its passage through legislative and executive branch obstacles made him a key asset for Solarz's exploration into a legislative remedy. Both Lewin and Solarz like to tell the story of how Lewin was able to overcome executive branch resistance to the 1972 amendment. Lewin joined the congressman for a visit with Stuart Eizenstat, the head of President Jimmy Carter's domestic policy staff, who indicated that the White House was not supportive of the legislation because it believed it would allow preferential treatment of one religion over another, thus violating the establishment clause. Lewin, who is Jewish, then told Eizenstat a story from his experience clerking for Justice Harlan, who allowed him to go home early on Fridays so he could get home before sundown. "I have to tell you," Lewin told him, "it never occurred to Mr. Justice Harlan that Mr. Justice Harlan was violating the Establishment Clause of the First Amendment." "I recall," said Lewin smiling, "that it ended up being pretty persuasive."

Lachmann spoke with Lewin about how to craft legislation to address *Smith*. Lewin explained, "I can certainly take some of the blame. It seemed that section five of the Fourteenth Amendment was the right vehicle. Precedent cases supported the notion that this was the right way for Congress to say, look, the Supreme Court has its responsibility, and we have our responsibility, and here's how we interpret this." With a green light from a religious liberty expert who had experience constructing legislation that protected religious freedom, Lachmann and Solarz drafted the bill.

At the same time these discussions were taking place in Solarz's congressional office, several other members of the coalition were also engaging in conversations about how to best address *Smith*. On May 16, 1990, Dean Kelley, general counsel for the National Council of Churches, an umbrella religious organization that includes thirty-two denominations and over forty million constituents in the United States, made a presentation to its 260-member general board in Pittsburgh. At the meeting Thomas and Walker from the Baptist Joint Committee and University of Texas professor Douglas Laycock pitched the idea that Congress could enact legislation modeled after the 1965 Voting Rights Act to protect religious liberty. Two days after the presentation, the general board enacted a resolution on "The Voiding of the Free Exercise Clause of the Constitution," which urged members to "alert their constituents to this incredible loss of protection for religious rights—of minority and majority—because of an aggressive and radical exercise of judicial activism not required by the case before the Court and not briefed or argued by the parties, sweeping away the 'compelling interest' standard that has been settled law for 27 years." However, the National Council of Churches did not endorse the idea of a specific legislative remedy at this time, deciding that it would be best to wait until the Court ruled on the petition for rehearing, which came several weeks later.

On June 5, 1990, the Supreme Court issued a brief ruling denying the petition for rehearing. With this opportunity closed, members of the Coalition for the Free Exercise of Religion did not waste time working on its legislative solution. That day, Halperin contacted Kim Yelton from Americans United for Separation of Church and State to arrange a meeting with members of the coalition and other interested parties three days hence to discuss the group's next step. The meeting, held in the Rayburn House Office Building, was attended by representatives from at least fifty religious and civil liberties organizations.

"We've got to legislate," Halperin told the group. He distributed the draft bill prepared by Solarz's office, and indicated that the congressman had been prepared to introduce the legislation the previous week. Several individuals present expressed reservations about whether Congress had the authority or the will to enact such legislation, but Halperin reassured them that the constitutional foundation for the legislation—section five of the Fourteenth Amendment—provided an appropriate avenue for the bill, and that members of Congress would likely back the effort if there was widespread support in the civil rights and religious liberty communities. The groups present ultimately agreed on the suitability of this legislative remedy. Thomas, Walker, and Laycock's visit to the National Council of Churches had already alerted some of the organizations to the viability and wisdom of such a solution, and at the meeting it was discovered that other coalition members had been working in this direction as well.

The group decided that the best strategy would be to restore free exercise law to where it existed prior to *Smith*. "We wanted to make it clear," Halperin stated, "that we wanted the Court to continue interpreting the meaning of the free exercise clause—we didn't want to lock it in—but that we wanted to undo this one decision." Two committees were formed; a drafting committee to refine the Solarz bill, and a legislative committee to spearhead the effort to gather cosponsors and lobby support for the measure. Organized and united, the coalition moved quickly to work out the finer points of the bill. The drafting committee met several days later to discuss changes suggested at the initial meeting. It agreed that the wording of the legislation had to be as neutral as possible to maintain the unity of the coalition. One member of the committee, David Saperstein, director of the Religious Action Center of Reform Judaism, noted, "From the beginning, the Coalition agreed very quickly on the ruling assumption that the only way to keep a Coalition this broad together was to restore the rule in

Smith and let the chips fall as they may on the particular issue that was brought to the table. We agreed that there would be no exemptions to the bill." The drafting committee understood that any exemptions would lead to requests for others, which could potentially divide the coalition and delay or kill the measure. The committee also decided that the legislation would avoid the issue of the sacramental use of peyote. Too much of a focus on peyote, or only on the rights of American Indians, it believed, could also divide the coalition because some of the more conservative religious organizations might characterize the measure as "a drug bill." However, the door was not closed to future efforts to enact separate legislation that specifically addressed the rights of American Indians to ingest peyote as a sacrament during religious ceremonies. Later, several members of the Coalition for the Free Exercise of Religion would also become involved in efforts to enact legislation to specifically protect the religious use of peyote.

On June 18 the Coalition for the Free Exercise of Religion met to discuss the draft bill, the Religious Freedom Restoration Act of 1990 (RFRA). Most members enthusiastically supported the measure, which would prohibit any federal or state action that burdened an individual's religious exercise unless it fulfilled a compelling government interest. An issue was also raised, however, that would later become a major obstacle to the bill. Several pro-life groups inquired about how RFRA would affect religious liberty claims to abortion rights. The concern was whether the measure would create a statutory right to abortion by allowing women to argue that they had a free exercise obligation to terminate a pregnancy. The issue was only briefly discussed, and most of the coalition members present, including some from the pro-life community, agreed that it was unlikely the legislation would be used to secure abortion rights because women already had a constitutional right to abortion under the Fourteenth Amendment. The drafting committee urged coalition members to resist any type of religious liberty exceptions, including a religious claim to abortion, and to support the generally written bill. The meeting adjourned with most members agreeing to back the measure as written.

At the same time the coalition's drafting committee was finalizing the bill, Solarz was working with the coalition's legislative committee to collect cosponsors for the measure. The first order of business was to secure support from Democrats and Republicans in leadership positions on the House Judiciary Committee, which would initially consider the bill. Solarz approached Don Edwards, a Democrat and the chair of the Subcommittee on Civil and Constitutional Rights, to join him in sponsoring the legislation, and then reached across the aisle to James F. Sensenbrenner, the ranking Republican on the same subcommittee, and Paul B. Henry, a conservative Republican and son of evangelical theologian Carl F. H. Henry. All three agreed to join the New York congressman.

The four representatives introduced the Religious Freedom Restoration Act at a news conference on June 26, 1990, only two months after the Court decided *Smith*. At the conference the chief sponsors declared that the proposed bill was a broad-based effort to restore religious liberty for all Americans, and that it was not a bill solely about peyote. At least twenty-five organizations from the coalition were present to support the bill. Thomas, who spoke for the group, stated, "Coalitions come and go but mostly—in the volatile field of church-state relations—they go. That's why this motley gathering of unlikely cohorts is historic. Although perennial adversaries, these groups are joining voices to say to the United States Supreme Court that religious liberty is not a luxury to be gratuitously bestowed by a beneficent majority." RFRA was clearly a response to the Court's decision in *Smith*. The "purpose" section read, "The purposes of this Act are to restore the compelling interest test set forth in *Sherbert v. Verner* (1963) and *Wisconsin v. Yoder* (1972) and to guarantee its application in all cases where the free exercise of religion is substantially burdened; and to provide a claim or defense to persons whose religious exercise is substantially burdened by government."

The next day the chief sponsors sent out a "Dear Colleague" letter to fellow House members requesting that they add their name to the list of cosponsors. As in the news conference, the letter emphasized that RFRA was a general bill to support all religious exercise, and steered away from the issue of peyote. One passage stated, "The bill will *not* ensure that Native Americans can use peyote, nor will it single out any other religious practice for special protection."

The Religious Freedom Restoration Act was introduced in the House of Representatives on July 26, 1990. By the time it was placed in the "hopper," the box on the bill clerk's desk where members put measures to be considered by the House, it had thirty-one additional cosponsors. The bill was assigned a number, HR 5377 and the Speaker of the House, with the assistance of the House Parliamentarian, referred the bill to the House Committee on the Judiciary, which is the committee responsible for constitutional and judicial matters. The chairman of the Judiciary Committee, in turn, referred the bill to the House Subcommittee on Civil and Constitutional Affairs, one of its five subcommittees, which then held hearings on the proposed legislation.

———

Most of the work in Congress takes place in committees, or "little legislatures" as described by Woodrow Wilson, who was a political scientist before being elected to the White House. The committee system allows Congress to consider thousands of often controversial bills and presidential nominations, and manage the oversight of the large federal bureaucracy at the same time. It also provides numerous points of access for members of the public, experts in the field, and representatives from organized pressure groups interested in a particular issue. The first stage of committee deliberations is a public hearing on a bill. Hearings usually take place in the subcommittees, which are smaller and more specialized than full committees, but they can and do take place in both forums. Hearings are orchestrated by the committee chair, who works with the ranking minority member to arrange the list of witnesses who will appear to discuss proposed legislation. A variety of witnesses may testify in a congressional hearing, including the sponsor of the bill, members of the executive branch, interest group representatives, and private citizens. Witnesses read prepared statements and committee members have limited time for questioning. Prepared statements from interested parties may also be submitted into the official record. The purpose of a hearing is to discuss the measure in detail and to examine its merits or problems. Hearings also allow the chair and other committee members to air their opinions on the proposals under consideration. As gatekeepers to the rest of the legislative process, how a bill does in committee is usually a good indicator of how it will fare on the floor of Congress.

The subcommittee hearing on the Religious Freedom Restoration Act was held on September 27, 1990. In his introduction, Chairman Edwards specified that the bill was in direct response to *Smith* and that the intention of the measure was to restore free exercise to the status that existed prior to the Court's decision. The purpose of the hearing, he announced, was to explore *Smith*'s impact on religious conduct in America, and to see if these consequences might be averted with passage of the legislation.

At the hearing, the bipartisan support for RFRA clearly matched the bipartisan nature of the Coalition for the Free Exercise of Religion. The witnesses represented a range of political and religious beliefs, and each lamented the negative effects of *Smith* and the need for Congress to pass legislation to protect religious liberty. Representative Solarz described the decision as a "devastating blow to religious freedom in the U.S.," and characterized RFRA as a "narrowly crafted, legislative response to the radical work of an activist Supreme Court majority." Reverend Robert P. Dugan, director of the Office of Public Affairs of the National Association of Evangelicals, an association of over fifty thousand churches from seventy-eight denominations, warned that the reasonableness standard mandated by *Smith* would lead to religious intolerance and an overall erosion of religious freedom. Reverend Kelley observed that the negative effects of *Smith* were already evident in state and federal court decisions.

Another theme running throughout the witnesses' testimony was the importance of congressional action to circumvent "mistakes" by the Court. Reverend John H. Buchanan Jr., chair of the People for the American Way Action Fund, a nonpartisan constitutional liberties organization, predicted that an increasingly conservative Supreme Court would lead Americans to Congress for the protection of rights and liberties. Members of Congress, he remarked, should learn to rely on legislative remedies to circumvent unpopular Court decisions.

Certainly I must say for those of us who are part of the civil rights and civil liberties community that everything I know about the present Court, and everything I know about the mindset of the Federal judiciary more generally, leads me to believe that not only in this matter, and in such matters as the Civil Rights Act of 1990, but in a series of cases over a series of years, I fear we shall have to come back to you, and to Congress for the sure protection of the constitutional rights and liberties of American citizens—and we shall.

The issue of whether Congress has the authority to act through the legislative process to protect constitutional freedoms was explained in detail in a letter Laycock wrote to Edwards, which was included in the subcommittee record. He explained how section five of the Fourteenth Amendment empowers Congress to enact "statutory protection for constitutional values that the Supreme Court is unwilling or unable to protect on its own authority." Laycock reviewed prior exercises of Congress' section five authority and provided a detailed case history of Supreme Court decisions that validated this type of congressional activity to reassure members that RFRA was constitutional and did not infringe on the Court's authority to interpret the Constitution. He observed that the legislation did not overturn the Court's constitutional ruling in *Smith*—its free exercise analysis in the decision would still stand—but that RFRA circumvented the decision by creating a statutory right to protect religious freedom.

At the end of the letter, Laycock reiterated the challenge that had been established throughout the hearing; that Congress act aggressively to ensure continued protection of the rights and liberties embodied in the Constitution. He stated that in this instance, it was not only entirely appropriate for Congress to act, but essential for the future protection of rights and liberties.

> By creating judicially-enforceable statutory rights, Congress can call on the powers of the judiciary that the Court feared to invoke on its own. Because the rights created would be statutory, Congress can retain a voice that it could not have retained if the Court had acted on its own. By legislating generally, for all religions, instead of case-by-case for particular religions, Congress can reduce the danger that it will not respond to the needs of small faiths. One function of section five of the Fourteenth Amendment is to provide for just such interbranch cooperation.

Members of the coalition were pleased with the subcommittee proceedings. There was bipartisan support for the Religious Freedom Restoration Act, and aside from the earlier nonpublic discussions about whether the measure might lead to religiously inspired claims to abortion rights, there was no vocal opposition to the measure in the coalition or the public. The coalition's legislative committee next focused its attention on gathering bipartisan support in the Senate. On October 26, Joseph R. Biden (D-Del), chair of the Senate Judiciary Committee, along with Orrin G. Hatch (R-Utah), the ranking minority leader, and six cosponsors introduced S 3254, a companion bill to HR 5377 in the Senate. It was assigned by the Senate Parliamentarian to the Committee on the Judiciary, but hearings on the Senate version of the bill were not held during the 101st Congress, which adjourned two days later. When Congress adjourns for the session and no formal vote has been taken on a bill in committee, the bill "dies" and must be reintroduced in the next session of Congress.

———

Both before and after the House hearing members of the Coalition for the Free Exercise of Religion reached out to religious and civil liberties groups to increase support for RFRA. Because most of the organizations belonging to the coalition have offices in Washington, D.C., and correspond regularly with like-minded groups, it was easy to get the word out through letters and informal meetings with group leaders. But not all of the feedback was positive. Some leaders and their general counsel expressed reservations about whether Congress had the power to enact such legislation, and if so, whether it was the best vehicle to circumvent *Smith*, but this did not stop consideration of RFRA as a viable alternative now that the opportunity for rehearing was closed.

One strategy used by the coalition to increase support for the bill was to ask constitutional law scholars who were familiar with religious liberty jurisprudence to persuade members of the religious community of the advantages of RFRA. Laycock joined colleagues McConnell and Edward McGlynn Gaffney, dean and professor of law at Valparaiso University School of Law in "An Open Letter to the Religious Community and Its Legal Counsel," sent in late November 1990. With their expertise and previous litigation efforts on behalf of religious liberty, the three scholars played an important role in the grassroots and legislative strategy. The letter emphasized their disagreement with *Smith* and endorsement of RFRA. They urged unified support behind the legislation, calling it "the best practicable means of correcting a grave interpretive error by the Supreme Court, and will help ensure that all Americans, whatever their religious faith, will be protected in their exercise of religion, as the framers and ratifiers of our Constitution intended them to be."

The year ended with coalition members intensively lobbying members of Congress and interest groups. The number of cosponsors grew, and the size of the coalition swelled as more groups backed RFRA. There was only one apparently minor concern that presaged possible problems on the horizon. The issue of abortion continued to be raised at coalition meetings by some pro-life groups as a possible obstacle to successful passage of the bill. One reason the issue kept coming up was because the same groups also expressed reservations about the ACLU's endorsement of RFRA. Because the ACLU is well known as a staunch supporter of reproductive freedom rights, some questioned its motivation for backing the bill. Chair of the coalition,

Halperin was the target of some of these concerns. As a result, he decided that it would be best if he stepped down and was replaced by an individual from a less "openly pro-choice" organization. Halperin's decision was supported by other coalition members who agreed that it had a better chance of sticking together and gathering additional support without the ACLU leading the RFRA battle. Oliver Thomas was selected to chair the coalition. The Baptist Joint Committee did not have a formal position on abortion, and that factor, combined with Thomas's friendly and easygoing style, made him a well-suited choice to head the diverse coalition.

As the 101st Congress adjourned, RFRA, with its growing list of cosponsors and support from a diverse, rapidly growing coalition, appeared to be headed toward passage.

———

But would the Religious Freedom Restoration Act be enough to protect religious liberty for American Indians? At the same time the Coalition for the Free Exercise of Religion was launching its effort to enact a general law to reinstate a high level of scrutiny to the judicial evaluation of religious liberty claims, Indian rights organizations were exploring legislation that would explicitly provide federal statutory protection for American Indian religious practices, including the peyote ritual. Some of these organizations were openly critical of CFER's efforts because RFRA did not specifically protect Indian religious practices in general, and the religious use of peyote in particular. To many, *Smith* represented a direct attack on the religious rights of American Indians. It was regarded as one of a series of Supreme Court decisions, including *Bowen v. Roy* (1986) and *Lyng v. Northwest Cemetery Association* (1988), that were overtly hostile to Indian religious freedom. Although sympathetic to the fact that the holding in *Smith* would have a negative effect on religious liberty for all Americans, as a minority group, American Indians had already suffered these kinds of losses in state and federal courts for years. As John Echohawk, executive director of the Native American Rights Fund, stated in the organization's newsletter shortly after *Smith* was decided,

Mistreatment of American Indian religion by federal courts has seriously weakened religious liberty for all Americans. Mainstream religious groups, who were previously unconcerned about the fate of Indian religious practitioners, are now deeply concerned about their own religious liberty. This irony gives meaning to Reverend King's statement, "Injustice anywhere is a threat to justice everywhere." *Smith* and its progeny demonstrate that when law cannot protect the basic freedoms of the weakest, it lacks vitality to protect the rest of society.

Furthermore, even if RFRA were enacted, it was very likely that American Indian religious rights would still be unprotected in the courts. The legislation would only subject state and federal actions that burdened religious liberty to a strict balancing test after the case wound up in court. Even then, judges might determine that a government action did not place a burden on an individual's religion, or if it did, that there was justification for doing so. For instance, in *Smith*, even if the Supreme Court used the higher level of judicial scrutiny demanded by the compelling government interest test, the respondents would have lost. O'Connor made this clear in her concurring opinion. Although she harshly criticized the Court for discarding the *Sherbert* rule, she used the compelling government interest test and concluded that the state's interest in eradicating drug abuse was compelling enough to outweigh the burden on Smith and Black's religious freedom. Also, in her majority opinion in *Lyng*, O'Connor resolved that the building of a road through federal land considered sacred by three Indian tribes for thousands of years did not place a burden on the free exercise of their religion because the government action did not coerce or penalize the Indians for practicing their religion. Because the high threshold requirement first introduced in *Bowen*, another Indian religious freedom case, was not met in *Lyng*, the high level of scrutiny was never triggered. There was also the danger that the Court might carve out an exception to the strict balancing test, as occurred in *O'Lone v. Shabazz* and *Goldman* when a majority determined that prisons and the military concerned "special circumstances" and that the

Court should employ the deferential reasonableness standard to evaluate religious liberty claims in these contexts.

A review of free exercise cases involving American Indians led to a foreboding conclusion. It was possible that even with the protection of RFRA, Indian religious rights would not be protected in the courts. In fact, if these past decisions were an indicator of how future cases would be decided, it was probable.

With this in mind, there was agreement among national Indian advocate organizations that outcome-specific legislation was needed to safeguard Indian religious practices. Existing federal laws were largely useless. The American Indian Religious Freedom Act, which was supposed to protect Indian religious freedom, had been relegated to a policy statement. Any possibility that the resolution could be used for protection of Indian religious freedom was lost in *Lyng* when O'Connor ruled that AIRFA did not create any judicially enforceable rights.

Support for national legislation initially centered around a law that would shield the religious use of peyote. By 1990, twenty-two states had no legislative protection for nondrug use of the sacrament, and the laws in the twenty-eight states that did provide cover were of varying degrees, with some laws granting a religious exemption to controlled substances laws to all individuals practicing peyotism, to an exemption only for members of the Native American Church, to the limited protection of an "affirmative defense." Such a patchwork of laws was seen as confusing and inequitable, resulting in similarly situated Indians being treated differently depending on where they practiced their religion. A federal statute could protect all American Indians, regardless of their state of residence, which would allow the exercise of religion without fear of violating the law. The legislation would be proactive, providing protection from the onset, rather than reactive like RFRA, which only provides protection, if at all, after an individual has been arrested, jailed, and prosecuted, and has fulfilled his or her responsibility of proving a burden on the exercise of religion.

This focus on federal legislation to protect the religious use of peyote also brought renewed attention to legislative efforts already being contemplated in the American Indian community. Prior to *Smith*, there was consideration of legislation to protect sacred sites, which became an issue after *Lyng*, and to protect the rights of American Indian prisoners, which were limited, along with the rights of all incarcerated prisoners, in *O'Lone*.

In light of the lack of specific national legislation currently on the books, and in response to an unsympathetic Supreme Court that refused to protect Indian religious practices under the free exercise clause of the Constitution, the strategy was to once again appeal to Congress and have it enact enforceable legislation that guaranteed religious freedom for American Indians.

———

The Native American Church, together with the Native American Rights Fund, played a leading role in this legislative effort. Soon after *Smith* was decided, the church approached Rueben Snake, a member of the Nebraska Winnebago tribe and lifelong Native American Church member, to lead the battle to protect the sacramental use of peyote. Snake was recognized nationally and internationally for his efforts on behalf of American Indians. After serving in the army as a Green Beret from 1954 to 1959, he attended college in Iowa and Nebraska, was involved in community service organizations that assisted Indian youth and their families, and helped organize tribal governments to appeal to the federal government for funding for Indian education. He later served as chair of the Winnebago Nation of Nebraska where he helped revitalize the tribe and was elected president of the National Congress of American Indians, where he helped enact national legislation to protect American Indians. He went on to serve as a board member on several national Indian organizations as well as the United Nations Committee on Human Rights. With his extensive grassroots organizing experience, knowledge of the legislative process, and respect in the Indian and non-Indian communities, he was the natural choice to lead the effort in fashioning a specific legislative remedy to *Smith*.

Snake worked swiftly with church representatives and NARF to coordinate a national plan to protect the religious use of the peyote sacrament. On May 11, 1990, less than a month after *Smith*, the Native American Religious Freedom Project was launched, headed by Snake, "to work to alert, educate and organize religious and moral leaders, and the media in this country, around the clear and present threat to the very existence of the Native American Church, and to basic religious freedom for all." From the onset, Snake actively solicited the endorsement and support of "all national and international religious, human and civil rights organizations to assist in this process."

The project was intended to be part of an even larger effort to protect Indian religious freedom, coordinated by the American Indian Religious Freedom Coalition (AIRFC). The coalition, which was established in 1988 soon after the Court announced *Lyng*, was founded by the Native American Rights Fund, the Association on American Indian Affairs, and the National Congress of American Indians to generally "develop and support legislation to resort the protections of the First Amendment to American Indian people." At the time *Smith* was decided, the coalition was actively working on legislative solutions to protect Indian worship on sacred lands and protection for Indians incarcerated in federal and state prisons. *Smith* galvanized these efforts. Within a few months, over one hundred Indian tribes and dozens of Indian, religious, civil liberties, and environmental organizations were coalition members.

The focus of AIRFC was in stark contrast to CFER, which purposely ignored focusing on the religious use of peyote, or the religious rights of any particular faith in its effort to enact RFRA. Although the American Indian Religious Freedom Coalition did support the Religious Freedom Restoration Act, it was also critical of CFER's inattention to Indian religious rights. On September 29, 1990, at a rally in Washington, D.C., in support of Native American religious freedom, Rueben Snake, discussing *Smith*, stated,

> But consider the implications of this case from our perspective. The United States Supreme Court reversed a long line of settled cases in order to rule that the use of the sacrament of

Native American worship, the holy medicine, peyote, is not protected under the First Amendment of the Constitution. They said, in our case, our religious exercise, our form of worship, the use of our holy sacrament, is not protected by the Constitution. The Court said that Native Americans, who have enjoyed religious liberty on this land since before the pilgrims fled here, are no longer entitled to religious liberty.

Snake criticized the Court for its "widespread fear, bordering on panic, about the tragedy of drug abuse" and urged national understanding about the practices of the Native American Church. "We are reduced to this posture," he stated, "because of laws passed and enforced in an atmosphere of almost total ignorance about Native Americans."

The rally had been timed to coincide with the House Subcommittee on Civil and Constitutional Rights congressional hearings on the proposed Religious Freedom Restoration Act. Although both the NAC and NARF were also members of the Coalition for the Free Exercise of Religion, American Indian leaders urged that the bill be either amended to protect Native American religious freedom or that separate legislation be written to reflect this concern. The rally culminated in an all-night Native American Church ceremony attended by hundreds of worshipers.

———

Back in Oregon, Democratic representative Jim Edmunson from Eugene worked with local civil rights and liberties organizations to draft legislation to protect the sacramental use of peyote in the state. He modeled the state bill after legislation in Arizona, which allows individuals to present their religious beliefs as an "affirmative defense" if convicted under the state law proscribing peyote. Although limited, the legislation did provide some legislative protection for members of the Native American Church. The bill was considered by the legislature in April and May 1991 and was signed into law by Governor Barbara Roberts on June 25, 1991. Roberts had replaced Neil Goldschmidt as the Democratic nominee for governor and the previous November defeated Attorney General Dave Frohnmayer in a three-way race. Frohnmayer had led Roberts in the early months of the campaign, but the dynamics of the race changed significantly in April 1990 when a third-party candidate from the Oregon Citizens Alliance, a conservative pro-life, anti–homosexual rights organization entered the race. The candidate, Al Mobley, who had never held elected office, decided to run for governor after Frohnmayer refused to make concessions to the conservative group. Mobley's candidacy played a significant role in Frohnmayer's defeat; Roberts won the race with 47 percent of the vote; Frohnmayer received 39 percent and Mobley received 13 percent of the vote. Political analysts watching the race estimated that 95 percent of the Mobley vote would have gone to Frohnmayer. At the end of 1991 Frohnmayer resigned his job as attorney general to become dean of the University of Oregon Law School. Several years later he would be selected as university president.

CHAPTER 11

Congress Responds to the Court

Shepherding legislation through Congress is a tricky, delicate process. It is best described as a "procedural obstacle course that favors opponents of legislation and hinders proponents." The defense has an advantage because legislation can be, and usually is, stopped at any stage in the process. Thousands of bills are introduced annually in Congress, and only several hundred ever become law. Before House Republicans adopted a rule in the 104th Congress that banned commemorative legislation, 35 percent of the laws that made it through the course were symbolic, noncontroversial pieces of legislation that honored an individual, product, or idea, such as designating a "National Pickle Week" or "National Tap Dance Appreciation Month." Even if the motivating principle behind a measure is shared by practically everyone, it is tremendously difficult to maintain a consensus on a bill. This is especially true if it is a bill that concerns religious liberty. To complicate matters, throw the issue of abortion into the mix, or suggest to powerful interest groups that access to federal lands might be limited to protect sacred Indian sites.

The four-year period following *Smith* would see a continuation of the two monumental legislative efforts initiated after the Supreme Court ruling; the Coalition for the Free Exercise of Religion's attempt to enact the Religious Freedom Restoration Act, which would provide statutory protection for religious adherents burdened by neutral, generally applicable state and federal laws; and the American Indian Religious Freedom Coalition's attempt to amend the American Indian Religious Freedom Act to preserve a range of traditional religious practices. Ironically, protection for the sacramental use of peyote would be the least controversial measure considered by Congress.

———

In the three-month recess between the 101st and 102d congressional sessions, several influential interest groups voiced opposition to the Religious Freedom Restoration Act. Soon, the issue of abortion would stop the legislation in its tracks. On January 18, 1990, James Bopp Jr., the general counsel for the National Right to Life Committee, an organization that represents approximately three thousand state and local pro-life chapters, issued memorandums arguing that RFRA "would provide pro-abortion groups with a powerful new weapon with which to attack state and federal restrictions on abortion." According to the argument, the legislation would create a statutory basis for pro-abortion litigation because women could argue that in certain circumstances their religious beliefs compelled them to terminate their pregnancy. NRLC argued that similar claims had been made in the past, and that pro-choice groups would likely exploit this "tremendous loophole," providing "a fertile field for pro-abortion litigation." In a news release Bopp remarked, "The abortion-on-demand movement is urgently seeking new moorings for a constitutional right to abortion because of the ongoing . . . judicial rejection of the *Roe v. Wade* abortion privacy analysis."

Bopp later sent letters to the sponsors of the bill, remarking that the National Right to Life Committee would continue to oppose RFRA unless it contained an "abortion neutral" amendment that ensured the legislation could not be used for any religiously motivated abortion claims. The NRLC then aggressively lobbied other pro-life groups to stall support for the bill. In its publication, the *National Right to Life News*, it insinuated that some of the drafters of RFRA, such as Representative Stephen Solarz and the American Civil Liberties Union, had a "sinister hidden agenda" to protect abortion rights. Bopp later released a thirty-four-page legal monograph on how RFRA could and would be used for this purpose.

Although a free exercise claim to abortion under the First

Amendment was unnecessary since the right was protected by the Supreme Court's 1972 *Roe v. Wade* ruling, pro-life groups were confident *Roe* would be reversed. This possibility was exaggerated because *Planned Parenthood v. Casey*, a case involving a challenge to Pennsylvania's restrictions on abortion, was pending before the Supreme Court. Moreover, two of George Bush's appointments to the Court, Clarence Thomas and David Souter, had replaced pro-choice justices Thurgood Marshall and William Brennan, and Court watchers counted five votes for a reversal. Several pro-life groups wanted to be certain they were not unwittingly opening an avenue for abortion rights under the guise of protecting religious freedom.

In light of this development, the coalition found it necessary to devote time and energy responding to these charges to avoid losing support for RFRA. In February 1991 law professors Michael McConnell, Edward Gaffney, and Douglas Laycock wrote a letter to RFRA sponsors refuting the charge that the measure would be used to secure abortion rights. Several weeks later, the Congressional Research Service, a nonpartisan support agency staffed with policy experts who assist members in their deliberation of legislation, released a memorandum concluding that use of RFRA in this manner was "extremely unlikely."

The pro-RFRA response from the pro-life community was led by William Bentley Ball, a prominent religious liberty advocate who had been involved in religious freedom cases for over twenty years, including representing Yoder in *Wisconsin v. Yoder*. In late February Ball distributed a memo that also discounted the RFRA-abortion connection. His involvement was significant; in addition to his advocacy efforts in support of religious liberty, Ball had been intensely involved in the pro-life movement for equally as long. Since Ball was a tireless advocate for the unborn, coalition members hoped his words might allay the fears of the pro-life community. His letter was followed by an "Open Letter to the Pro-Life Community" signed by five pro-life organizations that pledged support for the bill without the addition of the "abortion-neutral" amendment. Individual letters specifically addressing the NRLC's claims were also sent to RFRA's cosponsors.

March would be a disastrous month for RFRA supporters. On the 19th the NRLC stepped up its attack. With a $13 million budget for its Washington office and several thousand local chapters with individual budgets and large memberships, the organization had the money and the grassroots muscle to get its word out. It seized on a poorly timed RFRA endorsement by Pat Tyson of the independent Religious Coalition for Abortion Rights as proof of a hidden pro-abortion strategy. Although the group never claimed it would purposely use RFRA to protect a religious right to abortion or to undermine restrictive abortion laws, the NRLC drew its own conclusions and emphasized the "correlation between support for the Act and protection for abortion."

The claim prompted a flurry of activity. Later that day Ball sent a letter to Congressman Hyde indicating that he now opposed RFRA without an amendment addressing religious claims to abortion. By the end of the week he had formally withdrawn from the coalition. In a letter sent to Mark Stern of American Jewish Congress, Ball pointed out that seven organizations shared membership with the Coalition for the Free Exercise of Religion and the Religious Coalition for Abortion Rights. He stated, "I feel it is unrealistic to ignore the context in which the bill is appearing." With Ball's departure, support for RFRA began to disintegrate among members of the pro-life community. Concerned Women for America, Americans United for Life, the Christian Action Council, the Family Research Council, and Lutheran Church–Missouri Synod came out in opposition to the bill. John Neuhaus, a prominent religious leader and editor of the magazine *First Things*, labeled the bill "seriously flawed" and said it would be "dangerous in the extreme" to continue supporting the legislation. RFRA supporters started the year with high hopes that the measure would move quickly through Congress while it still had momentum; now they had to battle one of the most controversial policy issues of the day. As one Republican House aide stated, "I've seen this thing grow from a lovefest into a nightmare."

As bad as the situation appeared for safe passage of RFRA, it would get even worse. An even larger obstacle loomed on the horizon—the opposition of the United States Catholic Conference. The USCC, which sets social policy for the National Conference of Catholic Bishops, had been involved, albeit informally, in CFER's effort to enact RFRA from the beginning. Although it never expressed an interest in joining the umbrella group, Mark Chopko, the organization's general counsel, was kept abreast of RFRA developments and regularly corresponded with coalition members and Solarz's staff regarding the USCC's concerns about the measure. The conference was generally supportive of the effort to address *Smith*, but it had some reservations about whether RFRA was the best method for doing so. In addition to the issue of abortion, the USCC was concerned the measure might be used to challenge the tax-exempt status of religious organizations or to restrict the use of government funds for religious purposes. There was regular correspondence between the coalition chair and Chopko, however, and it was Thomas's understanding that the Catholic Bishops would remain neutral in their position— neither supporting or blocking passage of the bill. Because it is much easier to kill a bill than to enact it into law, it was the best the coalition could hope for. The USCC is a powerful organization with a great deal of influence in both the House and Senate, and Thomas knew that its active opposition could cripple the measure.

On March 20, at the same time pro-life groups were withdrawing their support for RFRA and CFER, the Administrative Committee of the National Conference of Bishops held a meeting to discuss the USCC's official policy regarding the Religious Freedom Restoration Act. The committee decided to continue to seek amendments to RFRA to ensure the legislation would not be used to allow the litigation of free exercise claims to abortion, or used by individuals to challenge a religious group's tax-exempt status or the right of churches to use government funds for religious purposes. However, it did not formally oppose the bill. It appeared as if Thomas's understanding with Chopko that the USCC would remain neutral and hold off its active opposition to the bill might hold. But this would soon change.

Reintroduction of the Religious Freedom Restoration Act in the House of Representatives was delayed until June 26, 1991, because of the coalition's wrangling over abortion. Nevertheless, there was still bipartisan support for the bill. The number of cosponsors had increased to 103 because of an aggressive grassroots effort on behalf of the coalition to lobby support for the measure. As Solarz recalled,

> In the case of RFRA, you had this incredible Coalition, and my feeling at the time was that given its extraordinary character, it had the potential for getting a better response lobbying for the legislation than I could. It was as if my efforts were not that essential because the Coalition was perfectly capable of making the case for the members, and it could demonstrate the political interests of its constituency at the grassroots level in districts across the country. And that, of course, is the best form of lobbying and is certainly the most effective.

There were casualties stemming from the abortion issue, however, and several names were notably absent from the list of supporters. Representatives Henry and Hyde had withdrawn as chief sponsors of the legislation, and there were very few pro-life members cosponsoring the legislation. Nevertheless, consideration of HR 2797 moved ahead, and the Subcommittee on Civil and Constitutional Affairs scheduled hearings the following year.

In the year between the reintroduction of RFRA and the hearings, coalition representatives continued to reach out to House members to increase support for the measure. They made little headway with pro-life groups, however, and some members of Congress were convinced there was a connection between RFRA and abortion. To make matters worse, in spring 1992 the U.S. Catholic Conference publicly announced that it would oppose the legislation. By the time the second subcommittee hearing was under way, it was evident that the Bishops had already been reaching out to seriously lobby pro-life and Catholic representatives to withdraw their support for the bill.

The second round of RFRA hearings was held in May 1992. From the start, it was evident that the widespread support and positive tone of the discussion from the previous year was gone. In this second hearing, there were three areas of intense debate: The bill's potential impact on religiously based abortion claims, its effect on the tax-exempt status and public funding of religious organizations, and whether Congress had the capacity to pass this legislation, and if so, whether it was an appropriate solution to *Smith*.

Because of its potential impact on abortion rights, opposition to RFRA dominated the hearing, led by Chopko and Bopp. Representatives from pro-life groups that supported the bill appeared to counter their testimony, such as Elder Dallin H. Oaks, a legal scholar and former Utah state supreme court justice, who testified on behalf of the Quorum of the Twelve Apostles, the Church of Jesus Christ of Latter-Day Saints. Other witnesses took the offensive. Nadine Strossen, president of the American Civil Liberties Union, criticized the Catholic Church and the National Right to Life Committee for allowing the abortion controversy to obscure the general benefits of the legislation. She ridiculed the scenario that would have the Court overturning *Roe* while allowing a free exercise claim to abortion under RFRA.

Several academics appeared before the subcommittee to address whether Congress had the authority to enact RFRA, a lingering doubt among some members of Congress. Legal scholars Gaffney and Laycock testified that Congress had the authority to act independently to protect religious freedom under section five of the Fourteenth Amendment because the Court had failed to do so. However, another scholar, Ira C. Lupu, expressed reservations about the constitutionality of the bill. Although he shared Gaffney and Laycock's disapproval of *Smith* and enthusiasm for a congressional response to the decision, he disagreed that RFRA, as drafted, was the proper avenue. He predicted that the Supreme Court, which was paying more attention to issues of state sovereignty, might be hostile to the bill. Lupu observed that a Court "on the verge of (re)protecting states against federal 'encroachments' on the operations of state government, can hardly be depended on to adopt an expansive view of congressional power to enforce the 14th Amendment in a context which overrides *Smith* and intrudes on state and local administration." In addition to the controversy over RFRA's potential impact on abortion and concerns about the bill's constitutionality, many witnesses that appeared before the subcommittee testified about the problems caused by *Smith* and the need for federal legislation. Several of the witnesses predicted that *Smith* would once again return the country to a time when minority religions were routinely persecuted. The Subcommittee on Civil and Constitutional Rights adjourned after two full days of hearings, and on June 24, 1992, approved the 1991 Religious Freedom Restoration Act for consideration by the full House Committee on the Judiciary by a five-to-three vote. Republican Representatives Hyde, Chris Smith (NJ) and Bill McCollum (FLA) voted against the bill primarily owing to the abortion issue.

On July 2, 1992, one week after RFRA was successfully voted out of subcommittee, the Religious Freedom Restoration Act of 1992 was introduced to the Senate Committee on the Judiciary by Senators Orrin Hatch and Edward Kennedy (D-MA). Twenty-one cosponsors signed on to the measure. Upon referral to the Senate Judiciary Committee, a hearing was held on September 18, 1992. As occurred in the House, the abortion issue dominated the discussion in the Senate. Most of the witnesses who appeared at the House hearing also appeared at the Senate hearing. A key addition was the testimony of Thomas, who provided the Senate Judiciary Committee with a memorandum prepared by his associate, J. Brent Walker, that listed dozens of cases in the lower courts that had been decided, because of *Smith's* new standard, against plaintiffs' religious claims. Thomas concluded, "While we have been haggling over a hypothetical abortion question, more than fifty cases have been decided against religious claimants. That is what we know." As the hearings ended, it appeared that the Religious Freedom Restoration Act of 1992 was hopelessly caught up in a divisive discussion over the issue of abortion.

Soon, another problem would further complicate the bill's progress. Several weeks after the Senate Judiciary Committee hearing, Senator Alan Simpson (R-WY) expressed concern that RFRA could be abused by prisoners raising frivolous free exercise challenges that would force prison officials to accommodate prisoners' religious practices to the detriment of penological interests. The issue threatened to peel off some conservative backers of the bill, and Simpson warned that if it was successfully reported out of committee, he would block the measure on the floor of the Senate. As a result of this potential, sponsors postponed putting RFRA to a committee vote until the bill's impact on prisons could be assessed. On October 9, 1992, days before the 102d Congress adjourned, the Religious Freedom Restoration Act died in committee. Later that afternoon the House Committee on the Judiciary, unencumbered by the prison issue, completed markup of RFRA and approved the bill by voice vote. Supporters in the House wanted to bring it to the floor for consideration before the end of the congressional session, but resisted any action because the measure had not been reported out of the Senate Committee on the Judiciary.

Another reason for the delay in moving forward was because the White House had not yet endorsed the legislation, and supporters were unsure whether President George Bush would veto the bill. Throughout the two-year debate over abortion, Bush resisted either vocally supporting or opposing the legislation, and coalition members did not reach out to the Executive Branch because they had their hands full in Congress. There was only speculation regarding the White House's lack of support for RFRA. Some believed Bush did not endorse the bill because of pressure from the National Right to Life Committee and the U.S. Catholic League; others suggested that the president allowed the bill to languish because he was caught between prolife groups that opposed the bill and evangelical groups that favored the measure. There were also unnamed sources in the Bush administration who stated that lawyers in the Justice Department were uncomfortable with legislation that appeared to directly attack a decision by Justice Scalia. Ultimately, the president dodged the issue.

After the bill died for a second time, things looked bleak for RFRA. The abortion issue had not been resolved, the Catholic Conference and National Right to Life Committee were becoming increasingly aggressive in their efforts to block the measure, and the White House refused to endorse the bill. Before the 103d Congress convened in January, however, two key events took place that ultimately paved the way for successful passage of the Religious Freedom Restoration Act.

The first event was the defeat of George Bush in November, which eliminated any threat of a presidential veto. William Jefferson Clinton, who previously endorsed RFRA as a candidate, was an enthusiastic supporter of the measure. Also important was the fact that high-ranking officials in the Justice Department, including Attorney General Janet Reno, endorsed the bill without an exception for prisoners. The second event was the Supreme Court decision in *Planned Parenthood v. Casey* (1992). Although it included exceptions to a woman's right to terminate her pregnancy, the decision also affirmed the central holding in *Roe v. Wade* that abortion rights were protected under a general right to privacy found in the due process clause of the Fourteenth Amendment. *Casey* eliminated the possibility of an imminent reversal of *Roe*, and future Clinton judicial nominees would make this even less likely, which significantly decreased the possibility that RFRA would replace *Roe* as an avenue for abortion rights.

Within a week after *Casey*, Thomas was on the phone to Chopko, trying to find a way to get the support of the Catholic Conference. "We were both ready to talk," said Thomas, "and we eventually agreed that we could write some legislative history into the bill to address the Catholic Conference's concerns about how the legislation would affect abortion rights and possible establishment clause issues." Before the bill was reintroduced for the third time, Thomas and David Saperstein met with Chopko and USCC's legislative director, Frank Moynihan, to draft the language to be included in the record. Saperstein recalls, "Buzz and I had a series of meetings that led to bringing them on. We locked ourselves in a room, literally at the end, for hours, thrashing out every piece, figuring how far we could go to accommodate their concerns, how far they could go to accommodate the organizing principles of the coalition . . . and eventually worked it out for them to come on board." The compromise language addressed the abortion concern without actually changing the wording of RFRA. It would later be introduced in both the House and Senate reports that addressed the legislative history of the bill. The report would indicate that the bill's application to abortion was "academic" in light of *Casey*, and that "the abortion debate will be resolved in contexts other than this legislation." Reports that accompany bills are significant; they clarify the purpose and effect of legislation, and may be used by courts to consider congressional intent. A section was also added to the bill that ensured RFRA would not be used for establishment clause claims against organizations that had been granted government funding, benefits, or tax exemptions. Based on these changes, the U.S. Catholic Conference and the National Right to Life Committee finally endorsed the bill.

The Religious Freedom Restoration Act of 1993 was reintroduced to the 103d Congress in March. Representative Charles Schumer (D-NY) replaced Steve Solarz as the chief sponsor in the House. Solarz had lost his seat to redistricting, and Schumer was the ranking minority leader. Additional hearings were not held on the bill; it was unanimously approved in the Subcommittee on Civil and Constitutional Rights and the House Judiciary Committee, and sent to the House floor on March 22. Under suspension of the rules, the full House passed RFRA in a unanimous voice vote on May 11, 1993. A companion bill introduced in the Senate was approved by the Judiciary Committee by a fifteen-to-one vote on May 6, 1993. The dissenting vote was cast by Simpson owing to the unresolved prison issue. It was a foreboding development this late in the process, particularly given his earlier threat to hold up the bill in the Senate.

––––––

In June another development illustrated the need for the Religious Freedom Restoration Act: the Supreme Court's decision in

Church of the Lukumi Babalu Aye, Inc. v. City of Hialeah, its first free exercise ruling since *Employment Division of Oregon v. Smith.* Although the Court unanimously ruled in favor of the church, at least six members of the Court reaffirmed the holding in *Smith.* The case involved a challenge by members of the Santeria religion to the constitutionality of several local ordinances enacted by the Hialeah City Council that prohibited the unnecessary killing, torture, or torment of any animal. Although the ordinances were facially neutral, the Court determined from a review of the record that they had been written to directly restrict the religious practices of members of the Santeria faith, which sacrifices animals as part of their religion. Members of the religious sect had been planning to build a church within the city limits when the ordinances were enacted. In the opinion of the Court, Justice Kennedy declared that laws specifically enacted to burden an individual's ability to practice their faith must be evaluated with the highest level of judicial scrutiny and must serve a compelling state interest, achieved by the least restrictive means. Because the ordinances failed this test, they were invalidated. He also concluded that the ordinances were overbroad and underinclusive. Thus, Kennedy differentiated *Lukumi,* which involved laws that targeted religion, from *Smith,* where the law was neutral and generally applicable. Neutral and generally applicable laws, Kennedy reiterated, did not trigger this heightened level of scrutiny, and the Court was not obligated to consider requests for accommodation of religious beliefs burdened by such laws. Justices Blackmun and O'Connor wrote a separate opinion reiterating their difficulties with *Smith,* and Justice Souter, new to the Court, wrote a lengthy concurring opinion explaining a need to revisit *Smith.* For members of the Coalition for the Free Exercise of Religion, *Lukumi Babalu* was evidence that six members of the Court endorsed the *Smith* rationale, and that the Religious Freedom Restoration Act was still needed to provide protection to individuals burdened by neutral, generally applicable laws.

———

The full Senate considered the Religious Freedom Restoration Act on October 26 and 27, 1993. The floor debate centered on a controversial amendment offered by Senator Reid (R-NV) that excluded prisoners from RFRA. Reid contended that RFRA would jeopardize prison safety and security. To illustrate support for his amendment, he presented a letter signed by every warden and prison director in every state in the Union supporting the prisoners' exception. Most Senate Republicans backed the amendment, and several presented colorful examples of prisoners' frivolous claims to illustrate Reid's point. Simpson warned his colleagues that prisoners would demand ritual animal sacrifice, and Jesse Helms (R-NC) reminded the Senate that some religions permitted the use of hallucinogenic drugs. Additional information was included in the *Congressional Record*. For instance, Simpson referred to a letter written by O. Lane McCotter, executive director of the Utah Department of Corrections, that included the example of members of the Church of the New Song (CONS) who made a free exercise argument that their religion required a special diet of Porterhouse steak and Bristol Cream Sherry. Supporters also argued that RFRA would encourage prisoners' free exercise litigation and ultimately clog the courts, even though the challenges would likely be unsuccessful.

Senator Orrin Hatch defected from his party and vigorously defended an unamended RFRA. He responded that all Americans were entitled to religious freedom and that concern over frivolous prisoners' claims were unfounded because a balancing test that incorporated the compelling government interest standard would almost always side with the interests of the state. This test, Hatch stated, allowed prison control yet protected prisoners' free exercise rights. "The bottom line is that prison administrators' interests in order, safety, security, and discipline are compelling, and the courts have certainly treated them as such, and have always done so." Furthermore, he noted, most of the frivolous claims would continue with or without the prisoners' exception. Senator Kennedy also spoke against the amendment, and presented a letter from Attorney General Reno supporting an unamended RFRA, and a letter signed by thirteen state attorney generals who observed that in the post-*Sherbert* years when the courts did use the compelling government interest balancing test, there had not been a significant increase in prison costs or compromises in prison security.

After two days of discussion, on October 27, 1993, the Senate defeated the Reid amendment in a forty-one-to-fifty-eight vote. The Senate then voted on RFRA, which passed by the overwhelming margin of ninety-seven to three. The Religious Freedom Restoration Act was sent back to the House as amended on November 3, 1993, where it passed in a unanimous voice vote. The measure was then sent to the White House for the president's approval.

President Clinton signed the Religious Freedom Restoration Act on November 16, 1993, on the South Lawn of the White House before over two hundred leaders of religious and civil liberty organizations. In a speech accompanying his signing of the measure, Clinton praised the bipartisan support of the bill, and emphasized that this new level of protection for religious freedom was necessary and more consistent with the framers' notion of free exercise of religion under the Constitution. President Clinton also mentioned the necessity of Congress to engage in this type of activity to protect constitutional rights.

> The power to reverse the Court by legislation . . . is a power that is rightly, hesitantly and infrequently exercised by the United States Congress. But this is an issue in which that extraordinary measure was clearly called for. . . . This act reverses the Supreme Court's decision *Employment Division against Smith* and reestablishes a standard that better protects all Americans of all faiths in the exercise of their religion in a way that I am convinced is far more consistent with the intent of the Founders of the Nation than the Supreme Court decision.

After a long, three-year battle, the Religious Freedom Restoration Act was finally law. Congress essentially nullified the broad ruling in *Employment Division v. Smith* that individuals suffering a burden on their religious exercise from neutral, generally applicable laws were unprotected by the free exercise clause of the First Amendment of the Constitution. The act provides federal statutory protection for the exercise of religion, ensuring that any local, state, or federal law that places a substantial burden on an individual's religion is subject to the high level of scrutiny found in the compelling government interest test. If government is unable to meet its burden, then the religious challenger will be granted an exemption to the law.

———

What about legislative protection for the sacramental use of peyote, the religious activity at the center of *Employment Division v. Smith*? The battle for religious freedom was far from over. At the RFRA signing ceremony President Clinton reminded the audience that the job was not done. "The agenda for restoration of religious freedom in America will not be complete until traditional Native American religious practices have received the protection they deserve. My administration has been and will continue to work actively with Native Americans and the Congress on legislation to address these concerns." Clinton was referring to the effort to specifically protect American Indian religious practices that was taking place at the same time RFRA was debated in Congress. The campaign resembled the RFRA struggle. It, too, was led by a diverse umbrella group, the American Indian Religious Freedom Coalition, and also faced resistance from outside pressure groups and members of Congress. To meet these challenges, some of the same strategies used by the Coalition for the Free Exercise of Religion were duplicated by the American Indian Religious Freedom Coalition, which was not surprising, given that some organizations belonged to both groups.

In 1991, shortly after Rueben Snake of the Native American Religious Freedom Project held the rally at the Capital in support of the first congressional RFRA hearing, AIRFC launched its national campaign on behalf of federal legislation to specifically protect Indian religious freedom. The campaign initially developed along two tracks; Snake gathered data from scholars and medical practitioners about the long history of peyotism and the safety and beneficial effects of the sacrament when used by members of the Native American Church, and AIRFC worked with members of Congress to draft legislation to protect the sacramental use of peyote and other Indian religious practices.

Snake sponsored several meetings to help educate the national and international community about the Native American Church's traditional use of peyote and the need for federal action to preserve this ancient ritual. In early August 1991 he organized a Native American Church summit on the Winnebago Reservation in Nebraska, where church leaders unanimously agreed to support federal legislation to preserve the sacramental use of peyote. The leaders drafted a resolution reflecting this need, which Snake later took to the United Nations Committee on Human Rights and the World Council of Churches in Geneva, Switzerland. He traveled to scores of meetings throughout the nation and worked with Native American Church leaders to gather support and educate others about the peyote ritual.

At the same time, other organizations in the American Indian Religious Freedom Coalition worked independently to draft resolutions criticizing the Supreme Court and appealing to Congress for legislation to correct *Smith*, *Lyng*, and *O'Lone*. Then, in the summer of 1991, Peterson Zah of the Navajo Nation and Patrick Lefthand of the Confederated Salish and Kootenai Tribes of the Flathead Nation, the cochairs of the Tribal Leaders Forum Committee on Cultural and Religious Rights, reached out to Senator Daniel Inouye (D-HI), chair of the Committee on Indian Affairs, to discuss the coalition's legislative strategy. In November, AIRFC, with Zah and Lefthand at the helm, held its first national conference, "The Religious Freedom Summit" in Albuquerque, New Mexico, to discuss amendments to the 1978 American Indian Religious Freedom Act. Over four hundred tribal members attended the conference. Prior to the meeting the coalition leaders visited Indian communities and reached out to spiritual and tribal leaders and members of national tribal organizations to raise consciousness of the legislative effort and to persuade people to attend the summit and later testify before Congress. The summit yielded a consensus on several areas in need of legislative protection: the preservation of sacred sites, the religious use of peyote, the religious use of eagle feathers and parts, and religious freedom for incarcerated Native Americans. Coalition members also believed that any other areas not specifically protected by legislation should be protected by a high level of judicial scrutiny. Borrowing language from RFRA, they concluded that any infringements on American Indian religious practices be subject to the compelling government interest test. Zah and Lefthand urged tribal members to push for legislation in their communities and to light a "prairie fire" of support to Washington, D.C.

Less than a month later the coalition formed a legislative technicians committee to work with members of Congress to specifically draft legislation that reflected these concerns. The committee worked primarily with Inouye, a Senator eager to work on a legislative solution to these restrictive Court decisions. Inouye had previously championed Indian issues in Congress, including sponsorship of the recent 1990 Native American Graves Protection and Repatriation Act, which established a process to monitor the excavation and removal of remains and cultural items and allowed American Indians to request the return of human remains or other cultural items held by federal agencies or federally assisted institutions. Inouye and the committee drafted a bill that addressed the four areas identified at the Religious Freedom Summit, and the Senator arranged field hearings to raise both public and congressional support for the measure. The first hearings were held in Portland, Oregon, and Los Angeles, California, in March 1992. They were followed by hearings in Scottsdale, Arizona, and Albuquerque, New Mexico, in February 1993, and a hearing in Minneapolis, Minnesota, the following month. The final field hearing was held in Honolulu, Hawaii, in May 1993. At each hearing, representatives from tribal communities across the nation and from national Indian advocacy groups testified about past infringements on Indian religious exercise, and the need for comprehensive federal legislation to put "teeth" into AIRFA. The coalition played a central role in organizing witnesses to appear at the hearing, and on more than one occasion at the hearings Inouye emphasized that this was a grassroots effort and the proposed legislation had been written in consultation with the American Indian Religious Freedom Coalition. Throughout this period of field hearings Inouye and other members of the Senate Committee on Indian Affairs, as well as representatives from the Clinton administration, met to refine the draft bill. On May 25, 1993, Inouye and seven cosponsors introduced Senate bill 1021, the Native American Free Exercise of Religion Act of 1992. The bill was referred to the Committee on Indian Affairs, which would later hold additional hearings in September.

———

Although the Senate was moving swiftly, action in the House was much slower. In February and March 1993 the Subcommittee on Native American Affairs, one of five subcommittees under the Committee for Natural Resources, held two hearings on the effectiveness of the 1978 American Indian Religious Freedom Act. The subcommittee chair, Representative Bill Richardson (D-NM), pledged to explore amendments to the toothless AIRFA, but he did not propose legislation at this time. The first hearing addressed the ineffectiveness of AIRFA and the need for congressional legislation to specifically protect sacred sites and the religious use of peyote. The second hearing focused on the need for access to sacred objects, particularly eagle feathers and parts, and protection for the religious needs of Native American prisoners. Clinton administration representatives, members of the American Indian Religious Freedom Coalition, and scholars from the legal community testified in both hearings and stressed the need for federal action. Supplemental material from the Native American Religious Freedom Project addressing the safety of peyote was also introduced into the record. Several of the witnesses that appeared, including Craig Dorsay, Al Smith's legal services attorney, testified about the ethnocentrism and insensitivity toward American Indians displayed by the U.S. Supreme Court.

The Senate hearing on S 1021, the Native American Free Exercise of Religion Act, was held six months later on September 10, 1993. It focused on the constitutionality of the proposed bill. Renewed attention to the need for protection of sacred sites during the earlier Senate field hearings and the House subcommittee hearings had fallen under the scrutiny of powerful interest groups that would be negatively affected by any federal legislation to protect sacred land. These groups, mostly from the forestry and mining industries, argued that legislation that only protected American Indian religious freedom would violate the establishment clause of the First Amendment by showing preference toward one religion. They also contended that it might violate the equal protection clause of the Fourteenth Amendment for the same reason, and the takings clause of the Fifth Amendment because the measure could potentially interfere with how people used their private property. Although these groups did not appear at the hearing, they had been in contact with representatives in Congress, and several letters making these claims were included into the congressional record. The correspondence also suggested that S 1021, particularly the provision protecting sacred sites, would result in more bureaucracy, procedural gridlock, delay, and abuse by nonreligious natives.

To address these concerns, witnesses appearing before the Senate included several legal scholars who defended the constitutionality of the measure, including Professor Milner Ball from the Georgia School of Law, Michael McConnell from the University of Chicago Law School, Robert Clinton from the University of Iowa School of Law, and history professor Vine Deloria from the University of Colorado. Each discussed Congress' broad plenary power under Article I of the Constitution in the field of Indian affairs. The relationship between the federal government and federally recognized Indian tribes is unique, these scholars testified, because Indian tribes enjoy a government-to-government relationship with the United States. Moreover, they observed, the United States has a special "trust" relationship with tribes that recognizes the cultural and political rights of tribal nations, and has a responsibility to work with Native Americans to protect these rights. The witnesses pointed to past legislative efforts where Congress exercised this plenary authority, such as the Indian Education Act (1972), the Indian Child Welfare Act (1978), the Native American Languages Act (1990), and the Native

American Graves Protection and Repatriation Act (1990). They also reviewed Supreme Court decisions that recognized the unique relationship between the United States and American Indian tribes. The legal scholars discounted each of the constitutional challenges and urged Congress to enact legislation to protect religious freedom for American Indians.

The second Senate hearing on March 23, 1994, switched focus to the Clinton administration's support for the measure. Appearing were representatives from the Department of the Interior, the Department of Justice, and the Drug Enforcement Agency. All testified in favor of S 1021 and praised members of the American Indian Religious Freedom Coalition for working with the Senate on the bill. Support for the Native American Free Exercise of Religion Act also received a boost on April 29 when President Clinton held a meeting with leaders from all the federally recognized tribal governments. He pledged to respect tribal sovereignty and support Native American religious rights. Clinton also specifically addressed the section of S 1021 that protected eagle feathers and parts with an executive memorandum to the heads of all executive departments and agencies asking for simplification of the process of collection and transfer of eagle carcasses and body parts for Indian religious purposes. The memo requested that the Department of the Interior streamline the process and expand efforts to work with Indian tribes and organizations, and state fish and game agencies and other relevant state authorities to facilitate accommodation of American Indians. The memorandum was a success for the Indian community, but it would be all that was accomplished this term. The congressional session was coming to a close, and further action on the Native American Free Exercise of Religion Act would have to wait until the next year.

After the 1993 hearings in both the House and the Senate, it became obvious to members of the American Indian Religious Freedom Coalition that support for a comprehensive federal law was mixed. Protection for the religious use of peyote was fairly uncontroversial at this point in light of the overwhelming evidence in the congressional record regarding the safety of the sacrament in Native American Church ceremonies and the approval and support of the Drug Enforcement Agency and Department of Justice. Congressional support transcended party lines, and there was no organized opposition to this part of the bill. There was similar support for the protection of eagle feathers and parts, but the need for federal legislation had diminished because of Clinton's action on this issue. Protection for the religious rights of incarcerated Indians had not received a great deal of attention, which was unusual given how controversial the issue had been during the RFRA battle. It is also likely that some members of Congress believed this protection was already provided in the 1993 Religious Freedom Restoration Act. On the other hand, it was very clear that the section of the bill protecting sacred sites did not enjoy broad-based support. The interest groups that earlier raised concerns about the constitutionality of the measure continued to contact members of Congress, and Republicans in both houses began to show signs that they would not support this part of the bill.

In light of this challenge, in spring 1994 Representative Richardson made a decision, with the support of AIRFC members, to introduce two separate measures, one to protect access to sacred sites, and the other to protect religious use of peyote. Such a strategy would allow for swift passage of at least the peyote measure, which might otherwise be held up by a controversy over the sacred sites provision. In March Richardson introduced HR 4155, which would amend AIRFA to protect federal lands considered sacred to Native Americans. The following month he introduced HR 4230, a bill to add a new section to AIRFA to allow the sacramental use of peyote in Indian religious ceremonies. The measure also protected Indians from discrimination for the use, possession, or transportation of peyote.

The House Subcommittee on Native American Affairs held a brief, favorable hearing on HR 4230 on June 10, 1994. At the markup of the bill, after the Department of Transportation raised some concerns about the effects of peyote on job performance, it was amended to allow for the more careful regulation of peyote use by individuals in safety-sensitive jobs. The subcommittee then approved the bill by voice vote on July 22, and the amended bill was approved by the Natural Resources Committee several days later. The measure later passed the House by unanimous voice vote on August 8, 1994. However, HR 4155, which would protect sacred Indian sites, died in committee.

At the same time HR 4230 was being debated in the House, Senator Inouye introduced S 2269, the Native American Cultural Protection and Free Exercise of Religion Act of 1994. Instead of an amendment to AIRFA, the measure was introduced as a statute to protect Native American culture and religion. It still contained the four major parts of the previous measure, but placed more emphasis on Native American traditional cultural practices in addition to religious liberty, and the bill applied to both recognized and unrecognized Indian tribes. The Senate Committee on Indian Affairs held a hearing on the bill in July and sent it to the Senate Energy and Natural Resources Committee, which considered the measure in August 1994. Before the bill was considered by the full committee, however, Senator Inouye amended the bill to remove the provision regarding the sacramental use of peyote; the House had just passed HR 4230, and it moved to the Senate for consideration. The strategy would pave the way for passage of the House bill.

The Senate then considered the revised S 2269, which was approved out of the full committee by voice vote in August. The vote was not unanimous; Senator John McCain (R-AZ) and seven other Republicans placed themselves on the record as opposing the law. The Republicans wanted to protect access to federal lands, and there were concerns about the bill's constitutionality. Because Inouye's new version applied to both recognized and unrecognized tribes, the Justice Department had testified that special protection for unrecognized Indians might potentially violate the establishment clause. With these issues unresolved, the Native American Cultural Protection and Free Exercise of Religion Act died in committee.

HR 4230 also ran into some unexpected problems in the Senate. The bill was reported favorably out of the Indian Affairs Committee, but was prohibited from moving to the floor of the Senate after several anonymous Republicans placed a "hold" on the bill. In order for a bill to be "called up" for consideration, the majority and minority leaders and relevant committee chairs must negotiate the Senate schedule and obtain a unanimous consent agreement that specifies the date the bill will be called up. This agreement requires a consensus, however, and a single senator can place a hold on the bill, thus delaying its consideration. The holds were later lifted after AIRFC members met with the Republican senators to discuss the measure, and consideration of the bill finally moved to the floor.

The Senate passed the measure on September 27, 1994, and it was signed into law by President Clinton on October 6, 1994. PL 103-344 added a new section to the American Indian Religious Freedom Act of 1978; it exempts Indian religious use of peyote in bona fide traditional ceremonies from state and federal controlled substance laws, and prohibits discrimination for use of peyote, including denial of benefits from public assistance programs. Under the bill, the Drug Enforcement Administration and State of Texas would continue to regulate the distribution of peyote. The only significant difference between the previous administrative regulation protecting religious peyote use was that the new law did not limit protection to members of the Native American Church, it allowed federal and state authorities to place "reasonable" limitations on the use of peyote by individuals employed in "safety sensitive" jobs, and it provided that any traffic safety regulations enacted by states to address peyote use be subject to the compelling state interest test.

Over four years after the U.S. Supreme Court used Al Smith's challenge to Oregon's prohibition against peyote possession as its opportunity to address the status of the free exercise clause in America, Congress successfully enacted comprehensive legislation that protected this ancient religious ritual in all fifty states of the Union.

John Echohawk, reflecting on the long battle, stated, "We got a bad Supreme Court case and this decision that ostensibly denies constitutional rights to practice the religion of the Native American Church, and it took a super effort on the church's part and our effort here to salvage a federal statutory right for the church to use peyote in their ceremonies. It was something we weren't at all sure we were able to get. But we were forced to do that, so at least we salvaged something. That is the most important thing in the end. But it was very tough."

CHAPTER 12

"An Endlessly Renewed
Educational Conversation"

Despite passage of the 1993 Religious Freedom Restoration Act and the 1994 amendments to the American Indian Religious Freedom Act, the two laws that essentially overturned the Supreme Court's ruling in *Employment Division v. Smith*, the conversation about religious freedom in America is far from over.

Even before enactment of RFRA, a lively debate was taking place in legal and academic journals over its constitutionality. Although many commentators defended the legislation as an appropriate and constitutional congressional response to an unwise and poorly reasoned Supreme Court decision that strayed from settled free exercise jurisprudence, a growing number questioned the wisdom of passing legislation that potentially interfered with the Court's role as the ultimate interpreter of the Constitution and the sovereignty of the states. Critics contended that the legislation violated the principles of separation of powers and federalism, and that these concerns overshadowed the commendable intention behind the RFRA—the protection of religious liberty. A constitutional challenge to the legislation was inevitable.

In the four-year period following passage of the Religious Freedom Restoration Act, over three hundred RFRA-related cases were decided in the lower federal courts. As predicted by some critics of the legislation, almost half of the cases involved inmates' religious challenges to prison regulations. The cases ranged from frivolous challenges to prison regulations prohibiting the use of illicit drugs to legitimate requests for the protection of religious liberty, such as Indian prisoners seeking access to sweat lodges, and Orthodox Jewish prisoners' requests for religious materials to practice their faith. Non–prisoner related cases included a religious challenge to a zoning ordinance that prohibited the operation of a homeless food program and a challenge to a state regulation that required community college employees to recite a loyalty oath as a condition of employment.

Several patterns were evident in these post-RFRA decisions. As occurred in the three decades prior to *Smith*, most religious claimants failed to prove that the government action placed a substantial burden on the exercise of their religion. Because this threshold requirement was not fulfilled in these cases, the courts did not apply the high level of scrutiny mandated by RFRA, and the religious claimant was denied the request for an exemption under the less stringent reasonableness test. However, in those cases where the religious challenger was able to prove a substantial burden on the exercise of his or her religion, the results were mixed; in some instances the government was able to illustrate that it had a compelling government interest that outweighed the request for an exemption to the law. In others, the requested exemption was granted because the government's interest was less than compelling. The outcome for each case was different, and the result largely depended on the strength of the individual's challenge and the persuasiveness of the government's case regarding its compelling interest in the uniform application of the law. Interestingly, religious liberty claimants were more successful under RFRA than they had been during the thirty years before *Smith*, when challenges were brought under the free exercise clause.

In several of the post-RFRA cases, the constitutionality of the federal law was challenged. The respondents argued that Congress did not have the authority to enact RFRA under section five of the Fourteenth Amendment and that the law intruded on states' rights, or that the legislation violated the doctrine of separation of powers because Congress was directly challenging the Court's interpretation of the free exercise of the Constitution, thus undermining the principle established in *Marbury v. Madison*. Members of the Coalition for the Free Exercise of Religion carefully tracked these cases. The coalition remained together after passage of RFRA; members knew it was likely the act would be challenged in court and wanted to ensure its correct interpretation. In cases where RFRA was challenged, CFER would file a generic brief drafted by Mark Stern of American Jewish Congress and University of Texas professor Douglas Laycock that addressed some of the constitutional and statutory issues being raised in the courts. In most instances, the law was upheld as constitutional, but it would be only a matter of time before the U.S Supreme Court would be asked to resolve the issue.

On June 25, 1996, the opportunity presented itself when the city of Boerne, Texas, filed a petition for a writ of certiorari to the U.S. Supreme Court to review the Fifth Circuit Court's decision in *City of Boerne v. Flores*. The case arose out of a zoning dispute that began several weeks after Congress enacted the Religious Freedom Restoration Act. In December 1993 the archbishop of San Antonio, P. F. Flores, requested a building permit to renovate and expand Saint Peter Roman Catholic Church to accommodate its growing parish. The city landmark commission lobbied against granting the permit because the church was located in a district protected by a historic landmark preservation ordinance, and the petition was denied. Flores appealed the decision to the city council, which upheld the denial, and the archbishop then filed suit in 1995 in the U.S. District Court for Western Texas under the Religious Freedom Restoration Act, charging that the denial placed a substantial burden on the church members' ability to freely exercise their religion. Attorneys for the city of Boerne originally decided to defend its compelling interest in historic preservation. However, after the case had already been set for trial, at the pretrial hearing the city amended its pleadings and argued that the Religious Freedom Restoration Act was unconstitutional. The attorneys had obtained a soon-to-be-published law review article on the issue by Cardoza Law School professor Marci Hamilton, "The Religious Freedom Restoration Act: Letting the Fox into the Henhouse under Cover of Section 5 of the Fourteenth Amendment," and decided to incorporate her arguments into their case.

The last-minute strategy worked. In a three-page decision, District Court judge Lucius D. Bunton ruled that RFRA, which was enacted to specifically overturn *Employment Division v. Smith*, was facially invalid because it infringed upon the "long-settled authority of the courts . . . to say what the law is," thus violating the principle in *Marbury v. Madison* that the judiciary has the ultimate authority to interpret the Constitution. Bunton also ruled that Congress had not appropriately invoked its power under section five of the Fourteenth Amendment when it enacted the legislation. The attorneys representing Flores, Thomas Drought and Patricia J. Schofield, accompanied by Laycock, who was recruited to assist in the case, then appealed the decision to the Fifth Circuit, which reversed. Writing for a unanimous court, Judge Patrick Higgenbotham determined that Congress had thoroughly considered its constitutional authority under section five of the Fourteenth Amendment, and that the principles of separation of powers were not violated because "the Executive and Legislative branches also have both the right and duty to interpret the constitution [which] casts no shadows upon Justice Marshall's claim of ultimate authority to decide. The judicial trump card can be played only in a case or controversy. The power to decide the law is an incident of judicial power to decide cases. There is no more." Higgenbotham concluded that Congress could legitimately assign a "higher value to free-exercise secured freedoms than the value assigned by the Courts," under section five of the Fourteenth Amendment to protect religion, and that this action did not subvert the doctrine of separation of powers or threaten the integrity of the Supreme Court.

The city of Boerne then appealed the case to the U.S. Supreme Court. After the city filed its petition for a writ of certiorari, Laycock, Drought, and Schofield, representing the archdiocese, and the Coalition for the Free Exercise of Religion, which was defending the act, had to plan their next step. Laycock recalled, "We had a major decision to make about whether to oppose the petition or not. And while it probably didn't matter in retrospect, we decided that we really needed a Supreme Court resolution on this issue. And so we urged the Court to take it." After a lengthy discussion, the Coalition for the Free Exercise of Religion also decided to support the petition for certiorari. According to Steven McFarland, director of the Center for Law and Religious Freedom at the

Christian Legal Society, the coalition believed it was a good case to defend. "We knew there would be a test case, and a landmark preservation case was about the best. Talk about the least compelling interest—architectural and aesthetic values versus the essence of free exercise. There wasn't space for people to worship. They couldn't get into church for Easter. And we were defending a victory." The CFER filed a brief in late August asking the Court to grant the petition for certiorari and remove "the cloud that continues to hover over the constitutionality of the law."

However, there was another party involved that disagreed with this strategy. The Justice Department, which can intervene to defend federal statutes in a constitutional challenge, did not want the Court to review the case, and filed a brief in opposition to the writ of certiorari. According to Laycock, "The Justice Department lawyers were scared to death of what the Supreme Court would do with this case. And I think the difference in our perspectives was that the Justice Department was looking at the case politically, and we were looking at the case in terms of doctrine. The cases were on our side and we didn't think the Court would take the step to strike down RFRA without calling into question all of Congress' previous civil rights legislation."

The Supreme Court granted certiorari on October 15, 1987, and the attorneys for both sides prepared the briefs on the merits. The city of Boerne argued that RFRA violates the rights of state and local governments because it forces a higher level of protection for religious beliefs than the Constitution requires, and it violates separation of powers because Congress was forcing the federal courts to use the high level of scrutiny mandated by the act. RFRA was characterized as "a bold and unprecedented example of federal social policy engineering that commandeers the states to accommodate religion more than the Constitution requires." There were five amicus curiae briefs from historic preservation and children's rights organizations filed on behalf of the city, and sixteen states and three American territories joined Ohio attorney general Betty D. Montgomery's amicus curiae brief contending that RFRA led to disruptions in prison operations with frivolous litigation.

The brief on behalf of Flores defended the constitutionality of RFRA as an appropriate exercise of congressional enforcement authority under the Fourteenth Amendment, and argued that Boerne's zoning laws placed a substantial burden on the church's ability to accommodate its parishioners and worship in an appropriate place. Under the balancing test required by RFRA, the attorneys argued that the zoning laws failed the compelling government interest test. Twenty amicus briefs were filed on behalf of Flores and the United States, including two briefs signed by thirty-four members of Congress, three briefs on behalf of seven states, and a brief from the Coalition for the Free Exercise of Religion representing seventy-eight religious and civil liberties organizations.

The U.S. Supreme Court heard oral arguments in *City of Boerne* on February 19, 1997. Hamilton and Jeffrey Sutton, solicitor general for the state of Ohio, served as advocates for the city of Boerne, and Laycock and Walter Dellinger, acting solicitor general for the Clinton administration, represented the archbishop of San Antonio for St. Peter Roman Catholic Church. The focus of oral arguments was whether RFRA violated principles of federalism and separation of powers. As one news report observed, "Many of the Justices seemed to think the act does all of those nasty things and then some."

Hamilton set the stage by focusing the case on the issue of federalism. She stated, "This case is not about religious liberty. It is about federal power. It's about the power of the U.S. Constitution to restrain Congress." She characterized the Religious Freedom Restoration Act as a "hostile takeover" of the free exercise clause, a "prophylactic law" not designed to remedy a known harm, but to "overturn a Supreme Court decision." Hamilton pointed out that the law was not remedial because Congress had not proven that government was hostile toward religion. She contended that the law represented "the worst of legislative overreaching," which reflected Congress' "brazen attempt to reinterpret" the free exercise clause. Hamilton told the Court, "It certainly can't get to the point where Congress gets to redefine the meaning of the Constitution instead of just enforcing it," adding that this would "shift the balance of power dramatically from the Court to Congress." She concluded that RFRA was an illegitimate exercise of congressional power under section five of the Fourteenth Amendment and that it violated the principles of federalism and separation of powers and should be ruled unconstitutional.

Sutton argued the states' rights position. He reminded the justices that the states could protect religious freedom on their own, and that they did not need Congress to instruct them with a "vast, intrusive, rigid law." Sutton observed, "There is an etiquette of federalism—that states will obey the Constitution without federal prodding." He depicted RFRA as a substantive rather than a remedial law, and a "nightmare for states [because] they cannot remedy what is not wrong." He characterized the legislation as "a constitutional amendment, disguised as a law." Congress did not have the authority, Sutton remarked, to override the Court's interpretation of the Constitution without violating the rule in *Marbury v. Madison*.

Laycock, representing the archbishop of San Antonio, addressed the concerns raised by Hamilton and Sutton about RFRA's constitutionality. In response to questions about the scope of Congress' section five authority, he noted that there was an "unbroken tradition" of congressional laws enacted under the enforcement clause of the Fourteenth Amendment, and that RFRA fit neatly into this tradition. "Congress has always had the right to make rights effective in practice that go beyond the floor set by this Court." It is not, he observed, "a dramatic power grab." Laycock also maintained that the law did not usurp the judiciary's role under *Marbury* because the courts would have the final word in the statute's interpretation. Not only will free exercise cases be decided in the courts, he noted, the Supreme Court would ultimately determine the constitutionality of the Religious Freedom Restoration Act. "This Court interprets [the Act] and this Court retains its power." Laycock reassured the Court it could safely rely on precedent and uphold RFRA.

Dellinger used his opportunity before the Court to downplay the expansiveness of the bill and to remind the Court that although RFRA mandates a higher level of judicial scrutiny for free exercise claims, this "doesn't mean that courts have to give in to every claim." He characterized the compelling government interest test as a workable standard that could be fairly applied to all legitimate free exercise claims, and stated that the Act "does not require the Court to break new ground." Dellinger also emphasized what the Justice Department believed was the most important aspect of the bill, that it protected minority religions that were not as "politically connected" as the mainstream religions. "We must," he stated, "ensure everyone's free exercise of religion gets the same treatment whether they're a powerful denomination or a small nondenomination." He added that RFRA was the only way to protect minority religions and prevent larger religions from getting preferential treatment. "Congress was concerned about marginal religious groups. What RFRA says is, everyone gets the same treatment—whether you're powerful, traditional or marginal."

Throughout the oral proceedings, the justices asked the attorneys a number of challenging questions. Most reports characterized the justices' questioning of the attorneys as hostile to the legislation. One account noted, "None of the Justices had anything nice to say about the protective goals of RFRA." In fact, practically every justice expressed reservations about its constitutionality.

———

The outcome of *Boerne* was difficult to predict. The Court had changed significantly since *Smith;* Justices Souter, Thomas, Ginsberg, and Breyer had replaced Justices Brennan, Marshall, Powell, and Blackmun, respectively. Because the case did not concern religious liberty, previous free exercise decisions were not a good determinant of the outcome. The Court's questioning during oral arguments illustrated that it was primarily concerned about the extent of Congress' power under section five of the Fourteenth Amendment and whether RFRA infringed on the Court's authority to interpret the Constitution. Although previous Court decisions on congressional actions under the Fourteenth Amendment had been upheld by the Court, its doctrine on the substantive power of Congress to enact legislation to go beyond what the Supreme Court requires was less than clear.

On June 25, 1997, the Supreme Court ruled that the Religious Freedom Restoration Act unconstitutionally violated the principles of federalism and separation of powers. It was a busy week for the Court; over the next two days it struck down two other popular Clinton administration measures: the Communications Decency Act in *Reno v. United States* and a section of the 1993 Brady Handgun Violence Prevention Act that required local law enforcement officials to conduct background checks in *Printz v. U.S.* Given that the Court had only declared approximately 140 federal laws unconstitutional at this point in its history, its use of the power of judicial review to strike down 3 laws enacted with broad, if not overwhelming bipartisan support, was extraordinary. Moreover, in both *Boerne* and *Printz* the Court specifically rejected an expansive interpretation of congressional powers, finding instead that the legislative branch had encroached upon states' rights.

Kennedy wrote the majority opinion in *Boerne*, joined by Rehnquist, Scalia, Thomas, Stevens, and Ginsberg. He determined that Congress exceeded its authority when it enacted RFRA because it attempted to substantively define the free exercise clause, inappropriate under section five of the Fourteenth Amendment, which only empowers Congress to pass remedial laws that enforce the amendment's guarantee of civil rights. Interpretation of constitutional rights, which RFRA attempts to do, stated Kennedy, is a power reserved for the judiciary. "Legislation which alters the meaning of the Free Exercise Clause cannot be said to be enforcing the clause. Congress does not enforce a constitutional right by changing what the right is. It has been given the power 'to enforce,' not the power to determine what constitutes a constitutional violation . . ." He acknowledged that Congress' section five authority does allow "remedial" and "preventative" congressional action, but that it could not pass legislation that alters the "substantive" meaning of constitutional rights. "Any suggestion that Congress has a substantive, non-remedial power under the Fourteenth Amendment is not supported by our case law." In the context of this discussion Kennedy compared RFRA to the Voting Rights Act, which he described as an appropriate exercise of remedial congressional power because Congress had a factual basis to determine "invidious discrimination in violation of the Equal Protection Clause." RFRA, on the other hand, was described as "so out of proportion to a supposed remedial or preventive object that it cannot be understood as responsible to, or designed to prevent, unconstitutional behavior." Kennedy established that there was no evidence of a "widespread pattern of religious discrimination in this country" that would warrant such a far-reaching law, which "ensures its intrusion at every level of government, displacing laws and prohibiting official actions of almost every description and regardless of subject matter." He concluded this portion of his decision with his statement that the action infringed upon states' rights, "this is a considerable congressional intrusion into the States' traditional prerogatives and general authority to regulate for the health and welfare of their citizens."

In the second part of the opinion Kennedy further explored the separation of powers question raised by Congress' attempt to substantively define constitutional rights and liberties. Kennedy cited *Marbury v. Madison* to reiterate that the Court alone has judicial supremacy over the meaning of the Constitution. He characterized RFRA as threatening this supremacy because it "was designed to control cases and controversies, such as the one before us," and, in striking down RFRA, concluded that it "is this Court's precedent, not RFRA which must control."

There were two separate concurring opinions; one by Stevens, who argued that RFRA was "a 'law respecting an establishment of religion' that violates the First Amendment to the Constitution," and an opinion by Scalia, who defended the legitimacy of his majority opinion in *Smith*. There were also three separate dissents. In her twenty-three-page opinion, O'Connor, joined by Breyer, dissented from the majority because *Boerne* was "premised on the assumption that *Smith* correctly interprets the Free Exercise Clause." An assumption, she added, "that I do not accept." She called for a reexamination of *Smith*, which she be-

lieved was not supported by "precedent," or "history," and included an extensive analysis of the history of the free exercise
clause in her decision. O'Connor concluded, "If the Court were
to correct the misinterpretation of the Free Exercise Clause set
forth in *Smith*, it would simultaneously put our First Amendment
jurisprudence back on course and allay the legitimate concerns of
a majority in Congress who believed that *Smith* improperly restricted religious liberty." Breyer also wrote a dissent, stating that
reargument of *Smith* was necessary but that reargument on section five of the Fourteenth Amendment was not. In his dissent,
Souter stated that he had "serious doubts about the precedential
value of the *Smith* rule and its entitlement to adherence." He
called for a reconsideration of the decision, but would not de-
clare whether it was improperly decided, waiting instead for reargument. Notably, each member of the Court explicitly or
implicitly endorsed Kennedy's very limited view of Congress' enforcement power under the Fourteenth Amendment.

———

Three factors are significant in *Boerne* beyond the immediate decision, which is that RFRA, as applied to state and local governments, is unconstitutional. First, although the Court did not
directly address this issue, RFRA still applies to federal laws,
which ensures that federal laws challenged under the act will be
scrutinized under the compelling government interest test if the
religious challenger can prove that the government activity substantially burdens their free exercise of religion. The other two
factors more broadly concern the balance of power between
Congress and the Court, and help explain why *Boerne* may be a
landmark decision in its own right. Significantly, the Court eliminated the "substantive rights" theory announced in Brennan's
1966 *Katzenbach v. Morgan* decision. This is notable because
Boerne limits congressional power under the enforcement clauses
of the Civil War Amendments to independently provide greater
protection for civil rights and liberties under the Constitution.
Under the rule established in *Boerne*, Congress' power under the
enforcement clause of the Fourteenth Amendment is limited to

remedial action. The Court illustrated that it would invalidate any federal attempts to provide greater protection for rights and liberties beyond what it believes is warranted if the congressional action intrudes on state sovereignty. Because the Court failed to persuasively delineate the difference between remedial and substantive action, however, this actually confuses the issue and increases the probability that *any* congressional action under its section five authority will be susceptible to a constitutional challenge. Kennedy acknowledged this difficulty in the opinion of the Court, conceding that "the line between measures that remedy or prevent unconstitutional actions and measures that make a substantive change in the law is not easy to discern."

Boerne is also significant for Kennedy's assertion of the Court's supremacy over Congress in the realm of constitutional interpretation. The Court, obviously stinging from Congress' rebuke of *Smith*, cited *Marbury v. Madison* to reiterate that the Court rather than Congress has the final say in the meaning of the Constitution, thereby jealously protecting its self-anointed role as the ultimate expositor of the Constitution. *Boerne* thus tries to silence Congress, essentially divesting a coordinate branch of government of its right to participate in a discussion about the protection of religious liberty in America. Unless, of course, the discussion is framed in terms of what the Court believes is the proper interpretation of the Constitution. The combination of these two factors effectively strips Congress of its right to engage in independent constitutional analysis and empowers only the Court, and not Congress, with the ability to protect liberty in America from abuses by state and local governments.

———

But would *Boerne* be the last word in this ongoing constitutional dialogue between Congress and the Court? Not at all. Days after the Court decided *Boerne*, Charles T. Canady (R-FL), chair of the House Subcommittee on Civil and Constitutional Affairs, announced that Congress would begin discussions about a new legislative effort to address *Employment Division of Oregon v. Smith* that would withstand scrutiny by the Supreme Court.

Within weeks after the Court ended its 1997 term, a subcommittee hearing was held on "Protecting Religious Liberty after *Boerne v. Flores.*" Similar to the hearings on the Religious Freedom Restoration Act, witnesses emphasized the need for legislation to protect religious freedom from neutral, generally applicable laws that burdened religious exercise. After the hearing, members of the Coalition for the Free Exercise of Religion met regularly to plan their strategy to protect religious freedom. They decided on a two-pronged attack: to rewrite federal legislation to avoid the constitutional problems associated with RFRA and to enact "mini-Religious Freedom Acts" in the states.

For the federal legislative effort, coalition members worked closely with staff from Canady's office and with David Lachmann, who was now working for Jerrold Nadler (D-NY). Lachmann previously served as a liaison between Solarz and the coalition during the RFRA battle, a role he was eager to repeat for Nadler, who was equally concerned about protecting religious liberty. A small group formed a drafting committee to write legislation that could circumvent *Smith* and withstand muster by a Supreme Court quickly becoming known for its restrictions on congressional power and protection of states' rights. The drafting effort was headed by Mark Stern of American Jewish Congress, who played a leading role in the drafting of RFRA, and Laycock, who defended the law before Congress and the Court. However, the drafting committee found it much more difficult to write legislation this second time around. Because the Supreme Court was closely monitoring federal-state relations, it was imperative that Congress carefully base any legislation on one of its enumerated powers. Laycock and Stern eventually decided upon Congress' Article I power under the spending clause and the interstate commerce clause, as well as its section five authority in specific instances where it could prove a pattern of religious discrimination, thus illustrating that the law was indeed "remedial." Under the proposed measure, titled the Religious Liberty Protection Act, government could not substantially burden a person's religious exercise, even as the result of a neutral, general applicability law, unless it demonstrates that the law furthers a compelling government interest. Section two of the bill applied to situations where the burden is a result of "a program or activity operated by the government that receives Federal financial assistance" and where the burden "affects interstate commerce." Section three provided additional protection for religious exercise, mandating that once an individual has made a "prima facie case" that their free exercise of religion has been burdened, that "government shall bear the burden of persuasion on all issues relating to the claim." This section also protected religious institutions and assemblies burdened by land use regulations under Congress' section five authority.

Some members of the Coalition were skeptical about use of each of these avenues of congressional authority. Several groups argued that reliance on the spending clause was inadequate because it would only protect religious liberty in those instances where federal money was spent, which would lead to situations where religion was unprotected. Others did not want to use the commerce clause because they believed it might exclude protection for smaller religions, and because they were ideologically opposed to widening Congress' authority under this part of the Constitution because it could potentially lead to federal regulation of religion in the future. Although only a small portion of the bill relied on Congress' section five authority to enact remedial legislation to address specific rights abuses, there was some reluctance about this avenue in light of *Boerne*. Despite these concerns, a majority of coalition members agreed that the best strategy was to base the measure on several parts of the Constitution in hopes that it would be approved by Congress and withstand review by the Court. However, there was tension in the coalition. According to Laycock, it took over a year "haggling over how to make sure the bill was neutral" and "finding language that members would agree upon," and several groups did withdraw from CFER over this matter, most notably Michael Farris, president of the Home School Legal Defense Association and a previous member of the RFRA drafting committee, over his disagreement with the use of Congress' commerce authority for a bill to protect religious freedom.

As RLPA was drafted, the House Subcommittee on the Constitution held two additional hearings on the need to protect religious freedom in February and March 1998. Coalition members assisted House Judiciary representatives in organizing panels consisting of individuals that could provide examples of how religious adherents were substantially burdened by neutral, generally applicable laws, especially in the area of land use regulations. The strategy was to build these examples into the congressional record to illustrate that the Religious Liberty Protection Act was remedial legislation. An extensive conversation about past abuses of religious liberty from such neutral laws was absent from the RFRA conversation, allowing Justice Kennedy to emphasize that RFRA was a substantive exercise of congressional power because there wasn't any evidence that Congress was attempting to remedy religious intolerance by state and local governments.

After a year of detailed discussions about how to respond to *Boerne*, on June 9, 1998, the Religious Liberty Protection Act of 1998 was unveiled at a press conference attended by members of Congress and the Coalition for the Free Exercise of Religion. Later that day HR 4091 was introduced in the House by chief sponsors Canady and Nadler, and a companion bill, S 2148 was introduced in the Senate by chief sponsors Orrin Hatch and Edward Kennedy, key players in the RFRA battle. Both bills had multiple cosponsors from both parties. A House subcommittee hearing and a Senate Judiciary Committee hearing were held within weeks after introduction, and an additional House hearing was held in mid-July. Some of the same individuals that had been active in the RFRA discussion seven years earlier testified in support of RLPA. The focus of the hearings was the constitutionality of the measure and concerns about unintended effects of the legislation on civil rights, environmental, and child welfare laws. In addition to Laycock, several constitutional scholars defended the appropriateness of the measure and discussed how this new version, based more carefully on Congress' enumerated powers, would withstand scrutiny by the Supreme Court. However, there was also opposition to the bill. Several academics discussed how

RLPA potentially conflicted with state sovereignty and the establishment clause, and others expressed reservations about using Congress' commerce clause authority for the legislation, thus further expanding Congress' power. As with RFRA, RLPA soon became a target for groups wanting exemptions from the law, such as the American Academy of Pediatricians, which believed children could be endangered by parents motivated by religious beliefs, and representatives from civil rights and environmental organizations who feared the measure could be used as a religious justification for violations of state and local laws that protected their interests. The religious rights of prisoners was also a minor issue, but RLPA drafters anticipated this potential roadblock and had added a section that required all prisoners' suits to be subject to the "Prison Litigation Reform Act of 1995," which targets frivolous claims.

Markup of the Religious Liberty Protection Act took place on August 6 in the House Judiciary Committee. Requests for exceptions to the legislation were considered and rejected. There were minor refinements to the section concerning land use regulation, which now more specifically provided that religious assemblies be treated equally as nonreligious assemblies and that religious institutions not be excluded from areas. More significant, however, was the deletion of the commerce section of the bill. After the introduction of the measure, several conservative groups led by Farris organized an intensive letter writing and phone bank campaign announcing their opposition to the use of the commerce clause because it could potentially lead to an expansion of government authority over religion. Farris's effort resulted in some reluctance on the part of Republicans to support the measure, and to ensure bipartisan support, Canady omitted the commerce section. However, there was no further action on RLPA. The day after the bill was marked up, the Starr Report was delivered to Congress, putting into motion events that would eventually dwarf this battle for religious freedom over the next six months: The effort to impeach and remove President Clinton from office.

In addition to the obvious delay in time, the impeachment hearings and Senate trial had an even more insidious effect on the debate over the Religious Liberty Protection Act. The hearings in the House were extremely partisan and there was a high level of distrust and anger between the Republicans and Democrats both during the proceedings and after the House voted to impeach Clinton on two counts. Although the Senate trial was a little less raucous, the heightened emotions and party-line vote to remove Clinton from office also dampened bipartisan spirits, even over an issue with broad support.

Canady and Nadler reintroduced the Religious Liberty Protection Act, retitled HR 1691, to the House on May 5, 1999. The measure retained the changes to the section on land use regulation and included the original section on the commerce clause. Hearings took place a week later. It was similar to the previous year, with a focus on the constitutionality of the bill and concerns about possible unintended consequences of the measure. Most of the discussion centered on how the bill might be used to undermine civil rights legislation. The American Civil Liberties Union, reflecting the concerns of several groups from the left, argued that RLPA could be used as a basis for a religious defense against enforcement of state and local antidiscrimination laws. Although the ACLU backed the 1998 version of the bill despite these concerns, it left the Coalition for the Free Exercise of Religion over this issue and actively opposed the measure.

RLPA was marked up with only minor changes in the House Judiciary Committee on June 15 and was approved by voice vote on June 23. RLPA supporters were thrilled, but a second news story about religious liberty that day dampened their spirits. On the last day of its 1998–1999 term, the U.S. Supreme Court issued a trio of rulings on federalism that significantly cut congressional power. The decisions concerned state challenges to federal legislation that allowed citizens to initiate private lawsuits against states in state courts. In each case, the Court ruled against Congress and in favor of protecting the states. In *Alden v. Maine* the Court considered whether state employees could use federal laws to sue states in state courts. The majority opinion by Kennedy, joined by Rehnquist, Scalia, Thomas, and O'Connor, generously interpreted the Eleventh Amendment to rule that

Congress did not have the authority to abrogate the "sovereign immunity" of states in state courts. In *Florida v. College Savings Bank* and *College Savings Bank v. Florida* the same majority ruled that two federal laws allowing lawsuits against states for patent infringement claims and trademark violations were an inappropriate exercise of Congress' section five enforcement authority under the Fourteenth Amendment.

The three cases follow a trend of decisions, beginning in 1992 after the appointment of Thomas, where the U.S. Supreme Court has cut back congressional power. In addition to *Boerne* and *Printz*, decided in 1997, in 1996 the Court handed down *Seminole Tribe of Florida v. Florida*, ruling that Congress was prevented under the Eleventh Amendment from allowing American Indian tribes to sue states. The decision invalidated part of the 1988 Indian Gaming Regulation Act passed pursuant to the Indian Commerce Clause, which gave Indian tribes the right to sue states over disputes over Indian casinos. In 1995 the Court decided *United States v. Lopez* where it invalidated the "Gun-Free Zones Act," ruling for the first time in six decades that Congress exceeded its authority under the interstate commerce clause. In 1992 the Court struck down provisions of the Low Level Radioactive Waste Policy Act in *New York v. United States* on the basis that it "commandeered" state lawmaking processes by forcing states to enact regulations to properly dispose of nuclear waste, or take "title" or possession of the waste.

The line of cases reflected the Rehnquist Court's intent to cut back federal power and devolve it back to the states. In terms of the RLPA discussion, the three decisions at the end of the Court's term cast doubt on whether any congressional action to protect religious liberty was safe from the Court's newfound interest in protecting states' rights.

———

Despite these possible concerns about the Supreme Court, several weeks after RLPA was voted favorably out of the House Judiciary Committee, the bill moved to the House floor for consideration. The measure received a much-needed boost on

July 14 when President Clinton endorsed the bill, and the House took up the bill the next day. Representative Nadler introduced the one major amendment to the legislation, to exempt the use of RLPA as a defense for violating civil rights laws, but it was defeated by a 234-to-190 vote, with most Democrats in favor of the amendment and most Republicans in opposition. RLPA then passed the House with majority support in both parties. One hundred and seven Democrats joined 199 Republicans to approve the bill. The 118 votes in opposition were primarily from Democrats, including Nadler, because of the failed civil rights exception, and from two dozen Republicans due to the commerce section of the bill. Senate consideration of RLPA stalled, and the measure has not been taken up again.

Even more foreboding than Congress' inability to enact legislation that protects religious freedom is the very high probability that such action would be struck down as unconstitutional by the Supreme Court. Several decisions handed down at the end of the Court's 1999–2000 term illustrate that its eagerness to cut back on federal power will continue. In January in *Kimel v. Florida Board of Regents* the Court invalidated a portion of the Age Discrimination Act that would have held states liable for age discrimination. And, on May 15, in its most significant ruling of the term, the Court handed down its decisions in *Brzonkala v. VIP University* and *United States v. Morrison*, two cases that involved constitutional challenges to portions of the Violence Against Women Act, which allowed women who were victims of gender-motivated crimes to sue in federal court. The Court upheld the decision of the 4th U.S. Circuit Court of Appeals, which ruled that the law was an unconstitutional exercise of Congress' commerce power. The five-person majority rejected the argument that Congress may regulate noneconomic, violent criminal conduct based solely on that conduct's aggregate effect on interstate commerce. The decision was based on the Court's *Lopez* ruling, illustrating that *Lopez*, where the Court invalidated a federal law based on Congress' commerce power for the first time in over sixty years, was not an anomaly. In *Brzonkala* and *Morrison* the Court also rejected Congress' argument that the law was justified under the equal protection clause of the Fourteenth Amendment.

It is likely, given the Court's federalism decisions over the last eight years, that the current trend in favor of states' rights will continue as the Court cuts back Congress' power vis-à-vis the states, jeopardizing any federal action to protect religious freedom.

––––––

The second prong of the coalition's response to *Boerne*, the effort to enact state Religious Freedom Acts, may prove to be the best long-term strategy to protect religious liberty in America. The effort was initiated shortly after *Boerne*, and took place at the same time RLPA was considered in Congress. The Religious Freedom Act task force, headed by Steve McFarland, coordinated the grassroots campaign. The Coalition for the Free Exercise of Religion agreed on three important principles to guide the state legislative effort. First, that the religious liberty bills should be enacted with no exceptions, not only because coalition members believed all Americans were entitled to religious freedom, but because exceptions for certain populations such as prisoners would lead to further exemptions to the legislation. Second, that the acts duplicate the stringent compelling government interest balancing test present in RFRA, and also include a definition of religion that describes conduct as behavior "motivated by religious beliefs or convictions" to ensure broadest support for religious exercise. Third, that acts focus only on correcting the problem in *Smith* and not contain additional measures that address church/state issues such as prayer in public schools and public funding for religious institutions. Because the coalition was divided on these issues, such an approach might create problems in the group and delay passage of state legislation. The task force made itself available to individuals and groups interested in enacting these bills and provided draft legislation and assistance in coordinating a statewide campaign.

In 1998 Religious Freedom Acts were introduced in nineteen states. The state acts were similar to RFRA in form, requiring that any state or local government action that substantially burdens an individual's religious exercise serve a compelling government interest in the least restrictive manner. As with the federal effort, one of the main stumbling blocks in the states was whether free exercise challenges by prisoners would threaten penological interests. There was also concern from the National League of Cities and the National Association of Counties that the acts would hinder municipal and state zoning and land use regulations, and increasing anxiety from some civil liberties organizations that the legislation could be used as a tool against local and state civil rights laws that prohibit discrimination. Nevertheless, in 1998 state religious liberty acts were passed in Connecticut, Florida, and Rhode Island. Alabama successfully amended its state constitution to protect religious liberty through a ballot initiative. State legislatures in Illinois and California approved similar measures, but each was vetoed by the governor because of the prison issue. Acts were also considered in Georgia, Louisiana, Maryland, Michigan, New Hampshire, New Jersey, New York, Oregon, Pennsylvania, South Carolina, Tennessee, Vermont, and Virginia.

In 1999 the Council on Religious Freedom, along with the Georgetown University Church/State Law Forum hosted a "Restoring Religious Freedom in the States Conference" to discuss some of the challenges faced by the state effort, such as the tension created between state religious liberty acts and speech regulation, zoning and land use issues, employment issues, prisoner issues, civil rights laws, and the establishment clause of the First Amendment. Panels also reviewed the need for state action and strategies on coalition building and legislative approaches. The conference kicked off another multistate campaign, and religious liberty acts were later passed in Arizona, South Carolina, and Texas. A bill was vetoed by the governor in New Mexico, and bills were withdrawn in light of opposition in Louisiana and Maryland. At the end of 1999, acts are pending once again in California, Connecticut, Hawaii, Michigan, Missouri, New York, Oregon, Pennsylvania, and Virginia. Requests for exemptions to the legislation, particularly for prisoners, and exceptions for antidiscrimination laws continue to dominate the conversations, but the battle for state legislative solutions continues.

Some states were assisted by their judicial branches as well. The coalition monitored free exercise cases in state supreme courts to see if state courts, unhappy with the limited protection provided to religious freedom under the *Smith* rule, might develop state constitutional doctrine on this issue. After *Smith* was decided, state supreme courts in Maine, Massachusetts, Minnesota, and Wisconsin rejected Scalia's rule mandating a low level of judicial scrutiny in cases involving neutral, generally applicable laws, and instead protected religious liberty through the application of strict scrutiny analysis in the interpretation of similar free exercise or freedom of worship clauses in the state constitution. However, reliance on the state supreme courts is limited at best—the Vermont state supreme court rejected this possibility, and in several other states, the courts' standard for evaluating religious liberty cases is less than clear.

———

This battle for religious freedom has also continued in the American Indian community, and there have been significant successes over the last several years. On May 24, 1996, President Clinton signed Executive Order 13007 to promote the protection of sacred Indian religious sites. Section one of the order requires federal agencies to "accommodate access to and ceremonial use of Indian sacred sites by Indian religious practitioners," and "avoid adversely affecting the physical integrity of such sacred sites." Section two provides that each executive branch agency with the responsibility for the management of federal lands promptly implement procedures for the purposes to carry out the order, and requires that they report back to the president to address any necessary changes to facilitate the accommodation and preservation of Indian sacred sites. Also, in the spring of 1997 the right of members of the armed forces belonging to the Native American Church to ingest peyote as a sacrament was secured when the Pentagon began implementing a rule on this issue. There are some minor restrictions to this right, such as notification and consent of commanding officer and a ban on peyote use or possession in military vehicles, but the rule finally gives the estimated five hundred to one thousand Native American Church members the right to exercise their religion while defending their country.

Currently, there is a continued effort for religious protection for American Indians incarcerated in federal prisons. In 1995 the National Native American Prison Rights Advocates Coalition, which includes groups such as the Native American Rights Fund, the National Congress of American Indians, the Association of American Indian Affairs, and the American Indian Movement, formed to fight for legislation to secure religious rights for American Indians incarcerated in federal prisons. The group lobbied Attorney General Janet Reno to issue a directive to provide religious services to native prisoners, to help train federal prison staff to recognize and respect religious worship and access to sacred objects, and to increase the federal government's commitment to monitor state and local prison conditions through its civil rights division. Although there has not been a resolution on this issue, the National Native American Prison Rights Advocates Coalition continues its efforts. Overall, Indian rights organizations carefully monitor future infringements on the religious freedom rights of American Indians. Given the U.S. history of targeting this minority population, particularly with respect to religious freedom, similar legislative efforts will be necessary in the future.

Lastly, it is important to note that the Supreme Court's decision in *Boerne* has not had an immediate impact on the 1994 amendments to the American Indian Religious Freedom Act, which provides protection for the religious use of peyote. However, this legislation could still be challenged in court.

———

Over a decade ago, Congress, unhappy with the Supreme Court's ruling in *Employment Division v. Smith*, entered into a constitutional dialogue with the Court over the meaning of the free exercise clause of the First Amendment to the Constitution. In this decision the Court revealed that it was unwilling to offer constitutional protection for religious exercise except for rare instances when government specifically targeted religion. Congress, believing religious exercise deserved greater protection under the First Amendment, responded by enacting the Religious Freedom Restoration Act to protect religious freedom generally, and amended the American Indian Religious Freedom Act to protect the sacramental use of peyote specifically. The Court then responded to RFRA in *City of Boerne v. Flores* by invalidating the legislation as it applied to the states, as well as reining in Congress' authority under section five of the Fourteenth Amendment to enact substantive legislation to protect civil rights and liberties. The Court also called up its landmark *Marbury v. Madison* decision to express its disapproval of Congress' foray into constitutional interpretation and to jealously defend its self-anointed role as ultimate expositor of the Constitution. Most recently, Congress responded to this rebuke by reasserting its role in this constitutional conversation and continuing its exploration into a legislative remedy to *Smith*.

It is important to note that *Smith* is only a decision, and it is not the final word on the meaning of the free exercise clause of the First Amendment to the Constitution. Congress has a right, indeed, a duty as a coordinate branch of government to respond to the Court when it believes the Court has erred and misinterpreted the meaning of the Constitution. Members of Congress did not set out to undermine the Court's role as one of many constitutional interpreters—rather, they have been fighting to take part in the conversation about the meaning of the Constitution. There has never been an exclusive interpreter of the Constitution, and the Court's perception that it alone provides meaning to the document is misleading and potentially destructive to the legitimacy of the Court. As judicial scholar C. Herman Pritchett announced long ago, a Court decision is final only "so long as the other branches of government and the political process allows it to stand." Overwhelming disapproval of *Smith* and widespread support for the Religious Freedom Restoration Act, the amendments to the American Indian Religious Freedom Act, and the Religious Liberty Protection Act provide evidence of this fact.

It is important to distance ourselves from the mistaken notion that only the Court has the responsibility to protect individual rights and liberties and instead embrace this constitutional dialogue taking place between the institutions of the federal government, the states, and the people. This discussion over the meaning of the free exercise clause, like all discussions about the Constitution, is best looked at as an interactive, perpetual debate. Although it is easy to focus on what happened at any one point on the continuum of this discussion about religious freedom in America—*Smith*, RFRA, AIRFA, *Boerne*, state Religious Liberty Acts, and RLPA—it would be unfortunate if one did not appreciate the fact that activity at each point was a reaction to a constantly evolving discussion taking place between a number of participants over the meaning of religious liberty in America. At the very least, there seems to be a consensus among Americans about the need to protect religious liberty in America, even though some may disagree with the means. The real story lies in the colloquy between the stakeholders as they interact over this volatile issue.

Congress has enjoyed a long history of substantive constitutional interpretation in its role as a coordinate branch of government, and its reaction to the landmark *Smith* decision is an example of its effort to engage in a colloquy with the Court. Significantly, Congress brings institutional strengths to this conversation about the Constitution that do not exist on the Supreme Court. For example, Congress has the added benefit, notably absent from the Court, of being a representative institution that has the ability to take the pulse of the American public and reflect the will of the people in its decisions. Furthermore, pressure groups such as the Coalition for the Free Exercise of Religion and the American Indian Religious Freedom Coalition, which have also played a historic role in the conversation over the meaning of civil rights and civil liberties, can act through these elected representatives to voice their concerns about the Supreme Court's interpretation of the Constitution.

The Court, as well as Congress, has been "wrong" about constitutional issues in the past, and each will be wrong in the future. Encouraging and recognizing the role of other constitutional interpreters provides the country with a fail-safe for correcting errors and for best protecting liberty. As a dynamic and interrelated process, the participation of different individuals and institutions involved in the process of constitutional interpretation will inevitably vary over the years. Dominance by one branch of government over another at any given time, for a variety of reasons, such as political circumstances, institutional competence, or external environmental factors, will always lead to times when one institution of government will be more vigilant than others in the protection of rights and liberties. As a result, having more participants involved in this process ensures the greatest amount of protection for constitutional freedoms. The fact that this dynamic is constantly changing should provide reason enough for multiple constitutional interpreters. The fact that one of those liberties being protected is religious liberty, the "first freedom" for most Americans, provides another.

Epilogue

On November 6, 1999, exactly ten years after oral arguments in *Employment Division v. Smith*, Al Smith observed his eightieth birthday. His wife, Jane Farrell, spent weeks organizing a celebration in honor of her husband. Smith and his family had spent the last three years in Germany, where Farrell worked in an Early Childhood Development program, and Jane saw this as an opportunity to celebrate Al's life and to reconnect with family and friends in the community.

The celebration was held at the Longhouse, a small, older building located on the University of Oregon campus next to the new Law School. The building is used by the university's Office of Multicultural Affairs to hold events, and it donated the space for the celebration. The office also used the occasion to arrange several panel discussions on the Chemewa Indian School, which still operates as a boarding school in Salem. The panels were held early in the afternoon at the Law School to coincide with Smith's birthday.

Farrell and a group of friends spent most of the day preparing the feast for the celebration. The menu consisted of traditional native food that would be served in a specific order according to custom: various vegetable roots, a mixture of corn and hominy, salmon, a variety of meats including elk and deer, and seasonal berries. Guests brought additional food to supplement the traditional fare.

People started arriving in the late afternoon, and by early evening, approximately 150 people—far too many for the small space—converged on the Longhouse. The building could only seat about 80 people, and so dozens of people sat outside, visiting with each other as the tables were set with the meal. A small fire burned outside and people drummed, chanted, and sang songs while the food was presented to the guests. Everyone was in high spirits, visiting with Smith, his family, and each other. The meal began with a prayer and a discussion of the food served that evening, and for the next several hours, people ate and visited, lingering over the feast. Additional guests also came during this time to join the celebration and to indulge in the good food.

After the feast, family and friends gathered in the commons area at the University of Oregon Law School and arranged a large "talking circle." The purpose of the circle was to provide the guests the opportunity to reflect on their relationship with Smith and to share their thoughts about this man and his impact on their lives. A man stood in the center of the circle, drumming and singing. A very faint haze of smoke from burning sage filled the air. Everyone sat quietly, listening as peyote songs filled the Law School.

After several songs, the man took a sacred eagle feather and handed it to Farrell, who initiated the talking circle. She held the feather, and spoke of her love, respect, and admiration for her husband and the joy he has brought into her life. She then handed the feather to the person on her left, who also shared thoughts in honor of Smith. The feather was slowly passed around the circle. Each person had something different to say. Some reflected on Smith's positive influence in their life—as a father, a friend, a drug and alcohol treatment counselor, a role model, an elder of the tribe. Others spoke of how Smith and Farrell helped create a sense of community in Eugene, and how happy they were that the family had returned. It was difficult for several of the guests to speak. Those who knew Smith before he embraced sobriety spoke of the hardships of the early days and the strength of character it took to overcome these challenges. Several people spoke of their personal struggles with alcohol or substance abuse, and commented on how Smith helped them with their sobriety. Many of the guests had known Smith for years, and reminisced about a loving memory or told an anecdote about their relationship. One young man, who had met Smith only days before the celebration, spoke of how thankful he was to be invited to honor Smith and how inspired he was by Smith's life story.

It was a celebration in honor of Smith, rather than a discussion about the Supreme Court case, *Employment Division v. Smith*, which only constituted a small part of his life. In fact, only two people mentioned the decision and the irony of how, ten years later, a group could gather to honor Al Smith and to sing peyote songs on the university grounds where Dave Frohnmayer currently served as president.

It was a moving, uplifting evening. A celebration of Smith's life. He sat quietly throughout the three hours it took to complete the talking circle. At times, he seemed embarrassed at the attention being lavished on him. At the end, Smith held the sacred eagle feather and thanked everyone for their kind comments and reminiscences. He smiled, and told the group he was looking forward to the next gathering. He, too, chose not to speak of the Supreme Court decision that bears his name and its role in this battle for religious liberty. It wasn't because of a lack of commitment to his religious faith; rather, it was because the significance of the decision was unimportant to him. After all, as far as he was concerned, he was only going to church.

CHRONOLOGY

1560	Peyotism first documented by the Spanish.
1620	The Catholic Church issues an edict prohibiting the use of peyote.
1891	The peyote religion is first documented in the United States.
1897	Antipeyotists begin their attempt to outlaw peyotism.
1918	The Native American Church is formally incorporated in the state of Oklahoma.
1919	Alfred Leo Smith is born in Modoc Point on the Klamath Indian Reservation.
1941	Smith is drafted into the army.
1954	The Klamath Indian tribe is terminated; the 1864 treaty between the U.S. government and the Klamath tribe is abrogated.
1957	After years of alcoholism, Smith embraces sobriety.
1964	The Civil Rights Act of 1964 is passed by Congress.
1968	Smith begins working for the Portland Alcohol and Drug Treatment Program.
1972	Smith is hired by the American Indian Commission on Drug and Alcohol Abuse.
1978	Smith is hired by the Sweathouse Lodge, and attends his first Native American Church ceremony.
1978	The American Indian Religious Freedom Act is passed by Congress.

1982	Smith is hired by the Douglas County Council on Alcohol and Drug Abuse Prevention and Treatment facility (ADAPT).
1982	Galen Black is hired by ADAPT.
September 10, 1983	Galen Black attends a meeting of the Native American Church, ingests peyote as a sacrament, and later is placed on indefinite mandatory sick leave and evaluated by a social worker, who concludes that Black has suffered a relapse into substance abuse.
October 3, 1983	Black is terminated from his job for misconduct for violating a company rule against the "misuse or abuse of substances." That day, the board of directors at ADAPT meet to discuss Black's dismissal and the company policy regarding the use of drugs and alcohol by recovering addicts. Black applies for unemployment compensation from the state of Oregon.
November 4, 1983	The Oregon Employment Division denies Galen Black's application for unemployment benefits, ruling that he was appropriately discharged for misconduct.
December 5, 1983	A hearing is held before an independent referee to review the state's denial of benefits. That day, ADAPT clarifies its company policy regarding the use of alcohol and drugs by employees in recovery, requiring that any "use of an illegal drug or use of prescription drugs in a non-prescribed manner is grounds for immediate termination from employment."

December 8, 1983	The independent referee sets aside the administrative decision and reinstates Black's unemployment benefits.
January 27, 1984	The Employment Appeals Board (EAB) sets aside the referee's decision and denies Black unemployment benefits.
March 3, 1984	Alfred Smith participates in a teepee ceremony at the Storm Ranch in Bandon, Oregon, and ingests peyote as part of his religious worship.
March 6, 1984	Smith is terminated from his job. He applies for unemployment compensation from the state of Oregon.
March 22, 1984	The Oregon Employment Division denies Alfred Smith's application for unemployment benefits.
June 6, 1984	A hearing is held before an independent referee to review the Employment Division's denial of benefits to Smith.
July 18, 1984	The Seattle District Office of the Equal Employment Opportunity Commission (EEOC) files a discrimination case on behalf of Smith against ADAPT.
July 23, 1984	The independent referee sets aside the administrative decision denying Smith unemployment benefits.
August 28, 1984	The Employment Appeals Board sets aside the referee's decision and denies Smith unemployment benefits.
August 31, 1984	Oregon Legal Services appeals for judicial review of the EAB decision denying Black unemployment compensation benefits.

June 7, 1985	Oregon Legal Services appeals for judicial review of the EAB decision denying Smith unemployment compensation benefits.
October 16, 1985	The Oregon Court of Appeals reverses and remands the EAB decision in *Employment Division of Oregon v. Black* and *Employment Division of Oregon v. Smith*.
January 9, 1986	The state of Oregon petitions the Oregon Supreme Court for judicial review of *Black* and *Smith*.
February 25, 1986	The Oregon Supreme Court grants the petition for review.
March 4, 1986	ADAPT and the EEOC negotiate an out-of-court settlement; ADAPT agrees to pay Smith and Black back wages and not engage in future employment practices which may deprive individuals of employment opportunities, and ADAPT is allowed to institute rules proscribing advocacy of the peyote ceremony in certain circumstances.
March 31, 1986	Smith and Black's Title VII challenge against ADAPT is resolved; the consent decree is filed in U.S. District Court in Eugene.
April 1, 1986	The Oregon Supreme Court hears oral arguments in *Black* and *Smith*.
June 24, 1986	The Oregon Supreme Court affirms the Court of Appeals decisions and reinstates unemployment compensation benefits for Smith and Black. The state of Oregon asks the Oregon Supreme Court to reconsider its decision in *Black* and *Smith*.

September 3, 1986	The Oregon Supreme Court denies the petition for reconsideration.
December 2, 1986	The state of Oregon files a petition for a writ of certiorari in *Black* and *Smith* to the U.S. Supreme Court.
January 5, 1987	Lovendahl files petitions opposing the writ of certiorari in *Smith* and *Black*.
March 9, 1987	The U.S. Supreme Court grants the writ of certiorari, and the two cases are consolidated under *Smith*.
December 8, 1987	Oral arguments are heard for the first time in *Employment Division v. Smith*.
April 20, 1987	The U.S. Supreme Court hands down its decision in *Lyng v. Northwest Cemetery Association*.
April 27, 1988	The U.S. Supreme Court hands down its decision in *Employment Division of Oregon v. Smith* (Smith I), but does not decide the free exercise of religion issue. Instead, it remands case back to Oregon Supreme Court to address the legality of peyote in the state.
May 1988	The American Indian Religious Freedom Coalition is established.
September 8, 1988	The Oregon Supreme Court hears oral arguments for a second time in *Employment Division of Oregon v. Smith*.
October 18, 1988	The Oregon Supreme Court rules that Black and Smith are entitled to unemployment compensation from the state of Oregon because they were unconstitutionally denied compensation for ingesting the peyote sacrament as part of their right to worship, which is protected by the free

exercise clause of the First Amendment to the U.S. Constitution.

January 17, 1989	The state of Oregon files a second petition for a writ of certiorari in *Employment Division of Oregon v. Smith*.
March 20, 1989	The U.S. Supreme Court grants the writ of certiorari.
October 10, 1989	David Frohnmayer, attorney general for the state of Oregon, announces that he is a candidate for governor.
October/November 1989	There is a behind-the-scenes effort, orchestrated by the Native American Rights Fund, representing the Native American Church, to settle the case and avoid having it go back to the U.S. Supreme Court. The negotiations fail when Smith decides to take his case back to the Court.
November 6, 1989	The U.S. Supreme Court hears oral arguments in *Employment Division v. Smith* for a second time.
April 17, 1990	The U.S. Supreme Court decides *Employment Division v. Smith*, ruling that because the law proscribing peyote possession is neutral and generally applicable, that Black and Smith's conduct is therefore not protected by the free exercise clause of the First Amendment, which only protects activity that is directly targeted by a government action. The Court decides the respondents were properly discharged from their jobs for misconduct, and remands the case back to the Oregon Supreme Court.
May 10, 1990	The Coalition for Free Exercise of

{ *Religious Freedom and Indian Rights* }

	Religion files a petition for rehearing in the U.S. Supreme Court.
May 11, 1990	Reuben Snake launches the Native American Religious Freedom Project to help enact federal legislation to protect the right of American Indians to ingest peyote as part of their religious freedom.
June 5, 1990	The U.S. Supreme Court denies the petition for a rehearing of *Employment Division v. Smith*.
July 26, 1990	The Religious Freedom Restoration Act of 1990 (RFRA) is introduced in the U.S. House of Representatives.
September 27, 1990	The House Subcommittee on Civil and Constitutional Affairs holds hearings on RFRA.
October 26, 1990	The Religious Freedom Restoration Act of 1990 is introduced in the U.S. Senate.
October 28, 1990	The 101st Congress adjourns, and RFRA dies in the House and Senate Committees.
June 25, 1991	Oregon governor Barbara Roberts signs a state law allowing for the use of a "religious defense" for people convicted under the state law proscribing peyote.
June 26, 1991	The Religious Freedom Restoration Act of 1991 is introduced in the U.S. House of Representatives.
August 1991	The Native American Church holds a meeting to plan a national legislative effort to preserve the sacramental use of peyote.
September 21, 1991	On remand from the United States

	Supreme Court, the Oregon Supreme Court decides that Black and Smith are not entitled to unemployment compensation.
November 1991	The American Indian Religious Freedom Coalition holds "The Religious Freedom Summit."
March 1992	The Senate Committee on Indian Affairs holds field hearings on the need to protect American Indian religious freedom.
May 13–14, 1992	The House Subcommittee on Civil and Constitutional Affairs holds additional hearings on RFRA.
June 24, 1992	The Religious Freedom Restoration Act is approved by the Subcommittee on Civil and Constitutional Affairs.
June 29, 1992	The U.S. Supreme Court decides *Planned Parenthood v. Casey*.
July 2, 1992	The Religious Freedom Restoration Act of 1992 is introduced to the Senate.
September 18, 1992	The Senate Judiciary Committee holds hearings on RFRA.
October 9, 1992	The House Judiciary Committee approves RFRA, but Congress adjourns before House consideration. RFRA dies in the Senate Judiciary Committee.
November 6, 1992	William Jefferson Clinton is elected forty-second president of the United States.
February/March 1993	The House Subcommittee on Native American Affairs holds hearings on the effectiveness of the 1978 American Indian Religious Freedom Act.

March 9, 1993	The U.S. Catholic Conference endorses RFRA.
March 10, 1993	The Religious Freedom Restoration Act of 1993 is introduced in the House and Senate.
March 17, 1993	The House Subcommittee on Civil and Constitutional Affairs approves RFRA.
March 22, 1993	The House Judiciary Committee approves RFRA.
May 6, 1993	The Senate Judiciary Committee approves RFRA.
May 11, 1993	The House of Representatives unanimously approves RFRA.
May 25, 1993	The Native American Free Exercise of Religion Act of 1992 is introduced to the Senate.
June 11, 1993	The U.S. Supreme Court hands down *Church of the Lukumi Babalu Aye v. City of Hialeah*, which reaffirms *Smith*.
September 1993	The Senate Committee on Indian Affairs holds hearings on the Native American Free Exercise of Religion Act.
October 27, 1993	The Senate approves RFRA by a 97–3 vote.
November 3, 1993	The House of Representatives unanimously approves RFRA.
November 16, 1993	President Clinton signs RFRA into law.
April 29, 1994	President Clinton meets with leaders of federally recognized tribal governments and issues an executive memorandum that protects access to sacred eagle feathers and parts.
March 1994	HR 4155, a bill to amend AIRFA to

	protect sacred sites, is introduced in the House.
April 1994	HR 4230, a bill to amend AIRFA to protect the sacramental use of peyote, is introduced in the House.
April 1994	S 2269, the Native American Cultural Protection and Free Exercise of Religion Act of 1994, is introduced in the Senate.
July 22, 1994	The House Subcommittee on Native American Affairs approves HR 4230 by voice vote.
July 25, 1994	The House Natural Resource Committee approves HR 4230 by unanimous voice vote, and the bill moves to consideration in the Senate. However, HR 4155 dies in committee.
August 8, 1994	The House unanimously passes HR 4230 by voice vote.
August 1994	S 2269 dies in committee.
September 27, 1994	HR 4230, which amends the 1978 American Indian Religious Freedom Act to protect the religious use of peyote, is signed into law by President Clinton.
May 24, 1996	President Clinton signs Executive Order 13007 to promote the protection of Indian religious sites.
June 6, 1996	The city of Boerne files a petition for a writ of certiorari in *City of Boerne v. Flores*, which challenges the constitutionality of the Religious Freedom Restoration Act.
October 15, 1996	The U.S. Supreme Court grants the writ of certiorari in *Boerne*.

February 19, 1997	The Supreme Court hears oral arguments in *Boerne*.
June 25, 1997	The Supreme Court hands down its decision in *City of Boerne v. Flores*, ruling that the Religious Freedom Restoration Act unconstitutionally violates the principles of federalism and separation of powers.
July 14, 1997	The Subcommittee on Civil and Constitutional Affairs holds a hearing on "Protecting Religious Liberty after *Boerne v. Flores*."
February/March 1998	The House Subcommittee on Civil and Constitutional Affairs holds additional hearings on the response to *Boerne v. Flores*.
June 9, 1998	The Religious Liberty Protection Act of 1998 (RLPA) is introduced in the House and the Senate.
July 1998	The House Subcommittee on Civil and Constitutional Affairs and the Senate Committee on the Judiciary hold hearings on RLPA.
August 6, 1998	Markup of RLPA takes place in the House Judiciary Committee.
August 7, 1998	The Starr Report is delivered to Congress.
December 19, 1999	President Clinton becomes the second president in history to be impeached by the House of Representatives.
January/February 1999	The Senate holds hearings on two articles of impeachment and the Senate votes to acquit President Clinton on both counts.
May 5, 1999	The Religious Liberty Protection Act is reintroduced to the House and

	Senate and hearings are held in the House one week later.
June 15, 1999	RLPA is marked up in the House Judiciary Committee, with minor changes.
June 23, 1999	RLPA is approved by voice vote in the House Judiciary Committee.
July 14, 1999	President Clinton endorses RLPA.
July 15, 1999	RLPA passes in the House; 107 Democrats join 199 Republicans to approve the bill. It later dies in the Senate.
November 6, 1999	Al Smith celebrates his eightieth birthday on the ten-year anniversary of oral arguments in *Employment Division of Oregon v. Smith*.

BIBLIOGRAPHICAL ESSAY

This work only scratches the surface of the scholarly research covering peyotism, the First Amendment religion clauses, the Religious Freedom Restoration Act, the American Indian Religious Freedom Act and its amendments, and other legislative efforts to protect religious liberty in America. Readers interested in these subjects will find the following book and journal citations useful for conducting further research. This essay also contains a review of the primary and secondary sources used for this volume.

A number of books have been written on the long history of peyotism in North America. For further information, I recommend Omer Stewart's *Peyote Religion: A History* (Norman, Okla.: University of Oklahoma Press, 1987), the definitive work on the subject. There are other excellent resources as well, including David F. Aberle, *The Peyote Religion Among the Navajo* (Chicago, Ill.: Aldine, 1966); Weston LaBarre, *The Peyote Cult* (Norman, Okla.: University of Oklahoma Press, 1989); James Sydney Slotkin, *The Peyote Religion: A Study in Indian-White Relations* (New York: Octagon Books, 1975); and Omer Stewart and David F. Aberle, *Peyotism in the West* (Salt Lake City: University of Utah Press, 1984). An excellent resource into the ethnology and pharmacology of peyote is offered in Edward F. Anderson's *Peyote: The Divine Cactus* (Tucson, Ariz.: University of Arizona Press, 1996).

Information on the Native American Church can be found in the works listed above as well as *One Nation Under God: The Triumph of the Native American Church* (Santa Fe, N.Mex.: Clear Light Publishers, 1996) edited by Huston Smith and Reuben Snake, which offers insight into the church and its legal struggles, and Silvester J. Brito's *The Way of a Peyote Roadman* (New York: Peter Lang, 1989), a detailed account of the life of the leader of this sacred ceremony. Two video productions are also useful: *The Traditional Use of Peyote*, presented by members of the Native American Church of North America (San Francisco: Kifaru Productions, 1993), which consists of detailed interviews with church members about their religion, and *The Peyote Road: Ancient Religion in Contemporary Crisis* (San Francisco: Kifaru Productions, 1993), which offers an explicit description of the peyote ceremony and a review of state and federal attempts to regulate the Native American Church. *The Peyote Road* was coordinated by the Native American Religious Freedom Project and won documentary awards at the National Educational Film and Video Festival and the Chicago International Film Festival.

If readers would like to explore more about the Klamath Indian tribe, I would suggest Theodore Stern, *The Klamath Tribe: A People and their Reservation* (Seattle: University of Washington Press, 1965); Carrol B. Howe, *Unconquered, Uncontrolled: The Klamath Indian Reservation* (Bend, Oreg.: Maverick Publications, 1992); and Patrick Mann Haynal, *From Termination Through Restoration and Beyond: Modern Klamath Cultural Identity* (Ph.D. thesis, Eugene: University of Oregon, 1996). Also useful are two videorecordings: *People of the Klamath* (New York: New Day Films, 1987) a short film that traces the history of American Indians on the Klamath Indian Reservation, and *Return of the Raven: The Edison Chiloquin Story* (Eugene, Oreg.: Barry Hood Films, 1984), a narrative of Chiloquin's life and battle to recover lands lost owing to the Klamath Termination Act.

More specific works on American Indian religious freedom, as interpreted and protected by Congress and the U.S. Supreme Court, includes Walter R. Echo-hawk, "Native American Religious Liberty: Five Hundred Years after Columbus," *American Indian Culture and Research Journal* 17 (1993): 33–52; David H. Getches, "Conquering the Cultural Frontier: The New Subjectivism of the Supreme Court in Indian Law," *California Law Review* 84 (1996): 1573–1655; Paul E. Lawson and C. Patrick Morris, "The Native American Church and the New Court: The Smith Case and Indian Religious Freedoms," *American Indian Culture and Research Journal* 15 (1991): 79–91; John Rhodes, "An American Tradition: The Religious Persecution of Native Americans," *Montana Law Review* 52 (1991): 13–72; and Jack F. Trope, "Protecting Native American Religious Freedom: The Legal, Historical, and Constitutional Basis for the Proposed Native American Free Exercise of Religion Act," *Review of Law and Social Change* 20 (1993): 373–403. John R. Wunder's edited volume, *Native American Cultural and Religious Freedoms* (New York: Garland, 1996) is an excellent compilation of works from several academics who specialize on this subject. A legal analysis of the American Indian Religious Freedom Act can be found in Christopher Vecsey, *Handbook of American*

Indian Religious Freedom (New York: Crossroad, 1991). Most of the more recent information on AIRFA and protection for the religious use of peyote, access to sacred sites and sacred eagle parts and feathers, and protection for religious freedom rights of prisoners was taken directly from the House and Senate committee hearings on this issue. These committee reports and the reports that accompany them can be found in the government document sections of most public and university libraries. Additional material on this legislative battle was supplied by the Native American Religious Freedom Project.

A great deal of the primary research on the court cases reviewed for this book is located in the Oregon and Supreme Court reports of the decisions associated with this landmark ruling. The Oregon Court of Appeals decision in *Smith v. Employment Division* and *Black v. Employment Division* can be found at 75 Or. App. 764 (Or. Ct. App. 1985) and 75 Or. App. 735 (Or. Ct. App. 1985). The Oregon Supreme Court opinions in *Smith* and *Black* can be found at 301 Or. 209 (1986) and 301 Or. 221 (1986). The decision of the U.S. Supreme Court in *Employment Division of Oregon v. Smith* (Smith I) is at 485 U.S. 660 (1988); the Oregon Supreme Court decision in *Smith v. Employment Division* on remand from the Supreme Court is at 307 Or. 68 (1988); and the decision of the U.S. Supreme Court in *Employment Division of Oregon v. Smith* (Smith II) is at 494 U.S. 872 (1990). All attorneys' briefs for these two cases while in the state court system are available at the Supreme Court Library for the State of Oregon, located in Salem, Oregon. These briefs include records from the hearings before the independent referee evaluating the denial of unemployment compensation for both Al Smith and Galen Black, records from the Employment Appeals Board's consideration of unemployment compensation for the two respondents, affidavits submitted by interested parties, and records of the Equal Employment Opportunity Commission's investigation of ADAPT. The consent decree in *EEOC v. ADAPT* (Civ. No. C85-6139E) is filed in the U.S. District Court in Eugene. Additional material on the Native American Church and the participation of the ACLU at the state court level was provided by the Eugene branch of the ACLU of Oregon. The official reports of these cases while in the state system was supplemented with interviews with two former Oregon Supreme Court justices, Hans Linde and Robert Jones.

The Supreme Court briefs of the attorneys representing Smith and Black and the attorneys representing the Employment Division, Department of Human Resources of Oregon, and the Douglas County Alcohol and Drug Abuse Prevention and Treatment (ADAPT) facility, as well as the numerous amici curiae participating in this case are available in microfiche form at most law school libraries. These briefs also contain additional supplemental material on Native American populations in the United States, the Native American Church, state drug laws proscribing peyote, and rules relating to the federal controlled substances law. Some information from the state judicial proceedings, including records of the unemployment compensation hearings and EAB deliberations, is repeated in these briefs. The petitions for the writs of certiorari in *Employment Division v. Smith* and *Employment Division v. Black* for *Smith I* and *Smith II* from the attorneys representing both parties and the several amicus curiae briefs filed in the case are also available in microfiche form at most law school libraries. Oral arguments in both cases can be accessed on audiotape at the National Archives in College Park, Maryland. A transcript of oral arguments for *Smith I* and *Smith II* is on file with the author. An edited version of oral arguments and transcribed excerpts in *Smith II* is available in Peter Irons, ed., *May It Please the Court: The First Amendment* (New York: The New Press, 1977). These official reports were supplemented with valuable information on the U.S. Supreme Court from the private papers of former justice Thurgood Marshall. Original votes on the petitions for certiorari, notes from Court conferences, and internal Court memorandums can be found in his papers on this case. Marshall's papers also include all of the drafts of the majority, concurring, and dissenting opinions. Materials from other relevant free exercise cases found in these papers were also used for this project. Marshall's private papers are open and available to the public for scholarly research in the manuscript division of the Library of Congress in Washington, D.C. The private papers of William Brennan are also available at this location, but files on this case are restricted until all of the justices who participated in the case are deceased, or have agreed to the release of the papers.

The bulk of the background information used for this book was obtained by in-depth personal interviews with the individuals associated with this case. At least one, and often several interviews were conducted with most of the key participants, and the information used from these discussions is present throughout the text of the manuscript. The interviews are available on audiotape and in transcribed form in the author's personal files. Most of the secondary material was gleaned from newspaper reports on the cases as they moved through the state and federal judicial process. Both the Eugene *Register Guard* and the Portland *Oregonian* have news articles on *Employment Division v. Smith* that can be accessed through standard newspaper indexes. I am indebted to Al Smith and his family, who participated in numerous interviews and provided access to their personal records and videos associated with this case.

A major part of this book concerns the Coalition for the Free Exercise of Religion and its effort on behalf of federal legislation to circumvent the decision in *Smith*. J. Brent Walker, general counsel of the Baptist Joint Committee, kindly granted me access to the archival records of the coalition's activities over the last decade, which are housed in its Washington, D.C., office. This information was supplemented by interviews with several key coalition members, including Morton Halperin, Steve McFarland, Mark J. Pelavin, David Saperstein, Oliver "Buzz" Thomas, and Walker. Interviews with two key players outside the coalition, Nat Lewin and Douglas Laycock, were also extremely helpful. Audio and transcribed reports of these interviews are on file with the author. Information on the discussion in Congress on the Religious Freedom Restoration Act and the Religious Liberty Protection Act is provided in the dozen House and Senate Judiciary Committee Hearings on this issue, and the House and Senate Committee reports accompanying the legislation, which are available in government document sections of most libraries. Also useful were the floor debates in both the House and Senate, which are printed in the *Congressional Record*. Interviews with Representative Henry Hyde and former representative Stephen Solarz complemented this material, and interviews with Shawn M. Bentley, Senator Orrin Hatch's majority counsel, and David G. Lachmann, Representative Jerrold Nadler's minority professional staff, provided an insider's look into the politics of the legislative process.

Well over one hundred articles have been written about the implications of *Employment Division v. Smith* and the constitutionality of the Religious Freedom Restoration Act. A selection of articles that provides critical analysis on both sides of this decision and the congressional reaction is listed for those who wish to explore this topic further: Thomas C. Berg, "What Hath Congress Wrought? An Interpretive Guide to the Religious Freedom Restoration Act," *Villanova Law Review* 39 (December 1994): 1–70; Jay S. Bybee, "Taking Liberties with the First Amendment: Congress, Section 5, and the Religious Freedom Restoration Act," *Vanderbilt Law Review* 48 (November 1995): 1539–1633; Daniel O. Conckle, "The Religious Freedom Restoration Act: The Constitutional Significance of an Unconstitutional Statute," *Montana Law Review* 56 (winter 1995): 39–93; Chris Day, *"Employment Division v. Smith:* Free Exercise Clause Loses Balance on Peyote," *Baylor Law Review* 43 (1991): 577–608; Robert F. Drinan and Jennifer I. Huffman, "The Religious Freedom Restoration Act; A Legislative History," *Journal of Law and Religion* 10 (summer 1994): 531–41; Christopher L. Eisgruber and Lawrence G. Sager, "Why the Religious Freedom Restoration Act Is Unconstitutional," *New York University Law Review* 69 (June 1994): 437–76; Edward M. Gaffney Jr. "Hostility to Religion, American Style," *De Paul Law Review* 42 (fall 1992): 263–304; Marci A. Hamilton, "The Religious Freedom Restoration Act: Letting the Fox into the Henhouse Under Cover of Section 5 of the Fourteenth Amendment," *Cardozo Law Review* 16 (December 1994): 357–98; Jonathan Kieffer, "A Line in the Sand: Difficulties in Discerning the Limits of Congressional Power as Illustrated by the Religious Freedom Restoration Act," *University of Kansas Law Review* 44 (May 1996): 601–32; Douglas Laycock, "RFRA, Congress and the Ratchet," *Montana Law Review* 56 (winter 1995): 145–70; "The Religious Freedom Restoration Act," *Brigham Young University Law Review* (1993): 221–58; "The Supreme Court's Assault on Free Exercise and the Amicus Brief that Was Never Filed," *Journal of Law and Religion* 8 (1993): 99–114; Ira Lupu, *"Employment Division v. Smith* and the Decline of Supreme Court Centrism," *Brigham Young University Law Review* (1993): 259–74; "Of Time and the RFRA: A Lawyer's Guide to the Religious Freedom Restoration Act," *Montana Law Review* 56 (winter 1995): 227–48; Kenneth Marin, *"Employment Division v. Smith*: The Supreme Court Alters the State of the Free Exercise Doctrine," *American University Law Review* 40 (summer 1991): 1431–76; William P. Marshall, "In Defense of *Smith* and Free Exercise Revisionism," *University of Chicago Law Review* 58 (winter 1991): 308–28; Roald Mykkeltvedt, "*Employment Division v. Smith*: Creating Anxiety by Relieving Tension," *Tennessee Law Review* 58 (1991): 603–34; Matt Pawa, "When the Supreme Court Restricts Constitutional Rights, Can Congress Save Us? An Examination of Section Five of the Fourteenth Amendment," *University of Pennsylvania Law Review* 141 (1993): 1029–1101; James E. Ryan, "*Smith* and the Religious Freedom Restoration Act: An Iconoclastic Assessment," *Virginia Law Review* 78 (1992): 1407–62; Luralene D. Tapahe, "After the Religious Freedom Restoration Act: Still No Equal Protection for First American Worshipers," *New Mexico Law Review* 24 (spring 1994): 331–63; and Harry F. Tepker Jr., "Hallucinations of Neutrality in the Oregon Peyote Case," *American Indian Law Review* 16 (1991): 1–56.

A review of major free exercise and establishment clause decisions can be found in most constitutional law casebooks such as Lawrence H. Tribe's *American Constitutional Law*, vol. 2, 3d ed. (New York: Foundation Press, 2000) or a book specializing in religion cases such as Terry Eastland's *Religious Liberty in the Supreme Court: The Cases that Define the Debate Over Church and State* (Washington, D.C.: Ethics and Public Policy Center, 1993). I would also recommend a book such as Louis Fisher's *American Constitutional Law*, 3d ed. (Durham, N.C.: Carolina Academic Press, 2000), which provides a more comprehensive look at how the various institutions of government engage in constitutional analysis, as well as Fisher's *Constitutional Dialogues, Interpretation as a Political Process* (Princeton, N.J.: Princeton University Press, 1988), which details, among other things, constitutional interpretation by members of Congress. Robert A. Licht's edited volume, *Is the Supreme Court the Guardian of the Constitution?* (Washington, D.C.: American Enterprise Institute Press, 1993) includes a number of essays on this issue. There are several books that specifically address free exercise jurisprudence, and Bette Novit Evans, *Interpreting the Free Exercise of Religion: The Constitution and American Pluralism* (Chapel Hill: University of North Carolina Press, 1997) might be useful. A good general book about the history of the religious clauses can be found in Francis Graham Lee, ed., *All Imaginable Liberty: The Religious Clauses of the*

First Amendment (Landham, Md.: University Press of America, 1995). The most detailed research on free exercise and establishment clause jurisprudence is found in legal periodicals. Articles one may wish to access include Russell Galloway, "Basic Free Exercise Analysis," *Santa Clara Law Review* 29 (fall 1989): 865–78; Philip A. Hamburger, "A Constitutional Right of Religious Exemption: An Historical Perspective," *George Washington Law Review* 60 (April 1992): 915–48; Philip Kurland, "Of Church and State and the Supreme Court," *University of Chicago Law Review* 29 (1961): 1–96; "The Irrelevance of the Constitution: The Religion Clauses of the First Amendment and the Supreme Court," *Villanova Law Review* 24 (1978): 3–27; Ira Lupu, "Reconstructing the Establishment Clause: The Case Against Discretionary Accommodation of Religion," *University of Pennsylvania Law Review* 140 (1991): 555–612; "Statutes Revolving in Constitutional Law Orbits," *Virginia Law Review* 79 (February 1993): 1–89; William P. Marshall, "The Case Against the Constitutionally Compelled Free Exercise Exemption," *Journal of Law and Religion* 7 (1989): 363–414; Michael McConnell, "Accommodation of Religion," *Supreme Court Review* 1 (1985): 1–59; "The Origins and Historical Understanding of Free Exercise of Religion," *Harvard Law Review* 103 (1990): 1409–1476; "Accommodation of Religion: An Update and a Response to the Critics," *George Washington Law Review* 60 (March 1992): 685–742; Steven Pepper, "A Brief for the Free Exercise Clause," *Journal of Law and Religion* 7 (1989): 323– 62; Leo Pfeffer, "The Supremacy of Free Exercise," *Georgetown Law Journal* 61 (May 1973): 1151–42; Geoffrey R. Stone, "Constitutionally-Compelled Exemptions and the Free Exercise Clause," *William and Mary Law Review* 27 (1986): 985–1009; Herbert W. Titus, "The Free Exercise Clause: Past, Present and Future," *Regent University Law Review* 6 (fall 1995): 7–63; and Ellis West, "The Case Against the Right to Religion-Based Exemptions," *Notre Dame Journal of Law, Ethics, and Public Policy* 4 (1990): 567–90.

background, 128–29
Braunfeld dissent, 55
Goldman dissent, 131, 205–6
Hobbie majority, 133
Hobbie memorandum, 114–15
Lyng dissent, 145–46
Morgan majority, 207
retires from Court, 229
Sherbert majority, 55–57
Smith I conference deliberation, 138–39
Smith I dissent, 142–43
Smith II dissent, 185, 194
Solarz and, 205–6
Breyer, Steven
Boerne concurrence, 261
Brzonkala v. VIP University (2000), 269–70
Buchanan, John, 216–17
Bunn v. North Carolina (1949), 51
Bunton, Lucius D., 253–54
Bureau of Indian Affairs
AICDAA and, 31–32
antipeyote campaign and, 11–13
assimilation and, 11–12
Klamath Termination Act and, 29
Smith and, 23–25, 31–32
Burger, Warren
Bob Jones majority, 60
Bowen plurality, 132
coercion test and, 132
compelling government interest test and, 57–61, 129–32
free exercise jurisprudence, 57–61, 129–31
Paty plurality, 58
retire from Court, 125
Sherbert concerns, 130, 132
Thomas reservations, 58
Yoder majority, 57–58
Burger Court
compelling government interest

test and, 57–61, 129–32
establishment clause decisions, 64–67
free exercise decisions, 57–61, 129–31
Bush, George H.
defeat, 236
RFRA and, 235–36
Supreme Court appointments, 229
Butler, Jerry, 44, 83

Caley, Eldon, 75, 88–89
Canady, Charles T.
Boerne reaction, 262–63
RLPA hearings, 265–68
Cantwell v. Connecticut (1940), 49–50
Cedarman, 1–2
Chemewa Indian School, 26
Chief justice of the Supreme Court, 137–39
Chiloquin, Edison, 32–33, 176
Chipps, Skinny, 25
Chopko, Mark
CFER discussions, 231
RFRA and, 231, 233, 236–37
Thomas and, 236–37
Christianity
American Indians and, 9, 11
antipeyote campaign, 7, 11–13
assimilation and, 7, 8
missionaries encounter peyotism, 7
Native American Church and, 14
peyotism, 7, 9–11, 14
Christian Legal Society, 203, 254
Church Council of Greater Seattle, 164–65
Church of Jesus Christ of Latter-Day Saints, 233
Church of the Lukumi Babalu Aye Inc. v. Hialeah (1993), 238

Smith and, 23, 25–26
Termination Act and, 22, 29, 33, 176
Kunz v. New York (1951), 50

Lachmann, David
Lewin and, 209–11
Nadler and, 263
RFRA and, 209–11
RLPA and, 263
Largent v. Texas (1943), 50
Law clerks
bench memos, 135
certiorari review, 108, 114
draft decisions, 139–40
Laycock, Douglas
brief on the merits in *Boerne*, 256
certiorari petition in *Boerne*, 254–55
Flores attorney, 254–57
Justice Department and, 255
letter to House subcommittee, 217–18
letter to pro-life leaders, 229
letter to religious leaders, 219
National Council of Churches meeting, 211
oral arguments in *Boerne*, 256–57
RFRA reply brief, 253
RLPA and, 263–65
Smith II reaction, 198
subcommittee testimony, 233
Lefthand, Patrick, 242–43
Legal Services Corporation, 68–69
Lemon v. Kurtzman (1970)
establishment clause cases and, 64–66
Lemon test, 64
Lewin, Nat
background, 209–10
enforcement clause of the Fourteenth Amendment, 210–11

Lachmann and, 210–11
legislative protection for religious liberty, 210
Solarz and, 210–11
Linde, Hans, 98
Linder, Virginia, 109, 116, 155
Lophophora diffusa, 4–5
Lophophora williamsii, 4–5
Lovell v. Griffin (1938), 48–49, 51
Lovendahl, Suanne
brief in the state supreme court, 96, 150–51
brief on the merits in *Smith I*, 118–20
counsel for Black and Smith, 112
Dorsay and, 150–52, 155
NARF and, 112, 118, 124
opposition to certiorari in *Smith I*, 112–14
oral argument in *Smith I*, 136–37
oral argument in state supreme court, 150–51
preparation for oral argument, 124
withdrawal as counsel, 155
Lupu, Ira, 233–34
Lynch v. Donnelly (1984), 66
Lyng v. Northwest Cemetery Protective Association (1988), 144–46, 162

Magnunson, John, 164–65
Marshall, Thurgood
background, 129
retires from Court, 229
Smith I conference deliberations, 139
Smith I dissent, 143
Smith II dissent, 185, 194
Marsh v. Alabama (1948), 50
Marsh v. Chambers (1983), 66
Martin v. City of Struthers (1943), 50

{ *Religious Freedom and Indian Rights* }